Patriotic Fire

Patriotic Fire

Andrew Jackson and Jean Laffite at the Battle of New Orleans

Winston Groom

Alfred A. Knopf, New York, 2006

THIS IS A BORZOI BOOK
PUBLISHED BY ALFRED A. KNOPF

www.aaknopf.com

Library of Congress Cataloging-in-Publication Data

Groom, Winston, [date]
    Patriotic fire : Andrew Jackson and Jean Laffite at the
Battle of New Orleans / Winston Groom.—1st ed.
        p. cm.
Includes bibliographical references and index.
ISBN 1-4000-4436-7
    1. New Orleans, Battle of, New Orleans, La., 1815. 2. Jack-
son, Andrew, 1767–1845. 3. Generals—United States—
Biography. 4. Laffite, Jean. 5. Pirates—Louisiana—
Biography. 6. New Orleans (La.)—History—19th century.
I. Title.

E356.N5G79 2006
973.5'239—dc22   2005051001

Manufactured in the United States of America
First Edition

❧ Author's Note ☙

At the same time this book was going to press, the destructive hurricane Katrina struck the New Orleans area. Among the most devastated parts of the city was St. Bernard Parish, where the Battle of New Orleans was fought. The battlefield itself, now a national historical site maintained and operated by the National Park Service, was, at the end of September 2005, under several feet of water. The historical papers, paintings, maps, and other original documents are apparently saved, having been moved before the storm to other parts of the state from the Historic New Orleans Collection, the Williams Research Center, the Louisiana State Museum, and other archival entities.

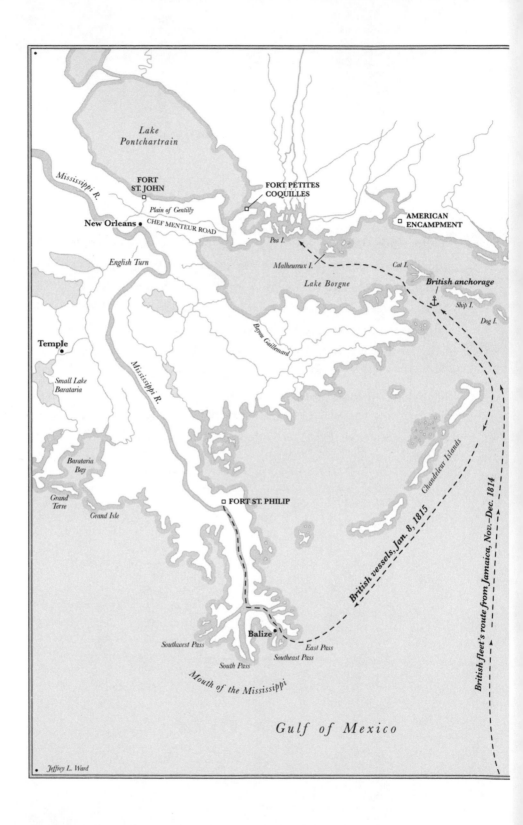

Lake
Pontchartrain

FORT
ST. JOHN

FORT PETITES
COQUILLES

AMERICAN
ENCAMPMENT

Mississippi R.

Plain of Gentilly

New Orleans • CHEF MENTEUR ROAD

Pea I.

Malheureux I.

Cat I.

British anchorage

English Turn

Lake Borgne

Ship I.

Dog I.

Bayou Gaillemard

Temple •

*Small Lake
Barataria*

Mississippi R.

*Barataria
Bay*

Chandeleur Islands

*Grand
Terre*

Grand Isle

□ **FORT ST. PHILIP**

British vessels, Jan. 8, 1815

British fleet's route from Jamaica, Nov.–Dec. 1814

Balize •

Southwest Pass

East Pass

Southeast Pass

South Pass

Mouth of the Mississippi

Gulf of Mexico

Jeffrey L. Ward

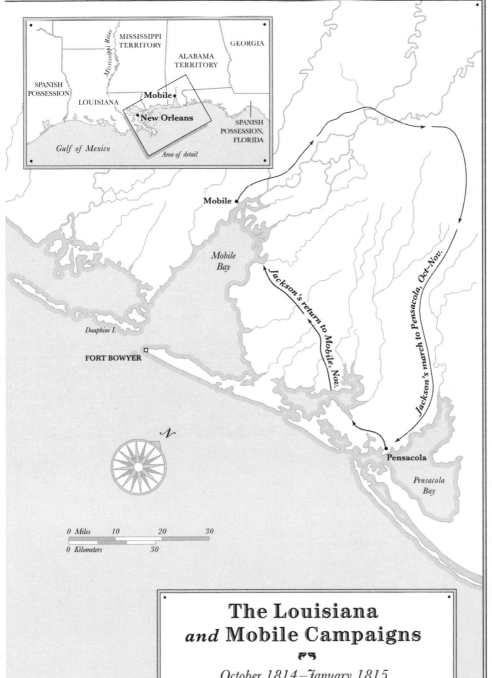

MISSISSIPPI
TERRITORY

GEORGIA

ALABAMA
TERRITORY

Mississippi River

SPANISH
POSSESSION

LOUISIANA

Mobile •

• New Orleans

SPANISH
POSSESSION,
FLORIDA

Gulf of Mexico

Area of detail

Mobile •

*Mobile
Bay*

Jackson's return to Mobile, Nov.

Jackson's march to Pensacola, Oct.–Nov.

Dauphine I.

FORT BOWYER □

N

Pensacola

*Pensacola
Bay*

0 Miles	10	20	30

0 Kilometers	30

The Louisiana
and Mobile Campaigns

༄

October 1814–January 1815

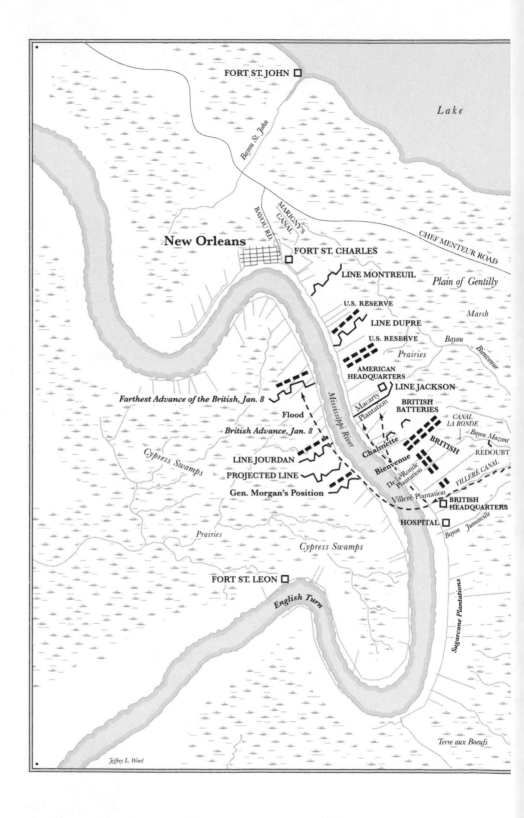

FORT ST. JOHN □

Lake

Bayou St. John

MARIGNY'S CANAL

CHEF MENTEUR ROAD

New Orleans

BAYOU RD.

FORT ST. CHARLES □

LINE MONTREUIL

Plain of Gentilly

U.S. RESERVE

LINE DUPRE

Marsh

U.S. RESERVE

Bayou

Prairies

Bienvenue

AMERICAN
HEADQUARTERS

Farthest Advance of the British, Jan. 8

LINE JACKSON □

Macarty Plantation

BRITISH
BATTERIES

CANAL
LA RONDE

Mississippi River

Bayou Mazant

Flood

British Advance, Jan. 8

Chalmette

BRITISH

REDOUBT

LINE JOURDAN

Bienvenue

De la Ronde Plantation

VILLERÉ CANAL

PROJECTED LINE

Cypress Swamps

Gen. Morgan's Position

Villeré Plantation

BRITISH
HEADQUARTERS □

HOSPITAL □

Bayou Jumonville

Prairies

Cypress Swamps

Sugarcane Plantations

FORT ST. LEON □

English Turn

Terre aux Boeufs

Jeffrey L. Ward

Pontchartrain

The New Orleans Battlefield *and* Vicinity

December 1814–January 1815

REDOUBT
Gov. Claiborne's
Command

□
FORT PETITES
COQUILLES

Marsh

BREASTWORK
BRITISH REDOUBT
Spanish Fishermen's Village

*British Advance,
Dec. 23*

*Cypress
Swamps*

Approach of British Barges

N

Lake Borgne

| 0 Miles | | 2 | | 4 | | 6 |
| 0 Kilometers | | | 4 | | 6 | |

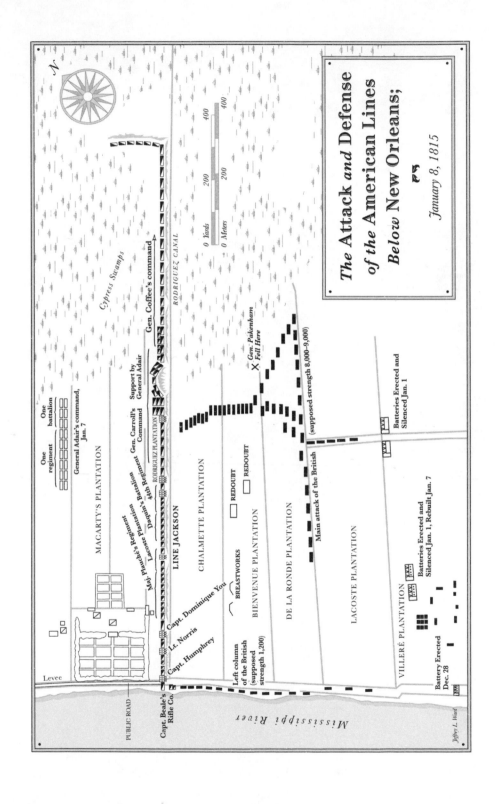

The Attack and Defense
of the American Lines
Below New Orleans;

January 8, 1815

⚘ Introduction ⚘

Most gratifying for any writer of histories is being able somehow to connect yourself to the events you're describing; it adds an extra impetus—the almost bone-shivering feeling that you might actually be a small part of it, a slender thread that binds. I remember how whenever the historian Steve Ambrose, a friend who lived not far from here, began a new project he would first of all collect every relic he could find from the era he was writing about and clutter his office with them, just to keep himself in the spirit. And when that book was finished he'd then clear them out and start all over again, getting up a new collection to suit his next topic.

The last time I saw him do this was when he was writing *Nothing Like It in the World,* about the construction of the American transcontinental railroad, completed in 1869. Steve had somehow acquired an old topographical tableau under glass, about six or eight feet long and taking up the whole center of his office, that laid out in bas-relief the entire Western United States from Omaha, Nebraska, to Sacramento, California, with mountains, rivers, plains, deserts, and so forth, and model tracks and trains with little tin men working on them, like those collections of toy soldiers children used to play with after World War I.

I've been lucky enough to have experienced this sensation myself, mostly through direct ancestral involvement, although my people have not by and large been professional soldiers. In *Shrouds of Glory: From Atlanta to Nashville: The Last Great Campaign of the Civil War* (1995), it was through my great-grandfather Fremont Sterling Thrower, who left college in 1862 to serve with the cavalry of the Confederate general Joseph "Fighting Joe" Wheeler.

In *A Storm in Flanders: The Ypres Salient, 1914–1918: Tragedy and Triumph on the Western Front* (2002), inspiration was drawn through my grandfather, who fought in France with an American infantry division, and who, after a few years and another visit to France, brought back a Michelin Company illustrated guidebook of those terrible battlefields, a book that impressed itself into my memory when I was a teenager.

In *1942: The Year That Tried Men's Souls* (2005), my father's service as a U.S. Army officer during World War II led to an even closer connection. I'd heard for much of my life his stories, and those of his friends, around the dinner table, stories of "Before the war . . . ," "During the war . . . ," and "After the war . . ."

Now here, to my surprise and delight, in this book on the dramatic and decisive end of the War of 1812, yet another ancestor has given me stimulus to recount the heroic events that occurred so long ago and far away. His name was Major Elijah Montgomery, of General Andrew Jackson's army at the critical Battle of New Orleans in late 1814 and early 1815, which forever crushed England's notion of reclaiming her dominant presence on American soil.

The source for these ancestral characters has been gleaned primarily from sheaves of old papers, letters, and other documents recovered nearly a quarter century ago in the attic of my parents' home. My family, all of them, were inveterate collectors, pack rats if you will, and over the generations a wealth of such information had been handed down. None of them, I imagine, had any real idea of what to do with it all, just that it oughtn't to be thrown away. Thus it was meticulously kept and stored in small packets tied with pink or blue ribbons, a quaint custom of the day, it seems, and saved in small metal strongboxes or wooden boxes. All of it at some point finally wound up in my parents' attic and, after their deaths, made its way into my own cabinets.

Major Elijah Montgomery was my great-great-great-grandfather, on my father's side of the family. He was born on the Northern Neck of

Virginia (near Yorktown) in 1777 and died on his plantation near Mobile, Alabama, in 1831, at the age of fifty-four. I had heard my grandmother speak of him, although he had died well before she was born in the 1880s, but she'd listened as a young woman when her own grandmother—Elijah's daughter—told her stories about him. As a young boy I heard some of my grandmother's tales repeated: that Elijah was an officer in the War of 1812; that he had accumulated substantial holdings; that he died leaving two young daughters who were swindled out of their fortune by an unconscionable guardian appointed by the courts; and so on. It's a shame, though, in retrospect, that I didn't listen more closely as a youngster.

After I decided to write this book, I returned to the old papers to see just who and what Elijah Montgomery had been and what he had done, on an outside hunch that he might have had some role in the Battle of New Orleans. Little did I know! Many of the documents are crumbling; those particular papers are now nearly two hundred years old and a few will break up in your fingers—living history half vanished in an instant. But as I carefully untied the bits of ribbon and string around the packets and laid out their contents on a table in my office, a life began to reassemble itself—the life of a soldier, a war hero, a Southern planter and father—a man born during the American Revolution who lived in the strange and distant times of ferocious Indians, of slavery and duels, of wars with Englishmen and the birth of a new nation among deep forests reminiscent of Cooper's *Leatherstocking Tales*.

It seems ironic that some of the papers most useful in reconstructing the life of Elijah Montgomery are court records concerning the disposition of his estate, following his death in 1831. You can learn a lot about a man by looking at these things, especially when the laws of probate were such as in bygone days. Anybody who feels a shudder over the so-called death tax today ought to go back and look at probate papers from the mid-1800s; that will really give you a fright—government people rummaging through your most private stuff. States had no income taxes then, and a principal way revenue was raised was to go after the property of the dead—every scrap of it—to collect the government's share.

Elijah must have had a lengthy final illness as the nineteenth century entered its fourth decade, given the medical bills paid out by his estate after his death. Then, within a few weeks, courts in Alabama appointed assessors and masters who rushed in to pick through and inventory every item of value he owned in this world, as well as to list (and tax) any moneys yet owed him and record and pay any of his legitimate debts so as to get it all settled—including $45 to the man who built his casket ($965 in today's dollars).

Samples of the property we know Elijah possessed, in no particular order, follow:

5	horses	$925
1	old horse	$21
	[presumably destined for the glue factory]	
1	stew pan	$1
10	satin sheets	$20
4	btls mustard	$1
9	feet rope ["at 14c per foot"]	$1.26
1	buff evening vest	$3
6	pair fine window curtains	$30
2	5lb bags of nails	$.75
16	saws ["three rust out"]	$12
4	loafs sugar	$1
13	qts. tea	$4

So it goes on page after page, but you get the drift: tables, sofas and chairs, items in the pantry or the bedroom or the closet, needles and spools of thread, rifles and shotguns, rings and cuff links, lumber, stands of bricks, pots and pans; the tax assessors overlooked nothing.

Elijah also had more important things for the state, city, and county to evaluate, taxwise, such as "1 large silver spoon $35," as well as china, silver flatware, crystal, vases, lace tablecloths and napkins, napkin rings, wagons, animal harnesses, several teams of oxen, blacksmith's tools, plows, shovels, wheelbarrows, 1,985 sap buckets, a piano, a fishing skiff, and a sailboat ("sloop rig, about 20 feet"); official value was stamped upon it all. The probate file I went through is nearly half a foot thick.

From the look of it, Elijah was a drinking man, too, or at the very least he liked to throw parties. This taxable inventory included:

3 bbls Scotch Whisky	$85
5 bottles Champagne	$11
5 casks Monongahela Whisky [likely riverboat moonshine]	$60
1 gallon whisky [local rot gut, no doubt]	$1

Then there were his home and his lands, all assessed to the last penny. The property was vast, some 8,866 acres (about fifteen square miles, much of it on the Dog River), which had been the dowry of his first wife, Carolina Hollinger, under a land grant to her family by the British government in 1767, eight years before the Revolution and ten years before Elijah was born. It was here—near Mobile, where I grew up—that after his service during the War of 1812 Elijah settled and established his plantation, where he grew cotton and produced turpentine, sap, and tars (for paints, corkings, and related things) from the great stands of native longleaf pines on the property.

There were also debts to be paid and debts to be collected by the estate. According to court papers, Montgomery owed $231 to a Mobile tailor shop and $120 to a man who had sold him a racehorse. In turn, his estate was owed various debts, including $50 from a man named Middleton who had written him a poignant letter dated October 28, 1829, and addressed to "My dear Major," saying, in part: "I am much in distress in making up a sum of money to pay [illegible] for fifty dollars [$1,000 in today's money] and in having buried my little daughter yesterday & am but poorly fitted to make an effort to raise any amt. in town. Make an effort, my good friend to let me have the amt. It would add another of the many favors for which I shall always feel under obligations to you."

Apparently Elijah sent Middleton the money he asked for, since the tax people were there to collect and tax it after he died. It's all set down in court papers, written in an exquisitely flourished ink-pen cuneiform unknown in what passes for calligraphy today.

Elijah also owned slaves, thirty-six of them to be exact, according to the probate records. They are all listed: "William, Edwin, Indiana, Alaria, Graham, Lizzy . . . twelve men, eight women, nine boys, six girls, one infant," collectively valued by the court at nearly $15,000 ($334,000 in today's dollars). The able-bodied male slaves were valued at $500 each, women at $400, and children not yet in their teens at about $250. There was one, Molly, "age about 60," who was valued at only $50, presumably because of her age and because the laws of the state obligated owners to provide care for their older charges.

I'm not proud that my ancestors owned slaves, but neither do I subscribe to the historic fallacy of assigning present-day ethics or morals to such a widely accepted practice by people who lived nearly two hundred years ago. Virtually every family of means in the South had slaves then (and many in the North, too—let alone slaveholders in Britain, France, Portugal, and elsewhere), including twelve of the first fifteen U.S. presidents and most of the nation's Founding Fathers, abominable as we consider it today. It has taken long years and countless deaths of men good and bad to arrive at our present state of morality about this matter.

From the papers of the probate, there's fragmentary evidence that Elijah took pretty good care of his slaves; at least one hopes so. Among the items paid out were $188 for "11 barrels of pork and 405 rashers of bacon," $64 "for medical services for negroes," as well as maintenance of a sort of nursery: $20 "for provisions and supplies for negro woman

Molly [she of the meager $50 value] who has charge of sundry children of the estate." There is also a bill for "$7 for burying the negro Ned."

One of the final and most heart-wrenching acts of the administrator of probate is recorded in these documents as well. This was the auctioning off of Elijah's slaves to liquidate his estate and settle the remaining taxes. On March 25, 1834, some twenty-eight slaves were divided into four lots and sold on the steps of the Mobile County courthouse. They brought $9,900—minus commission. (From the names and ages given in the papers, it would appear that they were sold off as families.)

One supposes that Elijah's widow, Adaline, did not feel up to running the plantation by herself and, with her two stepdaughters, wished to move into the city, some fifteen miles north. (Elijah's first wife, Carolina Hollinger, before she died in 1826 had borne him two girls, Mary Montgomery, nine at the time of his death, and Carolina Montgomery, seven.) At least some of the remaining slaves probably went with them as house servants.

One might question why, if Elijah was a relatively wealthy and decent man, he didn't simply free his slaves as George Washington had in his will upon his death in 1799. The answer is that by the 1830s, according to the "manumission laws" in Alabama, as in most other Deep South states, the state legislatures had made it illegal for an owner to free his slaves unless it could be proven in court that a particular slave had actually, and physically, saved the life of the owner or a member of his family, or had performed a similar service—and even then, the freed slave was required to leave the state within thirty days (but not with his or her family) under penalty of being sold off into slavery again.*

In any case, when all was said and done, the estate Elijah Montgomery left Adaline and his two young daughters—personal property, home, slaves, and acreage—was worth, in today's dollars, about $2.7

---

* This was because of the fear among many white Southerners that freed slaves would instill discord and disharmony among their brethren still enslaved, and/or undercut the wages of lower-class whites who sought positions on plantations. In addition, various periodicals of the day warned about the "glut" of freed slaves and the burdens they would impose on society.

million, minus taxes and lawyer's fees, of course. Still, not a bad windup for a boy from Virginia who had had to join the army to make a living.

How Elijah came to be at the Battle of New Orleans, and a hero at that, may likewise be pieced together from fragments found in the old attic strongbox. In the America of the eighteenth century, particularly in Virginia, where Elijah was born when it was still under British rule of law, the oldest male heir inherited the bulk of his family's estate. Of the others, it was anticipated that the girls would marry (and marry well) and that the younger boys would find themselves work suitable to their status. Often this entailed leaving their birthplace to seek opportunity and fortune across the Alleghenies in the rich and newly opened lands of Kentucky, Tennessee, Ohio, and Illinois.

Elijah most likely ventured forth on this course sometime in his early twenties. I could find no record of his schooling, but from the elegance of his signature and other of his scant writings in my possession, it can be reasonably deduced that he had a semblance of a proper education. At some point he settled in Kentucky, at Lexington, where, in 1808, at the age of thirty-one, he was commissioned as an officer of the newly organized 7th Infantry, a regiment of the regular U.S. Army.

This, and much of the other information on Elijah's military service, comes from a letter found in the strongbox from the adjutant general of the U.S. Army to my grandmother, dated July 8, 1931. Elijah's age at the time of his commissioning was rather old for a second lieutenant, and one can probably assume that whatever it was he was doing in Kentucky had not turned out very well, since applying for service as a professional soldier at the age of thirty-one was equivalent to spending the rest of your life's career in the military, starting out at the very bottom rung of the officer corps at that.

The 7th Infantry Regiment—about 400 to 600 men, depending on circumstances—remains to this day (according to its official Web site) the most decorated infantry regiment in the United States Army. In the early 1800s it was sent by the War Department to New Orleans, newly acquired in the Louisiana Purchase, as its permanent base, though the regiment was expected to operate up and down the Mississippi, on both sides of the river. By the time war with England broke out in 1812, Elijah had been promoted to first lieutenant, and the regiment was sent north to Ohio and Indiana, to fight hostile Indians who were being stirred up by the British from their bases in Canada.

By May of 1814 Elijah had been promoted to captain and the 7th Regiment was ordered back to New Orleans to defend it against a possible British invasion of Louisiana. There he remained six months later when Andrew Jackson rode into the city to take charge of all defenses. A month afterward, when the Battle of New Orleans broke out in earnest on December 23, 1814, Elijah rendered outstanding performance during the three bitter weeks of fighting.

There were no such things as military medals in the American army in those days—the little doodads that were scornfully thought to smack of the be-braided and be-decorated affectations of officers of the enemy, His Royal Britannic Majesty's imperial army. The "common" Americans wanted nothing to do with any of that. What served instead for medals and decorations in the U.S. Army was to be "Mentioned in Dispatches" by the commanding officer in his reports to the War Department in Washington.*

On January 8, 1815, the day on which the great battle culminated, General Andrew Jackson personally promoted Elijah to the rank of major on the spot, "for gallant conduct," and mentioned him in dispatches thusly, in a letter dated January 25, 1815, to Secretary of War James Monroe. Jackson wrote: "Captain's [sic] Montgomery, Vail and Allen, of the Seventh Regiment, acted well during the whole campaign. They are certainly good captains, and merit promotion."

Elijah remained in the U.S. Army for another seven years; then, on

---

* During the Revolutionary War, General George Washington had authorized the "Purple Heart" medal for those of his soldiers who had shown exceptional "military merit," but this medal was discontinued after that war's end and not reestablished until 1932 when General Douglas MacArthur revived it for soldiers wounded in combat, including those in World War I. The first official medal authorized for the United States military was the Medal of Honor, bestowed by an act of Congress during the Civil War.

June 1, 1821, he received an honorable discharge at Blakely, Alabama, a small army outpost across Mobile Bay from the city (ironically, the site of the last major battle of the Civil War, some forty-four years later). Obviously he had found something attractive about the place. Mobile was flourishing then, as both a seaport and a river port city, and with the same French-Spanish cultural heritage and architecture as New Orleans, but on a smaller scale.

Precisely when he met and married my great-great-great-grandmother Carolina Hollinger and when he began working his large plantation near the city is not known to me, though likely it can be found in Mobile's marriage and property record books. Nor do we know much else about his personal life. Had he fallen in love earlier? Fought duels? Started a business and lost it in those turbulent times? Elijah would have been about four years old when the famous surrender by Cornwallis to George Washington at Yorktown, Virginia, which ended the Revolutionary War, took place very near his family's home. Might he have witnessed it? At New Orleans, he met General Jackson and surely must have met Jean Laffite and his band of "pirates" as well; after all, he fought alongside them on a daily basis for several desperate weeks.

During his lifetime Elijah had crossed over from one century to the next, into an age of steamboats, railroads, and the telegraph, and saw his former commanding general elected president of the United States. From scraps of paper in the strongbox, it appears that Elijah in his later years was an esteemed citizen of Mobile, known universally as "Major Montgomery," who lived out the remaining ten years of his life amassing a fair fortune and leaving behind the wonderful legacy of two young daughters, one of whom, Carolina Montgomery, is the namesake for my own seven-year-old daughter, Carolina Montgomery Groom.

And what of all his property holdings, those 8,866 acres on the lovely Dog River? I know something about that, too. It was ever-divided among successive generations. Elijah's daughter Carolina Montgomery married Sterling Thrower and one of their sons, Fremont Thrower, my great-grandfather—the one who went off to fight in the Civil War—

inherited a small part of it, about 225 acres, which upon his return from the war he used as a hunting and fishing retreat. After his death in 1924, my grandparents built a home there on the banks of a creek off that lazy blackwater river, where I played as a little boy amid gardens of azaleas and camellias and mossy oaks and pines, and later as a young man hunted quail and fished the river's fertile waters. About half the remaining property was sold off in the 1950s and '60s, and the rest I myself inherited upon my father's death. Over the years I've donated it all as charitable gifts—to my father's college, to my old prep school, and to my own alma mater—all except for a few solitary acres, much of it marshland, which I keep for sentimental reasons. And upon which I still pay the taxes.

One more thing. I may have Elijah's sword from the Battle of New Orleans. It was the sword that always hung above my grandparents' fireplace in my earliest memories, and which now hangs above the fireplace in my own office; it was my great-grandfather's sword during his service in the Civil War cavalry—this much I know from my grandmother, who knew my great-grandfather Fremont well, since he lived until she herself was in her late thirties. When I inherited the sword in the 1990s, I took it to a dealer in antique arms to see what else could be learned about it.

"It's not from the Civil War period," he said authoritatively. "This sword was manufactured in the era of the War of 1812." Then he proceeded to explain why.

That was always puzzling until just lately when I got to thinking and began going through all the family papers. My great-grandfather Fremont left Springhill College in 1862 at the age of eighteen to join the 56th Alabama Cavalry Regiment, which, like all Southern cavalry, was expected to arm, equip, and mount itself, not relying on the Confederate government at Richmond. Might it not be too far a stretch to assume that the sword probably had been handed down to him from his own grandfather Elijah Montgomery—the same sword that Elijah had worn at the Battle of New Orleans in 1814—and that Great-grandfather Fremont took it along himself into the Confederate army? After all, the South didn't have many sword factories then, and a sword was just a sword in those days, wasn't it? At least it's interesting to think so.

And by the way, this was a *working sword*, not a fancy dress-up ornament for parades and balls. There's a dark, long-dried, brownish-red substance on the top crease of the sword that family tradition has long had it must have been the blood of some Yankee, hacked out in Civil War combat.

Might it not instead be the "blood of an Englishman" from fifty years earlier—"Fee, Fie, Foe, Fum"? It's sometimes said there were giants of men at that time, too. Which brings me back to the subject at hand.

Point Clear, Alabama
MARCH 11, 2005

Patriotic Fire

Prologue

History is strewn with stern and peculiar endings, and were it not for the tenacity of Andrew Jackson and his makeshift army, the whole American experience might have been different. The Battle of New Orleans was fought in a thunder of electric-like flashes, of swords, cannon blasts, and rifle fire that became almost Shakesperean in its final, epic crescendo. When the battle ended, the American civilian-soldiers from the Southland had held the field against a trained and experienced British army, a force conceded by everyone to be the best in the world: men who had arrived riding the crest of recent victories over Napoleon's fabled legions, men who had run over the feeble American militia and burned down the American capital at Washington—an enemy that had crossed the Atlantic with all the accumulated knowledge of its civilization to crush the upstart Americans.

This great force was defeated by men wearing rags, derided as "dirty-shirts," men without proper military training and weapons, scorned as scum of the earth, men who had no mirror to hold up against a future as they faced the Duke of Wellington's smartly attired red-coated veterans, who marched against them with the attitude of soldiers who owned the very ground they trod upon.

The American Founding Fathers, nearly forty years earlier, were never quite sure that democracy would work, especially during wartime, and the British were absolutely convinced that it wouldn't. In their country, the king still more or less called the tune and his subjects danced the dance (and paid the piper, too). Their very Englishness had instilled in them a heightened sense of the rightness and superiority of their own way, and had provoked their fear and hatred of outlandish notions such as "democracy" and "republics."

Into this mix entered Andrew Jackson, a backwoods country lawyer and politician who commanded the American forces. He was a man ripe for the task, despising the British with a hate that was almost ignoble, having been brutalized by them during the Revolutionary War and with most of his family having been killed by them in one way or another. If history ever beckoned a man into a crisis, it was during this confrontation.

That same moment propelled another man onto the stage, one reviled by some as a pirate, the Frenchman Jean Laffite, who had had his run-ins with the law. But in this case the "pirate" turned patriot and sent his fierce crews into the fray at precisely the right time, and with the very real danger of finding himself swinging from a British hangman's rope.

The outcome reverberated across the globe, and in the process rekindled the spirit of America for generations to come.

One

By late autumn 1814, the United States of America, a nation barely thirty years old, was shaky, divided, and on the verge of dissolving. The treasury was empty, most public buildings in Washington, including the Capitol, the White House, and the Library of Congress, had been burned to ashes by a victorious and vengeful British army. New England, the wealthiest and most populous section of the new country, was threatening to secede from the still fragile Union. After two years of war with Great Britain, it appeared to many Americans that their experiment in democracy—the likes of which the world had never seen—might only have been some strange, nonsustainable political trial and, worse, that a return to the unwelcome fraternal embrace of the English kings seemed inevitable.

American seaports from the Atlantic to the Gulf of Mexico were blockaded by the British navy and the economy was in ruins because of it, with goods and crops piled up and rotting on the wharves. The U.S. Army was stymied and stalemated; the navy, such as it was, had fared little better, except on the Great Lakes. There was finger-pointing, recrimination, and torment everywhere, from the Congress to the press to ordinary citizens; no one was spared.

Then, as autumn leaves began to fall, a mighty British armada appeared off the Louisiana coast with the stated purpose of capturing New Orleans, America's crown jewel of the West and gateway to all commerce in the great Mississippi River Basin, a misfortune that would have split the United States in two. New Orleans was as nearly defenseless as a city could be in those days, with only two understrength regular army regiments totaling about 1,100 soldiers and a handful of untrained milita to throw against the nearly 20,000 seasoned veterans of the British army and navy who were descending upon it as swiftly and surely as a tropical cyclone.

As word of the impending invasion reached decimated and burned-out Washington, President James Madison and Secretary of War James Monroe sent urgent pleas for the Western states to come to the aid of their stricken countrymen west of the Mississippi. Backwoodsmen from Tennessee and Kentucky were thus recruited into makeshift army units, but they were far off—as much as seven hundred miles by land and two thousand miles by water—and river transportation was mostly by slow river rafts and flatboats. It was doubtful they could get there in time. Orders from the secretary of war also went out to the legendary Indian fighter Andrew Jackson, then in nearby Mobile, Alabama, after having defeated the large tribe of Creeks who had just perpetrated the bloodiest massacre in American history. Would he go immediately to New Orleans and take charge?

Yes, of course—but of what? Jackson must have wondered. The British fleet contained more than a thousand heavy guns against the perhaps three dozen cannons New Orleans could muster, and what of powder and shot, or flints for muskets and rifles? Assuming that the British didn't overrun them outright, to Jackson's knowledge there was little or nothing in the way of equipment, munitions, or manpower in New Orleans for a sustained siege. There were more than 10,000 trained, first-rate British redcoats bearing down, plus the larger roster of the British navy's marines and sailors to support them—all this against fewer than a third that number of untrained and poorly armed Americans, even assuming the rubes from Tennessee and Kentucky did somehow arrive in time for the show. Jackson's task was daunting, to say the least.

This was arguably the gloomiest moment in American history before or since, it being almost universally believed that Britain, still smarting from defeat at the hands of the upstart colonies three decades earlier, now seemed determined to crush, humiliate, and retake her lost possession. And as Britain at that time was the wealthiest and most powerful nation on earth, there was little doubt among many Americans that the British could do it—considering what they had done so far—and not a few United States citizens prepared, however grimly, to return hat in hand to the iron fists of His Royal Britannic Majesty and life again under the British lion.

"I expect at this moment," declared Lord Castlereagh, the British foreign secretary, "that most of the large seaport towns of America are laid in ashes, that we are in possession of New Orleans, and have command of all the rivers of the Mississippi Valley and the lakes, and that the Americans are now little better than prisoners in their own country."

As it turned out, of course, this was not to be, but no one could have known or even expected it at the time. What they hoped for, but did not count on, was the courage and tenacity of a small band of American warriors, probably the most disparate and slapdash army ever assembled on earth. It consisted of Frenchmen, Spaniards, Germans, Irishmen—and their descendants—infantry battalions of freed black men, a handful of gunboat sailors, some displanted Acadians ("Cajuns") from Nova Scotia, a regiment of pirates and smugglers, a convent of Catholic nuns, companies of prominent New Orleans lawyers and merchants, stranded seamen of all nations, leftover adventurers and soldiers of fortune from the Revolutionary War era, numerous women of New Orleans from high society dames to prostitutes, the two small regiments of U.S. Army regulars, plus the aforesaid backwoodsmen from Tennessee and Kentucky—but what an army they became!

All of this in due time, but first let us focus on the broader picture of just what the fledgling American nation had become by that time, how its people lived, and what they thought of themselves.

By 1812 America had grown into a huge but unwieldy economic giant, shipping foodstuffs and raw materials throughout the world. In the more than two centuries since the first colonists settled at Jamestown, huts had been replaced by homes, some of them palatial, and roadways and riverways connected its great cities, which flourished at Philadelphia, Baltimore, New York, Boston, Charleston, and, of course, New Orleans—all of them busy harbor ports. A vast westward expansion had begun, carrying settlers into the fertile lands across the Alleghenies, in the process pushing the Indians out of western New York and Pennsylvania, Ohio, Indiana, Kentucky, and Tennessee, which were now becoming dotted with farms raising corn, grains, cotton, and other cash crops.

The U.S. population had doubled in the three decades since the end of the Revolutionary War, so that by 1812 there were some eight million Americans, many of them recent immigrants from Great Britain, Ireland, and Germany, with a smattering of French and Spanish, many of these last settling in New Orleans, Mobile, and Charleston—all adding to the simmering melting pot that was coming to define the United States.

By the standards of today, transportation and communications were rudimentary, and the sailing vessel remained the most efficient mode of travel. Railroads and steamboats had recently been invented but were not yet in any significant use in the United States. Thus, for instance, it took about a month to send a message by sea or on horseback from New Orleans to Washington City, as the nation's capital was then called, and another month to receive a reply. The telegraph was still two decades into the future, as were the reaping and threshing machines that took so much of the backbreaking work out of farming. However, Eli Whitney's cotton gin had opened up the Southern states to abundant cultivation of that fabulous crop, and with it the widespread introduction of slavery into the region.

In the large cities, gas lighting for homes and streets was just being introduced. Among the wealthier classes, most furnishings, fancy dress, and other high-end items were still imported from Europe and England; the less affluent used cheap local goods or made their own. Newspapers and broadsheets thrived as the principal means of information, and a number of magazines of opinion such as the *Niles Weekly Register* and *Debow's Review* were also widely circulated.

The cities had immediately become hotbeds of political activity, much to the disappointment (and even disgust) of George Washington, who had consistently warned against it. After the Revolution ended, Americans had quickly divided up into two "factions," or political parties, as they are now called, which reflected—as they do today—the same two natural divisions of liberal and conservative human philosophy that have dominated political thought ever since the days of ancient Greece and Rome.

The Federalist party, exemplified by the first U.S. treasury secretary, Alexander Hamilton, a transplanted New Yorker, arguably more closely resembled today's Democrats, advocating big government and federal involvement in regulating the economy, including government sponsorship of manufacturing, industry, and public works, as well as a national monetary system and a standing army—in short, more federal control—and, of course, higher taxes to support it all.

On the other hand, the Democratic Republican party, as it was known and defined by Thomas Jefferson and the other Southern presidents, wanted as little government as possible from Washington and, instead, preferred that the various states assume the brunt of governmental activities, including national defense, banking, and, of course, little or no taxation from authorities in Washington. (Plus, there was the ever vexing question of slavery, which Southern states were beginning to suspect was becoming target zero of the small but growing abolitionist movement in the North.)

To that end, members of both factions had conducted for years a relentless discourse in the nation's newspapers, treating the reading public to snide, confrontational, and often libelous "letters" published anonymously and signed with pen names usually taken from Greek and Roman classics. This practice sometimes led to duels in which either the offender or the offended was often dispatched to his reward.* In truth, Americans have always been such a fractious people that it remains something of a wonder democracy has survived at all.

* One of the most infamous of these being the 1804 confrontation between former U.S. treasury secretary Alexander Hamilton and Aaron Burr on the New Jersey Palisades, resulting in Hamilton being shot to death by the vice president of the United States.

Those citizens who tired of political controversy during the era could indulge in a wealth of literary works by the famous authors and artists of the day. The poems of Lord Byron, William Wordsworth, Samuel Taylor Coleridge, and Percy Bysshe Shelley found their way across the Atlantic and into American parlors and libraries. So did the novels of Jane Austen and Sir Walter Scott. If Americans wanted to read the literature of their own countrymen, Washington Irving was widely known—he was America's first internationally acclaimed author—and soon thereafter arose James Fenimore Cooper. For those who craved the visual arts and could make the transatlantic voyage, there were the latter-day European masters Francisco Goya and William Blake, or, if not, there were American artists and portrait painters such as Benjamin West, Charles Willson Peale, Gilbert Stuart, and John Singleton Copley.

Americans of the 1812 era ate pancakes, which had been around since the time of the ancient Egyptians, and mayonnaise was popular, but they ate no tomatoes, which were widely regarded as poisonous. There were, of course, no potato chips, Wheaties, hamburgers, or hot dogs, and much of the main-course table fare was still wild game: turkey, duck, deer, quail, and squirrel; there was domestic pork, chicken, mutton, beef, and seafood as well. They drank tea and coffee when they could get it and otherwise washed down their meals with wine, cider, or whisky.

Sudden death was an omnipresent reality, and medicine was in its primitive stages ("bleeding," for example, was still a widely accepted medical practice, as were blood-sucking leeches, and, as a sort of cure-all for many ailments, patients were commonly fed mercury, one of the most dangerous elements on earth for human ingestion). The average American life span in the early 1800s was forty years or so; frightful epidemics of typhoid and yellow fever ravaged the country every year, as did scourges of cholera, typhus, tuberculosis, diphtheria, influenza, smallpox, dysentery, measles, and uncontrollable staph infections—not to mention things like shipwrecks, horse throws and kicks, house fires, the sudden and unpredictable arrival of natural disasters such as hurricanes, and, of course, duels. If you ventured outside the cities there was always the chance of getting eaten up by bears or mountain lions or being scalped by Indians. All in all, America was a fairly dangerous place, and many if not most families lost a heartbreaking number of children before they had even reached their teens. Complications from pregnancy and childbirth were the leading cause of death for women of childbearing age.

Nontheless, by 1812 those eight million Americans—except for the dwindling population of Indians and the ever increasing number of slaves—had surrounded themselves with eight million pleasurable dreams of "life, liberty and the pursuit of happiness" in their brave new world. They believed that they were part of a land of progress and bounty unknown across the far reaches of the Atlantic Ocean. Since the end of the Revolution the U.S. merchant shipping fleet, like the population, had doubled in size, and American exports had tripled. Grain and corn from Pennsylvania, New York, New Jersey, and the newly opened lands to the west were transported across the North Atlantic to feed the peoples of Europe. Virginia, Maryland, Kentucky, and North Carolina provided Europe's nicotine-addicted with tobacco aplenty. The vast cotton plantations of the Deep South were churning out hundreds of thousands of bales of cotton to stoke the looms of the New England states, and those of Manchester, England, and the coastal millworks of France. (Always a bit oddball, New Orleans had become a major supplier of refined sugar from its great sugarcane plantations.) Beneath all this ebullience and prosperity, however, by the time 1812 rolled around America seethed.

The cause of its indignation was the flagrant and long-standing depredation and bullying by the British, who had not forgiven the upstart American colonists for defeating their army at Yorktown thirty years earlier and setting up their own sovereign nation. All this became exacerbated with the rise of Napoleon and the subsequent war between Britain and France. That decade-old conflict had drained Britain of manpower, and especially of trained seamen, so in order to make up the losses the British navy, acting on orders from London, began intercepting American merchant ships and searching their crews for

"British subjects," whom they then "impressed" into their navy. This immediately became a sore point with the Americans, since the British policy was that anyone who had been born in Great Britain was still a British subject and always would be, whether he was now an American or not.

Among those who chronicled one such outrage was the French-born American naturalist and artist John J. Audubon, who, on a return trip from France, encountered one of these impressment interceptions. "We were running before the wind under all sail, but the unknown gained on us at a great rate and after a while stood to the windward of our ship about half a mile off. She fired a gun, the ball passed within a few yards of our bows; our captain heeded not, but kept on his course, flying the American flag. Another and another shot was fired at us; the enemy closed upon us." When the captain hove to, the English ship sent over a boat containing two officers and a dozen armed sailors, who demanded all the captain's papers and then ransacked the ship.

"Every one of the papers proved to be in perfect accordance with the laws existing between England and America," wrote Audubon, but the English "robbed the ship of almost everything that was nice in the way of provisions, took our pigs, and sheep, coffee and wines and carried off our two best sailors."

True, some impressed seamen were deserters from the British navy, but most were legitimate American citizens, which led to fractious confrontations, the most outrageous of which was the so-called *Chesapeake* Affair in 1807. In this incident, the new captain of an American frigate-of-war, the *Chesapeake*, took the ship prematurely to sea before all her guns were installed and, just off the Virginia coast, was jumped by the British fifty-gun warship *Leopard*, out searching for crewmen. An unequal fight ensued in which some twenty of *Chesapeake*'s seamen were killed or wounded, and the British carried off four others—three Americans and one Briton—claiming they were deserters.

In this way, more than six thousand Americans found themselves suddenly impressed into British service, a development that did not sit well at all with the American people, and which no amount of U.S. diplomacy could seem to rectify.

Further, both the British and the French put a clamp on the Americans' right to trade with their enemies (meaning each other), and that drove a tremendous hole in America's burgeoning economy. U.S. merchant ships were seized wherever found and impounded in English or French ports and their cargoes confiscated. The United States might have gone to war with both Britain *and* France over this issue, but ultimately chose war with England because, after a series of victories over the French navy, England was by far the strongest maritime power and thus was causing most of the trouble. For their part, the Americans wanted nothing to do with the fighting that was going on in Europe, and the slogan "Free Trade and Sailors' Rights" was quickly taken up by newspaper editors and pamphleteers.

As America's anger festered, her citizens became even more incensed by the treatment they were receiving in the British press; their country and its president were constantly lampooned and belittled as second-rate and cowardly. The British view was that while they themselves were engaged in a war of survival against the greatest menace the world had known (Napoleon), the timid and greedy Americans—instead of joining with them in this noble cause—had chosen to remain neutral.

When all the jawboning diplomacy produced no effect, the Jefferson administration began pushing economic sanctions through Congress in the hope that England would come to her senses and start respecting American rights on the seaways. First, in 1806, was the so-called Non-Importation Act, which forbade importing British goods but, by necessity, included so many loopholes to keep American manufactories going that it did little good. Next came the far more damaging Embargo Act of 1807, which forbade imports and exports into or out of America to or from *any* nation at all. The problem was, most of the resulting damage was done not to the British but to the U.S. economy. In 1807 Americans exported some $108 million worth of goods (more than $1 trillion in today's dollars); within a year that figure had sagged by 75 percent and the nation sank into a severe economic depression. Britain quickly found other export markets in South America. One political critic compared Jefferson's laws with "trying to cure corns by cutting off the toes." These two measures would still rank near the very top of "stupid and shortsighted legislation" were such an analytic list ever kept. Clearly something else had to be done.

In the meantime, out in what was referred to then as the West— Indiana, Ohio, Illinois, Michigan—the British, from their strongholds in Canada, were stirring up the Indians to prey on American settlers. This produced, of course, no idle fear; many remembered all too well the ravaging of British-backed Indian tribes during the Revolution. For instance, a letter from a British officer to Canada's governor-general had been widely circulated in the press, in which the Englishman informed his boss that "at the request of the Seneca Chiefs I send herewith to your excellency under the care of James Boyd, eight packs of scalps cured, dried, hooped and painted with all the Indian triumphal marks."

He then went on to inventory this grisly gift: Box no. 1 contained "43 scalps of congress soldiers killed in different skirmishes . . . also 62 farmers killed in their houses, the hoops red, the skin painted brown and marked with a black hoe, a black circle all around to denote their being surprised in the night and a black hatchet in the middle to denote their being killed with that weapon."

The other boxes held even more ghoulish relics: "93 farmers killed in their houses. White circles and suns shew they were killed in the daytime; 97 farmers, hoops green to show working in fields . . . 102 farmers, 18 marked with yellow flame to shew that they were burned alive . . . 81 women, long hair, those braided to shew they were mothers . . . 193 boys scalps various ages . . . 211 girls scalps, big and little, small yellow hoops marked hatchet, club, knife, etc. . . . Mixture 122 with box of birch bark containing 29 infant scalps small white hoops. Only little black knife in middle to shew they were ripped out of mother's body."

It is not recorded how the British governor-general received this macabre present, but publication of the accompanying cover letter, whether it was authentic or not, had the effect of galvanizing both terror and disgust among Americans who learned of it, and the notion that the British were back at it again incited grave indignation.

As if that weren't enough, a charismatic forty-three-year-old Shawnee Indian chief named Tecumseh went on a warpath of his own, which threatened dire consequences for Americans all over the southern and western states and territories.

After having suffered the death of his father at the hands of Americans when he was six years old, Tecumseh (or "Shooting Star," as the name has been translated) developed a blinding hatred for the white race, which, when he grew older, turned into rage as settlers pushed deeper into his homeland of Indiana, Ohio, and other nearby states. It was recounted by a friend that Tecumseh said he "could not look upon the face of a white man without feeling the flesh crawl on my bones." As he grew into adulthood, Tecumseh became a natural leader with a dignified bearing that even white men remarked on. Tall, handsome, intelligent, and brave, Tecumseh was remembered by a British officer this way: "In his appearance and nobel bearing one of the finest-looking men I have ever seen."

The only atmosphere that the myriad of American Indian tribes had known in their history was eternal war—mostly with each other but recently, of course, with the settlers, too; and with the relentless American push westward, Tecumseh concluded that unless this expansion were stopped, the Indians would soon become extinct in a world dominated by whites. Thus he embarked on a stupendous undertaking: he would visit all the major tribes in what is today the Midwest and the South and persuade them to join a vast, warlike "Indian Confederation," extending from the Great Lakes to the Gulf of Mexico, backed and supplied by the British, to bring the Americans' westward movement to an abrupt halt.

In the late summer of 1811, with about two dozen of his braves, Tecumseh set out in canoes from his village on the Tippecanoe River in

Indiana and traveled down the Mississippi to convert the southern tribes: the great Choctaw, Chickasaw, Creek, and Seminole nations.* Tecumseh's party had painted its war clubs red, for which they were soon given the sobriquet "Red Sticks," but their first encounters were something less than successful. The Choctaws under Chief Pushmataha were unreceptive, the Chickasaws less so, but with the Creeks of Alabama Tecumseh struck a chord.

As an entranced audience of Creeks listened earnestly by their campfires, Tecumseh urged them to join with all the other tribes and drive the white man out; to kill his hogs and cattle and burn his crops and houses; to throw away their own looms and plows, abandon their livestock, and rejoin the Indian traditions of their ancestors; to kill the white man and his wives and children and even to "kill the old chiefs, friends of peace!" He told them that after the whites had cut down all the trees to make farms and stained the rivers with silt, they would then force the Indians into slavery as they had the Africans. Before he left the Creeks, Tecumseh issued a warning to those who were unconvinced that his voice had come directly through the Great Spirit in the Sky. "When I return to Tippecanoe," he is reported to have said, "I will stamp my foot, and the earth will tremble!"

For those disbelievers among the Creeks, their epiphany arrived less than a month later when, on December 16, 1811, the New Madrid fault near Cape Girardeau, Missouri, lurched apart in an earthquake so tremendous that it was said to have changed the course of the Mississippi River and caused it to flow backward for a while. It was the most severe quake America has ever experienced, and its terrible tremors were felt as far away as the Creek Nation's encampments on Alabama's Tallapoosa River, north of Montgomery.

Not all Creeks had been able to agree on Tecumseh's proposals, but among the audience the night Tecumseh spoke was young William

---

* These were known as the so-called civilized tribes for their gradual adoption of the white man's ways—farming; raising cattle, hogs, and sheep; and keeping slaves. Many had taken to living in houses instead of teepees, and their women sometimes fraternized or intermarried with whites.

Weatherford—a "half-breed" who went by the name of Chief Red Eagle—the son of a Scottish-American Alabama trader and a one-quarter-Indian mother. He was impressed (though not completely convinced) by the notion of Tecumseh's great Indian confederation, but the impression stuck, especially after the prophetic earthquake of 1811. In the not too distant future Weatherford's actions would have a distinct bearing on the Battle of New Orleans.

Two

During his terms in office (1801–1809), President Thomas Jefferson and his Democratic Republican majority in Congress had allowed the U.S. armed forces to deteriorate almost into oblivion. True to his pacific nature, Jefferson—along with most of his fellow party members—wished to avoid a large standing peacetime army, which, in addition to being an unnecessary government expense, they saw as a possible threat to the new republic itself. Therefore, the U.S. Army was cut by nearly one-third, to only 3,300 men, and, according to General Winfield Scott, later of Mexican War fame, was officered by "imbeciles and ignoramuses."

The U.S. Navy was likewise neglected, due not only to concern over expenses but to Democratic Republican suspicions in those days that a large navy, roaming the world, would somehow always find a way to get a nation into war. Despite Jefferson's temporary strengthening of the navy during his first term to fight the Barbary pirates in the Mediterranean, by the end of the decade the American sea arm consisted of only seven small frigates, a few sloops of war, and no ships of the line (which would correspond to modern-day battleships or aircraft carriers).

Proponents of these stingy military policies, Jefferson foremost among them, argued that in times of crisis America was better off relying on its citizen soldiers, that is, militias from the various states. So far as sea power was concerned, it was maintained by the largely Southern majority in Congress that Great Britain, with the world's most powerful fleet, could simply overwhelm anything the United States might send against it and thus the expense of a large navy would be wasted. The theory went instead that so-called privateers—armed ships privately owned but operating under government sponsorship—would serve in place of a regular navy. Not everyone was happy with this; John Adams later wrote Jefferson that he wished more frigates had been built. "Without this our Union will be a brittle china vase," he said.

That's how things stood in 1809 when Jefferson's Virginia colleague and fellow pacifist James Madison became the fourth U.S. president, but now war clouds were gathering as England continued its humiliating depredations at sea (some eight hundred American merchant vessels had been seized over five years) as well as agitating the western Indian tribes to strike against American settlers. By 1812 Tecumseh and his followers had scalped and tomahawked so many citizens in the Indiana Territory that Governor William Henry Harrison wrote the secretary of war that most of the people had fled their farms for collective safety in various forts and blockhouses.

Nothing seemed to be working in Madison's diplomacy. It didn't help matters when the prince regent, after assuming the responsibilities of his father, the now-gone-mad King George III, appointed as Britain's minister to the United States a rabid, America-hating thirty-one-year-old junior diplomat named Augustus John Foster. In letters home to his mother (published more than eighty years afterward), Foster complained that "corruption, immorality and self-interest" on the part of most Americans had "corroded" the democracy he loathed, and then went on to evaluate American women as "spying, inquisitive, vulgar and ignorant." Not surprisingly, Foster's arrival in Washington would not bode well for amicable diplomatic relations between the two countries.

By 1812 the ruinous embargo had been lifted, and the Non-Importation Act repealed, but the seizings and searchings by British men-of-war went unabated and the Indian horrors continued. Congress, still dominated by the party of Jefferson and Madison, was now beginning to clamor for war against England. Party-affiliated newspapers and pamphlets were pushing for a showdown: American honor is at stake . . . The United States would never gain the respect of other nations by allowing itself to be humiliated by the British . . . Interruption of oceanic trade is ruining the economy . . . British ships are kidnapping American citizens . . . British-incited Indians are scalping helpless women and children. And so on.

Also by now Congress was led by a group headed by the redoubtable Henry Clay of Kentucky. These were the "war hawks," who had an agenda of their own. They argued that because Britain was presently entangled on the European continent in the great war against Napoleonic France, she would be unable to send significant numbers of soldiers and ships to fight in America three thousand miles away. As the rationale went, the only troops the British were likely to employ would be those from her Canadian colony, which in turn would give the United States a perfect excuse to drive the British out of that vast territory and perhaps even to annex it to the new republic. Thus the war hawks were able to persuade Congress to authorize the recruitment of a standing army of 35,000 regulars plus a call for 50,000 volunteers, as well as the federalizing of 100,000 state militia.

This was a tremendous force on paper but a tall order in reality, since the American army at that time had barely been able to recruit 5,000 officers and men despite a bounty for enlistment of $31. Also in the months leading up to the declaration of war Congress authorized some $3 million for equipment, ordnance, and the building of fortifications to protect cities on the Atlantic and Gulf coasts.*

When all these well-publicized measures failed to yield any concessions from the British Parliament, Congress produced a war bill that passed 79–49 in the House and 19–13 in the Senate—"the closest vote on any declaration of war in American history," the historian Donald R. Hickey points out—which was signed into law by President Madison the following day, June 18. The panorama of what would become the War of 1812 had rolled forward on a tide of dark, irresistable forces: pride, greed, resentment, hauteur, insult, revenge, and some intangible notion that the Americans should be rid of the British once and for all.

---

* In fact, some fortification was begun on the Atlantic Coast, but the Gulf Coast was practically ignored.

Yet now all the follies of the past three decades of isolationism, laxity, and unpreparedness would come home to roost.

At first the news of war with their old archenemy was greeted with enthusiasm by many Americans, but this did not last long. When the immensity of the undertaking began to sink in, a great many people started having second thoughts, which led to much domestic trouble. Especially distressed were the New England states, predominantly Federalist in their politics (and even pro-British, according to some), whose great seafaring trade would be seriously restricted (given that America had no navy to speak of) if not completely curtailed by a British blockade. Farmers began to realize that the crops—cotton, tobacco, sugar, grains, and wheat—they counted on for cash by selling them overseas would probably soon rot in barns or on wharves; men subject to the militia call worried that they would be snatched from their peaceful farms or jobs to fight seasoned British redcoats; even well-to-do women began to comprehend that the latest fashions from London or Paris would no longer be arriving. It was in this atmosphere that the malignancy of war was again perceived to be visited upon the American homeland.

Federalist newspapers quickly decried the declaration of war as a dangerous and unnecessary measure—"President Madison's War," it was called—that had put the country's future in jeopardy by inviting battle with the most powerful nation on earth. All over New England, state legislatures condemned the declaration as hazardous folly for a country so unprepared as the fledgling United States. As the conversation heated, the cry of *treason!* rang out from both sides, and people were beaten and tarred and feathered; naturally, in some instances duels were fought. In Baltimore, then the country's third-largest city, ferocious riots erupted when a mob of Democratic Republicans attacked a local Federalist paper. Shots were fired, people killed, homes and businesses burned. Violence swept the city amid looting and talk of hangings.

Into that fray stepped old Henry "Light-Horse Harry" Lee—father of future Confederate commander Robert E. Lee—who had fallen on hard times since his exemplary service in the Revolutionary War and was in Baltimore trying to peddle his memoirs to raise cash. At the outbreak of violence the aristocratic Lee offered his service as mediator and was in return stoned by a mob, suffering severe injuries from which he later died. All in all, the War of 1812 had not gotten off on a good footing.

Nor did things go any better on the military front. By midsummer of 1812 the United States had organized three major army expeditions against Canada, hoping to drive the British out of that country for good. The operations were conducted at points running from just below the Canadian border along the line of the St. Lawrence River near Montreal, westward to Niagara on Lake Ontario, and thence farther west to Detroit on Lake Erie. All failed miserably.

The Detroit fiasco was conducted by Michigan governor William Hull, a fifty-nine-year-old relic of the Revolutionary War, who led some 2,000 U.S. Army regulars in an attempt to occupy Fort Detroit, in Canada, and force the retreat of British forces in the region. After numerous mishaps—including a savage attack by Tecumseh's Indians—Hull reached Fort Detroit, but, after an abortive foray a few miles farther north, there he remained, horrified by a fraudulent document the British commander had let fall into his hands. This ruse claimed that a great swarm of uncontrollable, hostile Indians was descending upon him, setting visions of a horrible massacre dancing in the American commander's head.

Then a British army—not nearly as strong as Hull's—arrived and laid siege to Fort Detroit, occasionally lobbing an artillery shell at it. As the weeks passed Hull succumbed to increasing attacks of anxiety and worried publicly about the fate of a number of settlers' families who also occupied the fort. It was said that he could frequently be seen skulking between the buildings, his mouth stuffed with large twists of chewing tobacco, brown spittle staining his clothes and beard. In any event, on August 16, still fearful of an Indian massacre and without a word to anybody, the wretched Hull suddenly surrendered the fort and his whole army along with it. British officials paroled him* a few weeks later, but when Hull returned to the United States he was arrested, tried by court-martial, convicted of cowardice and neglect of duty, and sentenced to death.† Thus ended Operation Detroit.

Next was the operation against Niagara, designed to drive the British from the southern end of Lake Ontario. In the autumn of 1812 a force of 6,000 Americans led by an inexperienced political appointee, forty-eight-year-old militia general Stephen Van Rensselaer, encountered an army of British redcoats and Indians about one-third its strength on the opposite bank of the Niagara River. Van Rensselaer's plan for an amphibious operation to cross the river and attack them was foiled when for some reason an American officer vanished downriver toward the falls in a boat carrying all the oars for the expedition, and was not heard from again. (Theories yet abound as to whether this officer was a traitor or somehow got swept up in the current and went over the falls.) On October 13, however, a second try was successful, and some 1,000 American soldiers landed on the British side of the river, driving back the redcoats and Indians and in the process killing their commander, the very talented English general Isaac Brock.

Here was a perfect opportunity for Van Rensselaer to seize the initiative, to bring his entire force into Canada and drive the British armies back on themselves, but it was not to be. The army Van Rensselaer commanded was made up in large part not of regulars but of militia who became fainthearted when they saw the dead and wounded soldiers being returned in boats from the site of the battle. With no apparent shame, they piously invoked a clause in their original enlistment contracts with their various states, claiming that as militia they were not authorized to fight outside U.S. territory. Thus the campaign failed

---

* Parole was a custom of the era whereby opposing armies swapped captured prisoners man for man on the theory that it was less expensive than having to guard, house, feed, and care for them. Parolees were required to take an oath not to fight again, but many did, especially officers. The practice largely fell into disuse following the Civil War.

† Because of his age and his service during the Revolution, Hull had his sentence commuted by President Madison, and he was sent on his way in shame.

entirely, and the remainder of the American soldiers who had at least clawed their way to the British side of the river were captured.

Van Rensselaer resigned and his command was given over to General Alexander Smyth, who did no better, and probably worse. Instead of attacking immediately, he cravenly took a vote of his officers on the question of assaulting the British-held Fort Erie just to the south; when they demurred, Smyth canceled operations and slunk back to his native Virginia (taking "back roads," according to one historian), where he was cashiered from the army. So concluded Operation Niagara.

Next came the assault against Montreal, which was planned as the prize pearl of U.S. military strategy. To lead this vital mission the secretary of war resurrected yet another Revolutionary War retread, Henry Dearborn, who himself had been secretary of war in the Jefferson administration. Old and fat at sixty-one, Dearborn was also agonizingly slow. He dithered away the summer fooling with coastal forts in New England and complaining to Washington that he couldn't find enough troops for the invasion. Finally, in November, just before the Canadian winter set in, the War Department found it necessary to *order* the newly promoted major general to march his army north and strike at Montreal. With about 8,000 troops, Dearborn moved from Albany up to the shores of Lake Champlain and thence into Canada, where his army—or at least part of it, the militia again refusing to leave American soil—engaged in a desultory and unsatisfactory nighttime fight with a British force about half its size. After this puny effort Dearborn marched them back south again, his mission a failure and a disgrace. Ironically, Dearborn later sat on the court-martial board that sentenced the unfortunate General Hull to death for the Detroit fiasco.

The Federalist press naturally had a field day with all this bad news, especially in populous New England, where antiwar sentiments ran high and a movement was already afoot to end the fighting. Gloomy expressions were thrown about in the press: "degrading," "dismal perfidy," "ruin and death," "abysmal misfortunes," and the like—perhaps somewhat extreme, but in truth much of the criticism stuck. Results of the 1812 campaign along the Canadian border running from New York to

Michigan had left the Americans with nothing to show but a cataract of inglorious defeats that rendered the British stronger than ever, not only still holding Canada but comfortably ensconced on United States soil. With that disgraceful situation to contemplate, the U.S. Army retired to winter quarters, praying for better fortunes in the spring of 1813.

The American campaign of 1813 opened along the lines of the previous year, with attacks again planned along the Canadian border, except this time they were designed more to drive the British back into Canada than to actually conquer Canada itself, as had originally been intended.

Over the winter Madison replaced his incompetent secretary of war, William Eustis, with an even worse choice, New Yorker John Armstrong, a political waffler and intriguer who, during the Revolution, had conspired to oust George Washington and incite mutiny among the Continental Army by secretly authoring an infamous correspondence known as the Newburgh Letters. Armstrong liked no one in the present administration (including Madison), and no one liked him either. About the only thing that might be said in his favor was that, unlike his predecessor, who was a mere politician, Armstrong at least had some genuine military service under his belt. But as the months moved on it became apparent to almost everyone that John Armstrong had been a perfectly awful choice for the job.

By the time the ice thawed in the early spring of 1813, Tecumseh had persuaded British colonel Henry Procter, who had replaced the slain Brock, to attack a newly built American fortification near the western end of Lake Erie, south of Detroit near the Michigan border. Known as Fort Meigs (named after the then Ohio governor with the unusual name of Return J. Meigs), this edifice was defended by only 600 men under the command of General William Henry Harrison of Indiana, who had been fighting Tecumseh and his people for years, and who had recently been appointed to command the Western army after Hull's debacle at Detroit.

The British laid siege to Fort Meigs on May 1, but so strongly was it built that little damage was done and even the flaming arrows shot by

Indians did not affect it. Four days later a relief force of 1,200 ardent Kentuckians arrived and soon attacked Procter's army. In their "ardor," however, the Kentuckians got themselves cut up in a wild melee, and many of those captured were massacred by the Indians, who, not understanding the principles of siege warfare (or, for that matter, the European rules of military conduct), soon afterward disappeared into the forest with their collection of scalps and booty.* Not only that, but to illustrate that militia problems were not confined to the American army, the Canadian militia—comprising nearly half of Procter's force—declared that it was planting time back home and returned to their farms. Procter then gave up and marched his men back north with some 600 Kentuckians as prisoners, leaving behind another 450 dead and wounded (not counting Indians), including about 100 of his own men.

Two months later Procter returned with a larger army consisting of 5,000 regulars, Canadian militia, and a large body of Indians, and on August 2 attacked Fort Stephenson, about thirty miles east of Fort Meigs. Here, however, he suffered a shocking reversal of fortune at the hands of the vengeful Kentuckians, who, in addition to blasting them with cannon fire, mowed down the British and Indians with their long rifles "like wheat in a hailstorm." Complaining that this was "the severest fire I ever saw," Procter called it quits and once again marched back north. Finally, things seemed to be looking up on the Northwest front.

A month later, his army now grown to 5,500 men with the arrival of another large contingent of Kentucky volunteers, Harrison determined not only to chase the bothersome Procter out of U.S. territory but, if possible, to destroy him. This he did on October 5, when he finally caught up with the British at Moraviantown, Canada, about five days' march northeast of Detroit. Procter had formed up his lines between the Thames River and a swamp where he was determined to make a stand, counting on the discipline and massed firepower of his trained regulars and the ferocity of Tecumseh's Indian tribes.

---

* In addition to the Shawnee of Tecumseh's tribe, the combined Indian force included Ottawas, Wyandots, Chippewas, Potawatomis, Kickapoos, Winnebagos, and Iroquois.

This proved to be a mistake, because the Americans mounted a surprise cavalry charge (with militia from Kentucky, made of sterner stuff than other U.S. militia) that broke Procter's lines in less than five minutes and put the British in a deadly crossfire. Concluding that the battle was lost, those redcoats who could—including Procter*—fled down the road toward Moraviantown. This left Harrison's army with only Tecumseh's Indians to subdue, since they did not fight in lines like infantrymen but (more effectively) from behind bushes and shrubs on the edges of the forest. The mounted Kentuckians quickly plunged into these thickets, and fierce hand-to-hand fighting broke out, with Indian tomahawks against Kentucky hatchets.

During the melee the courageous Tecumseh was shot through the heart and killed, and his body later mutilated by soldiers bent on revenge, so they said, for Indian depredations going back two centuries or more. Accordingly, Tecumseh was skinned and pieces of his preserved hide were parceled out to the Kentucky troops, who took them home as relics for the edification of friends, sweethearts, wives, and children. With the death of this most charismatic of American Indians also died his dream of a great Indian Confederation—almost, that is, except for one final act in that drama, which was soon to be played out a thousand miles away in Alabama and would set the stage for the spectacular conclusion to the War of 1812.

If the war in the West finally seemed to be going well, back east it was only more of the same. To replace the hapless Dearborn, Secretary of War Armstrong had chosen a commander with even worse credentials and certainly fewer scruples. He was General James Wilkinson, whom the ever pithy Winfield Scott described as an "unprincipled imbecile"; his assignment, handed down by Amstrong's War Department, would be yet another attempt to take Montreal.

Wilkinson's very presence on the Canadian border belied his well-deserved reputation as a conniver and an incompetent. He had previously been commander of the Seventh Military District, headquartered

---

* Procter was later convicted by court-martial for bad conduct during the battle.

at New Orleans, which encompassed the Louisiana, Mississippi, and Alabama territories, as well as Tennessee and Arkansas. So inept and loathed was he that his own Louisiana troops refused to serve under him. Yet Armstrong's idiotic solution to this thorny problem was to send Wilkinson north and put him in charge of the most difficult and important campaign of the war.

Not only was Wilkinson incompetent; it later turned out that he also had been a spy and traitor on the payroll of Spain, selling whatever secrets the United States had vis-à-vis that shaky Mediterranean kingdom. Furthermore, Wilkinson had been mixed up in the treasonous scheme by Aaron Burr, the former U.S. vice president then in disgrace for the duel that resulted in Alexander Hamilton's death, in which Burr sought to detach the lower Mississippi Valley from the Union, kick the Spaniards out of Mexico, and form a new nation with himself as king, emperor, president, or what have you. Amid all these strange machinations, as historian Marquis James has pointed out, "for some time [Wilkinson] had been confronted with the necessity of deciding whom he could most profitably betray—the United States, Spain, or Aaron Burr." In the end Wilkinson betrayed Burr, but not before waiting two weeks to do it so that he could extort $100,000 from the Spanish for revealing this supposedly valuable information. (In 1808 Wilkinson was court-martialed for his role in the affair but acquitted.) In any event, he was the man Armstrong put in charge of the new Montreal operation.

It started out badly, in part because Wilkinson didn't want to attack in the first place. The operation was designed as a two-pronged affair, with his 7,500 men moving on Montreal from the west down the St. Lawrence River and another force, under General Wade Hampton (grandfather of Wade Hampton III, one of Robert E. Lee's Civil War cavalry commanders), attacking from the south with an army of 4,500. Hampton went first, but no sooner had he crossed the border than he ran into a much smaller British force of Canadian militia, which should have been an easy obstacle to overcome. Yet when the Canadians commenced a great howling, firing, and blowing of horns, Hampton was fooled into thinking they were much superior to him in numbers and, after some minor skirmishing, he returned to the American side of the river, set his army into winter quarters, and refused to obey any further orders from Wilkinson, whom he found contemptible. For his part, Wilkinson ran into a British beehive just as he crossed into Canada. At Chrysler's Farm another inferior British force drove Wilkinson's army back into the United States, after inflicting casualties at a ratio of three to one. By this point, apparently due to illness, Wilkinson had become addicted to the then popular drug laudanum (an opiate) and had taken to babbling incoherently and singing to himself all the time, according to one of his generals.

By the following spring, after a wretched term in winter quarters during which many soldiers froze to death or died of disease, Wilkinson had pulled himself together enough for another go at it, though without the services of Hampton, who still refused to have anything to do with him. This time Wilkinson took 4,000 of his men toward Montreal, but as soon as they had cleared Lake Champlain and crossed over into Canada they encountered a small, squat blockhouse with fewer than 200 British soldiers inside. Wilkinson besieged it, but when the small cannons he brought up failed to dent the little fort's stone walls, he reversed tracks and marched his army back to the United States, where he was relieved of command, this time for good.

There was, however, one military front upon which the United States *had* achieved success thus far in the war. This was at sea, which is almost astonishing since the British navy could count on one thousand ships in its war fleet while the pitiful American navy could muster only seven frigates, a handful of sloops of war, and a few gunboats. The problem for the British was that most of their navy was tied up fighting Napoleon's ships, blockading the French coast, or attacking French-held colonies in the Caribbean. Even so, the British navy had a force in North American waters more than twice the size of the U.S. fleet. It is all the more remarkable that this inferior collection of American naval ships not only battled the great British navy to a standstill but, in doing so, their heroics produced a number of historically celebrated slogans and mottoes, such as "Don't give up the ship," which even today easily roll off the tongues of Americans.

In the closing months of the previous year, the few American frigates gave a very good account of themselves against the British navy. Frigates, though not nearly as large as ships of the line, were nevertheless formidible warships. Fairly typical of an American frigate of the day was the *Constitution*, a 204-foot-long, oak-sided three-master built in 1798. She could do more than thirteen knots (about fifteen miles per hour) under a full acre of sail, and at that rate travel about 350 miles in a twenty-four-hour period, providing the winds were perfect (which they usually weren't). The *Constitution* carried a crew of 450, including 50 marines and 30 "cabin boys," some as young as nine, who fought too.

In battle, the marines manned the "fighting tops"—wooden shooting platforms at various levels up the masts—from where they could bring a murderous rifle fire down on an enemy in close quarters. *Constitution* was armed with thirty-two twenty-four-pounder long guns with an effective range of twelve hundred yards, nearly three-quarters of a mile (most cannon in those days were identified by the weight of their projectile), twenty thirty-two-pounder short guns (with a range of four hundred yards), and two twenty-four-pounder "bow chasers" with a range of a thousand yards. She was not equipped with stern guns, on the assumption that she was there to fight, not to run.

On August 19, 1812, the *Constitution* encountered the British frigate HMS *Guerrière* two days out of Boston, and a sea fight ensued. Captained by Isaac Hull (nephew of the odious army general William Hull), *Constitution* opened fire first with a double-shotted broadside that seemed to cause *Guerrière* to leap out of the water. Within thirty minutes the British ship was dismasted, her hull torn to pieces, and many of her crew dead or dying. Being without masts from which to strike her colors, she fired a gun to leeward (recognized as a sign of maritime surrender), and, after removing the remainder of her crew, the sailors aboard *Constitution* watched *Guerrière* slip slowly beneath the waves.

So sturdy was the oak from which *Constitution* was planked that at one point during the battle a sailor watched a solid shot literally bounce off the ship, and exclaimed, "Her sides are made of iron!" The name stuck, and not long afterward *Constitution,* now nicknamed "Old Ironsides," chased down another British frigate, *Java,* and gave her the same treatment.*

Then, on the morning of October 12, the American frigate *United States* was spotted in the mid-Atlantic by the British frigate *Macedonian,* which immediately moved in for a fight. The *United States*—captained by Stephen Decatur, one of America's foremost naval heroes—obliged. What the captain of *Macedonian* didn't realize was that he was outgunned by the *United States* (fifty-four guns to forty-nine) and that the Americans were expert gunners, a fact he quickly learned, to his regret. Decatur luffed into the wind to slow the ship and unleashed a series of broadsides that cut away *Macedonian's* rigging and much of her mastage.

More than a hundred solid shots penetrated the Britisher's hull and more than a hundred sailors were killed or wounded—nearly a third of her crew. *Macedonian* struck her colors barely an hour and a half after the fight had begun and was taken as an American prize. A year and a half later, while conducting treaty negotiations, Decatur authored one of the aforementioned famous slogans that have found their way into the American lexicon: "My country, right or wrong."[†]

War at sea was not always so successful for the Americans, though. On the first day of June 1813, Captain John Lawrence was in Boston Harbor trying to refit and reman the *Chesapeake,* the same ill-fated American frigate that had been attacked by the British off the Virginia coast some six years earlier in an attempt to impress crewmen, an incident that contributed significantly to the outbreak of war.

Outside the harbor cruised *Shannon,* a thirty-eight-gun frigate; spying

* The USS *Constitution,* Old Ironsides, is on permanent display in Boston Harbor as a popular tourist attraction of the U.S. Navy.

[†] Ever since his notable service in the Tripolitan Wars (beginning in 1801) Decatur had become one of America's best-known naval heroes. In 1820, at the age of forty-one, he was killed in a duel with one of his fellow officers. His home, the Decatur House—now a museum—stands on Lafayette Square in Washington, D.C., across the street from the White House.

Chesapeake's masts, she sent ashore a boat carrying a challenge to battle. Lawrence was at a definite disadvantage, since his crew was almost entirely without experience and included a large number of Portuguese of dubious commitment who spoke no English. Nevertheless, he ordered them to make sail and man the guns.

Just before six p.m. the two ships closed for battle. They were about evenly matched in armament, but the British ship had a far better trained crew. The cannon fire that tore into both vessels produced frightful effects. Theodore Roosevelt, an admired naval historian, described the action this way: "*Chesapeake*'s broadsides were doing great damage, but she herself was suffering even more than her foe; the men in the *Shannon*'s tops could hardly see the deck of the American frigate through the cloud of splinters, hammocks, and other wreck that was flying across it, [but] man after man was killed at the wheel; the fourth lieutenant, the master, and the boatswain were slain."

After only fifteen minutes the two ships were so close that *Shannon*'s captain ordered grappling hooks thrown across and told his crew to prepare for boarding. At this unpleasant prospect, many of *Chesapeake*'s green sailors "became disheartened" and ran belowdecks. As this was happening, Captain Lawrence, who had made himself conspicuous by standing on the quarterdeck in full-dress uniform, was fatally shot by one of the British marines in *Shannon*'s fighting tops. Lawrence fell to the deck crying, "Don't give up the ship!"—another of the memorable exclamations from the War of 1812 that soon found a permanent home in the language.

The fighting from then on was at close quarters and extremely savage—*Chesapeake*'s chaplain had his arm nearly severed by a blow from "a broad Toledo blade" wielded by *Shannon*'s captain—but soon it was over and the British victorious. One hundred and forty-eight Americans had been killed or wounded, and the *Chesapeake* was claimed as a British prize and taken to Nova Scotia.

Nevertheless, the Americans by this point were not just holding their own against the British in naval actions, they were actually ahead. Yet the strong presence of the British navy on the Great Lakes continued to hamper American operations on the Northern frontier, since the most efficient way to move men, ordnance, and matériel was by water, which the British could do with impunity, while the Americans could not. It was thus determined by the War Department to attempt to rectify the situation.

To that end, a twenty-seven-year-old naval officer, Captain Oliver Hazard Perry,* was ordered in mid-1813 to the shores of Lake Erie, where five American warships were in the process of being built: two twenty-gun brigantines and three smaller two-gun schooners.[†] Perry immediately conducted a surprise raid on a British-held harbor at the westward end of the lake, which contained two of His Majesty's brigantines, and he captured both; although one ran aground and had to be destroyed, the other was joined to the growing American fleet. Perry also was able to purchase several merchant craft, which he armed and manned for warfare, bringing his squadron to a total of nine ships of one description or another. Then, on September 10, 1813, Perry sallied out of Presque Isle (now the harbor of Erie, Pennsylvania) in hopes of doing battle with the six warships of the British Lake Erie fleet.

His hopes were quickly fulfilled, though not without some trepidations. Like Lawrence on the *Chesapeake,* Perry suffered from a critical lack of trained seamen. Fortunately, the army commander in the area, General William Henry Harrison,[‡] scoured the ranks of his soldiers for experienced seamen, cannoneers, and marksmen and sent them to Perry with the foresight that if Perry and his navy could rid Lake Erie of the British, then his (Harrison's) own job would be that much easier.

Under sail since dawn, Perry finally spied the British squadron on the western end of the lake just before noon, and the two adversaries began

* Perry's brother, Commodore Matthew C. Perry, was commander of the U.S. fleet that sailed into Tokyo Bay in 1853 and "opened" primitive Japan to Western trade, leading, inadvertently, to the subsequent modernization of Japan and her consequent militarism, which culminated in World War II.

[†] The big frigates, which drew seventeen to eighteen feet of water, could not operate in the shallowness of the Great Lakes.

[‡] Harrison would be elected the ninth president of the United States in 1840, but he died after only one month in office.

to close. Perry had the wind to his back, giving him a tactical advantage, and, as well, he could throw nearly a third more metal. The battle was fierce and ardent, but after two hours Perry's flagship, *Lawrence,* had suffered some 80 percent casualties out of a crew of 136 and was turning into a wreck. Instead of striking colors, however, Perry had himself rowed over to the brig *Niagara,* where he continued the fight. Soon the heavier American firepower began to tell. By three p.m., four of the British ships struck colors, their commanders either killed or wounded, and two others that tried to escape were seized and captured. According to historian Hickey, "When the victors boarded the *Detroit* they found a pet bear lapping up blood on the decks and two Indians hiding in the hold."

Temporarily, at least, Perry's victory became a restorative tonic for an American public presently accustomed to bitter and disappointing news. As a military objective it was a brilliant success, since the British had been driven from Lake Erie altogether. Once again a significant literary sidelight occurred when Perry's communiqué to Harrison was published: "We have met the enemy and he is ours."*

---

* These War of 1812 slogans—ranking with such memorable wartime mottoes as "Remember the Alamo"—were familiar to every American schoolchild until recently. Despite the current academic trend of deconstructing U.S. military history, many such slogans have survived through usage in popular culture and product advertisements, often relying on twists on the original verbiage; among the best known of these is Walt Kelly's memorable takeoff on Perry's "We have met the enemy and he is ours" in his comic strip *Pogo:* "We have met the enemy and he is *us.*"

Three

In June 1812, just a few days after the declaration of war, Andrew Jackson, major general of Tennessee militia, dispatched from the Hermitage, his magnificent home in Nashville, a letter to President Madison offering to transport his 2,500-man division of Tennessee infantry on an immediate invasion of British Canada with the intention of conquering Quebec "in ninety days."

The offer was accepted by Secretary of War Armstrong, but orders never arrived. As the months passed, Jackson became infuriated that commanders such as Wilkinson and Dearborn—whom he rightly considered incompetent—were being tapped to lead campaigns up north while he languished in Tennessee with a full division of trained militia eager to get into the fight. Soon Jackson was able to conclude that he'd become persona non grata at the War Department as the result of stepping on too many toes, a habit long since perfected and honed. Still, the fiery militia general gnashed his teeth at Washington's inaction, because it is doubtful that anyone in America loathed the English more than Andrew Jackson, and not without good cause; he was perfectly ripe for hating.

Like the new nation in which he lived, Jackson was suspended between a difficult past and an uncertain future. He had no formal military training, but as a leader of military men he had few peers; he was smart, honest, brave as a lion, and, like the lion, he could be a cold-blooded killer.

Jackson was born on March 15, 1767, in the scrubby Waxhaw District of eastern South Carolina,* a child of Scots-Irish immigrants who had come to America two years earlier. Andrew's father died only a few days before his new son's birth, after "straining himself" lifting a log, and now Andrew's mother abandoned the farm, which the Jacksons had hoped would provide their living and fortune, and moved with the baby and his two siblings to a relative's house nearby, where she took up duties as a housekeeper and babysitter.

To say that young Andrew grew up precocious would understate the case. He was more like a terror—fighting, swearing, gambling, smoking, and drinking, traits that would stay with him a lifetime—dashing the fond hopes of his mother that he would one day become a Presbyterian minister. Yet he was also smart and received a fair education, though he never quite mastered the skills of spelling and grammar.

By the time Andrew was thirteen the American Revolution had swept into the Upper Carolinas, spearheaded by the cruel and remorseless Scottish cavalryman Colonel Banastre Tarleton and his infamous green-coated dragoons, who ruthlessly raised the level of violence and brutality: hanging, burning, raping, and looting, and, in the process, touching off a civil war between patriots and Tories of the region that pitted neighbor against neighbor.

Andrew's older brother Hugh died fighting the British at the Battle of Stono Ferry in 1779, and the following year the two remaining Jackson boys, Robert, sixteen, and Andrew, thirteen, signed up to fight with the cavalry of Colonel William Davie. By then the fighting in the Carolinas had turned so ferocious that no quarter was generally given by either side and massacres were commonplace. Because of his age and riding prowess, young Andrew was made a courier, but he certainly saw his share of war and developed a lifelong loathing of the British practice of it.

---

* Some say North Carolina; the boundary then was very close and subject to change with each new survey.

The following year both boys were captured by a British raiding party. When Andrew refused an "imperious" order to clean a British officer's boots, the man struck him with his saber, slashing him savagely on his head and hand, leaving scars, both physical and mental, for the rest of his life. The raiders then looted the house, raped the women, and burned the place down, barn and all. Andrew and Robert were thrown into a filthy, bedless British prison in Camden and put on a diet of bread and water; a Tory stole Andrew's pistol, shoes, coat, and hat, and both boys contracted smallpox, a scourge that had already wreaked havoc across the nation.

Plucky Elizabeth Jackson, hearing of her boys' capture, rode into Camden and persuaded the British commander to include the two youngsters in an exchange of prisoners that was being negotiated. Robert was so weak from disease that he had to be strapped on a horse, while Andrew, barefoot, hatless, and coatless in the rain, walked the forty miles it took to get home. Robert died two days later, and it looked as though Andrew, too, was doomed, but nursed by his mother he pulled through.

Several months later, when Andrew seemed to be on the road to recovery, Elizabeth journeyed to Charleston to minister to her two nephews, who were ill aboard British prison ships in Charleston Harbor. At their parting, his mother gave young Andrew some advice: "Make friends by being honest and keep them by being steadfast. Never tell a lie, nor take what is not your own, nor sue for slander—settle them cases yourself!"

These words, like his scars, remained hard and dear to Andrew Jackson all his life, for it wasn't long before he learned that his mother had died of cholera contracted aboard the prison ships. She was buried in an unmarked grave in Charleston, leaving him little to remember her by except those parting words and the pitiable bundle of her belongings that had arrived along with word of her death. Andrew Jackson, at the age of fifteen, was alone in the world—as he vividly remembered it, an orphan of the British war.

For the next three years, by all accounts, Jackson lived a dissolute life with no one to guide him or take care of him. He became a sort of glorified Huckleberry Finn, gambling, smoking, drinking, and, in his case, racing fine thoroughbred horses acquired with a small inheritance that his grandfather in Ireland had left him. Two years after the war ended, Jackson decided he wanted to be a lawyer and "read" law with a prominent attorney in Salisbury, North Carolina, where he lived above a tavern and, according to local residents, merrily dissipated himself, as the saying goes, with wine, women, and song.

Despite all this, in 1787 Jackson, now twenty, received his license to practice law. He had grown into a man just short of handsome, above six feet tall, lean and somewhat gaunt with deep, piercing, steel-blue eyes and a great shock of reddish-brown hair on his forehead. Perceptively, Jackson concluded that the Tennessee territory on the western side of the Alleghenies was a smart place to start a legal practice. Tennessee was still largely Indian land,* settled by Americans just eighteen years earlier—and then by just one person, a man named William Bean. But raw new territories often provided spectacular opportunities for men learned in law, since there were always boundary disputes and property sales to be settled, wills and deeds to be drawn up, even the territorial laws themselves had to be written—all this in addition to the defense or prosecution of the abnormally large number of killers, thieves, and other miscreants who tended to inhabit such wildernesses.

Within a year Jackson was appointed to the post of territorial prosecutor and within another he was made United States attorney general for the territory. He settled in a dingy little hamlet consisting of about fifty primitive log houses on the Cumberland River at what is now the city of Nashville.

Tennessee was where Jackson fought his first duel, also within a year of his arrival,† and within yet another he met and married his wife, twenty-two-year-old Rachel Robards. The circumstances of this last

---

* And technically, then, still a part of North Carolina—but that's another story.
† It was with a fellow lawyer in a dispute over legal fees. Neither man really wanted to kill the other, so, by a prearrangement reached by their seconds, when the command to fire was given, both men shot into the air, a perfect example of the silliness of dueling.

were to cause Jackson much trouble (and dueling) throughout his life, because both he and Rachel had relied on reports from Kentucky—where her first husband had gone after he left her—that a divorce had been granted there. When that news proved to be untrue, occasionally rude comments were circulated by the ambitious Jackson's growing number of detractors to the effect that he was an adulterer and she a bigamist, and Jackson spent no small amount of time challenging any and all of these assertions.

As time went by Jackson progressed from prosecutor to judge, at the same time acquiring vast amounts of land in the area, upon which, using slave labor, he raised cotton, corn, and wheat and eventually built his splendid mansion, the Hermitage. He also built up one of the finest stables of racehorses in the South, winning (or losing, as the case some-times was) large sums of money. Almost from the moment of his arrival in Tennessee Jackson's career was meteoric. In 1796 he was elected to the U.S. House of Representatives; in 1797 he was elected to the U.S. Senate; in 1802 he was elected major general of the Tennessee militia.*

By this time the Jacksons had a growing brood in their household. After Rachel lost a number of infants in childbirth, the couple began taking in orphans or children whose parents were unable to properly care for them; one of these was legally adopted and christened Andrew Jackson, Jr.

During this period there were, occasionally, unfortunate vicissitudes. In 1806 Jackson became, arguably, the best pistol shot in Tennessee after killing a man named Charles Dickinson (whom everybody had *said* was the best shot in Tennessee) in a duel over a horseracing bet. In 1803 he had gotten into a dispute with then Tennessee governor John "Nolichucky Jack" Sevier, an old rival whom Jackson had publicly exposed for perpetrating large real estate frauds. When Sevier retali-ated by insulting Mrs. Jackson regarding her alleged adultery, he was promptly challenged to a duel.

---

* After having served for six years as the judge advocate general (lawyer) of that organization.

The governor did not wish to fight a duel with Jackson, however, pleading old age, his service in the Revolutionary War, and the likely resultant poverty of his large family, should he lose. But neither would he apologize for making a crack about Jackson's "taking a trip to Natchez with another man's wife [Rachel]," so Jackson promptly published a screed on the front page of the local newspaper in which he called Sevier all the ugly things that were fit to print, including a "coward." Jackson then set out for the appointed dueling grounds to await the governor, who was not at all punctual. What happened next, by the account of Marquis James, one of Jackson's biographers, is worth quoting in its entirety:

"For five days they encamped at the Point and had started to leave when Sevier appeared with several armed men. Andrew Greer rode ahead and addressed Jackson, who suddenly left off speaking and drew a pistol, dismounted and drew a second pistol. Turning, Greer perceived Sevier off his horse with pistols in his hands advancing on Jackson. Twenty steps apart they halted and began to abuse each other, the governor damning him to fire away. After a little of this both put away their arms. There were more words and Jackson rushed at Sevier saying he was going to cane him. [Then] Sevier drew his sword, 'which frightened his horse, which ran away with the governor's pistols.' Jackson drew a pistol and the governor went behind a tree and damned Jackson: 'Did he want to fire on a naked man?' he asked. George Washington Sevier, the governor's seventeen-year-old son, then drew on Jackson and Dr. Van Dyke [Jackson's second] drew on Washington.

"Members of the Sevier party rushed up making amicable signs. They got the three men to put away their guns and suggested that the governor relinquish the field, which he did, swearing at Jackson and receiving [Jackson's] comments in return as long as either could hear."*

* Versions of this encounter differ somewhat. For example, some writers give the time that Jackson waited for Governor Sevier as two days, others say a single day, some report it was the same afternoon, while still others say five days. I have chosen to use the account by James because it seems well researched, makes better sense, and is also the most lively.

So it sometimes went on dueling days, but Jackson's next encounter was not to be so uneventful.

With the War of 1812 four months old and still going terribly for the Americans, and with Jackson still brooding in Nashville with his militia division, something finally seemed to be happening. Washington had sent out its call for 50,000 volunteers from the various states. Unlike militia, these would come directly under the authority of the War Department, as would their commanding officer. The governor of Tennessee, William Blount, appointed Jackson to the post of major general of U.S. volunteers, certainly an exalted regular army slot for a mere militia officer. Tennessee's quota had been 1,500 men, but 2,500—including the famed frontiersman Davy Crockett—joined up from mid-October until the end of December, walking or riding out of the canebreaks, mountains, and backwoods communities to form up in Nashville on the banks of the frozen Cumberland River. Jackson personally mortgaged much of his fortune to supply and equip them.

Unfortunately—or so concluded Jackson—his orders were not to march his force to the fighting fronts along the Canadian border, but instead to go to New Orleans and reinforce the despised Wilkinson, who had not yet left for his unsatisfactory performance in the north, and who was supposed to march on Spanish West Florida, where the Spanish and British were stirring up the Indians against the United States. Accordingly, Jackson moved his men eight hundred miles by river rafts down to Natchez, just above New Orleans, where he received a further communiqué from the War Department canceling the whole mission and telling him to disband his army and go home. Jackson did no such thing, at least not the part about disbanding his army. He believed that the new orders were nothing more than a smarmy ploy to get rid of him and to have his volunteers serve under Wilkinson. Instead, he vowed to march his men all the way back to Nashville himself, which he did, acquiring in the process the nickname "Old Hickory," when somebody watching the general leading his men out of the wilderness remarked, "He's tough as hickory," after the toughest wood he knew. The name stuck, but it was also along this arduous march that serious trouble began to fester.

The Benton brothers, both officers in Jackson's army, were from a prominent and wealthy family in Franklin, just outside Nashville. The younger Benton had become friends with one Lieutenant Littleton Johnson, who had developed a grudge against Lieutenant Colonel William Carroll, the brigade inspector. Johnson sent Jesse Benton to Carroll with a challenge to a duel. Carroll refused on grounds that Johnson was not a gentleman;* Benton then declared that if that be so, he himself was one, and promptly challenged Carroll personally to the duel.

Carroll asked Jackson to be his second, but Jackson demurred and tried to patch things up. When this proved impossible, he reluctantly accompanied Carroll to the dueling grounds. Jesse Benton fired first and nicked Carroll on the thumb, then, "in a fit of panic," he turned and bent over, exposing his rear end to Colonel Carroll, which was precisely where Jackson's brigade inspector shot him.[†]

Having his little brother humiliated in this way did not set well with now Lieutenant Colonel Thomas Hart Benton, who had once been

---

* Just what constituted a gentleman in those days is not easily defined, but there was obviously more to it than money, fine clothes, and nice table manners. Most people seemed to take an "I'll know one when I see one" attitude. In any case, under the *code duello* duels were to be fought only between gentlemen; lesser figures, presumably without honor at stake to begin with, were expected to settle their differences by beating each other with canes or by knife- or fistfighting.

† The Bentons later became for a time one of the most famous families in America. After the Nashville shoot-out, both Thomas and his brother Jesse left Nashville for St. Louis, Missouri, where they felt safe from Jackson and his friends. Thomas became one of the nation's most powerful senators and was close to the Lincoln administration during the Civil War. His daughter Jessie (named for her uncle Jesse, of gunfight notoriety) married Colonel John Frémont, the "Pathfinder," whose western explorations led him to fame and fortune and a shot at the White House. Jesse himself had a lesser career, but his Greek Revival home still stands in Nashville, a shrine, and was used during the Civil War battle in that city as a soldiers' hospital; it was later bought and restored in the 1920s by a descendant of another of Jackson's old enemies, onetime Tennessee governor John "Nolichucky Jack" Sevier. A grand-nephew, Thomas Hart Benton, was celebrated as an American artist and muralist of the naturalist-regionalist school beginning in the 1920s.

Jackson's friend and envoy to Washington, and he stated to Jackson that it was a "very poor business for a man of [Jackson's] age and standing" to be involved in a duel between two of his young officers. There things might have rested but for Nashville gossips and troublemakers who kept hinting to each of the ruffled parties that one or the other was saying something impolite about him. Things finally got so bad that Jackson publicly stated he would "horsewhip" Thomas Benton the next time he encountered him.

This occurred six weeks later, on September 4, 1813, when the Bentons rode into Nashville and checked into the City Hotel, across the courthouse square from the Nashville Inn, where Jackson and his associates customarily hung out. News of the Bentons' arrival quickly got to Jackson, who retrieved his horsewhip and marched over to the hotel to fulfill his promise. There he accosted Thomas Benton in the doorway and, calling him a "damned rascal," brandished the whip, at which point Benton reached into his pocket for what Jackson thought was a pistol. Jackson outdrew him with his own, backing Benton through the hotel doorway with his pistol leveled. But brother Jesse, hearing the encounter, had sneaked around to the side of the barroom, from which vantage point he fired two shots at Jackson, which smashed into his arm and shoulder. Jackson, toppling, fired at Thomas and missed; then Thomas drew and fired twice at Jackson's prone figure in front of him, but he missed, too.

Jesse had reloaded and was about to put an end to Andrew Jackson on the spot when two of the general's friends came bursting into the room. A melee ensued: Stockley Hays, Jackson's nephew, began stabbing at Jesse with a sword cane, while Jackson's faithful cavalry commander, John Coffee, brutalized Thomas with the butt of his pistol. Both Bentons managed to make their getaway, but Andrew Jackson was left in very bad shape.

At first it was feared he would not live; his blood soaked up two mattresses before the bleeding stopped. Every physician in Nashville attended the general, and all but one agreed he'd have to have the arm amputated lest gangrene set in and kill him. Jackson would have none of it, though, saying, "I'll keep my arm." He remained bedridden for more than three weeks, until momentous news arrived from Alabama.

Following Tecumseh's visit to the Creek Nation there two years earlier, a band of about two dozen Creek warriors trekked all the way up to Indiana to meet with Tecumseh about the great Indian Confederation he had planned. They accompanied him on several raids against white settlers and also participated in the massacre of U.S. prisoners at the River Raisin in Michigan Territory. Afterward the Creeks returned to Alabama more bloodthirsty than ever, massacring settlers all along the way. When they got home they found that something even larger was in the wind: William Weatherford, the powerful Creek chief now known as Red Eagle, had put on his warpaint.

Weatherford's ancestry is so unusual that it begs amplification. Nearly a hundred years earlier, in 1722, an officer named Captain Marchand was ordered by French authorities in New Orleans to take a body of troops and establish an outpost on the upper reaches of the Coosa River where it joins the Alabama near present-day Montgomery. Once there he built Fort Toulouse, constituting thereby a French presence against encroachments by the English from their colonies to the east, or by the Spanish, who controlled Florida to the south.

There Marchand met an Indian girl, who produced for him a lovely child they named Sehoy. Shortly afterward, Marchand's troops mutinied and killed him, which is the end of his story, but the soon-to-be legendary Sehoy grew into a beautiful woman who, when the British encroached into Alabama, just as the French had feared, began consorting with one of their officers, and producing children, until a handsome and wealthy Scottish adventurer by the name of Lachlan McGillivray turned up and "repaid his host's hospitality" by running away with Sehoy. McGillivray then built a fashionable home on the Coosa River and established an Indian trading post, which soon made him a very wealthy man.

One of their sons, Alexander McGillivray, whom Lachlan had sent away to boarding school in Charleston, returned to the Coosa and promptly disavowed both his education and his three-quarters-white blood by joining the Creek "Clan of the Wind," of which he soon became head chief. The younger McGillivray also disliked Americans, and during the Revolution he became a colonel in the British army, after which he worked in Pensacola for Spain, before changing allegiances once again and winding up at his death, in 1793, "a brigadier-general in the United States Army, worth one hundred thousand dollars, and . . . buried with Masonic honors in a Spanish gentleman's garden at Pensacola."

Before Alexander died, however, another Scottish trader named Charles Weatherford happened along and married Alexander's half sister, whereupon, like the elder McGillivray, this new Scotsman built a fine house for himself and his wife and went on to make a fortune in the Indian trade. Of Weatherford's two sons—themselves only one-eighth Indian by now—Robert chose the way of the white man (and was never heard of again), but William, like his famous uncle Alexander McGillivray, chose the path of a Creek warrior and soon became known as the ferocious Chief Red Eagle of the Clan of the Wind.

The visit to Alabama by Tecumseh in 1811 had left a murderous impression on Weatherford, which was further exacerbated by the recent construction of the controversial Federal Road through Georgia and Alabama; this road, in addition to facilitating the delivery of mail as it was intended to do, brought more and more settlers into what until then had been an Indian wilderness. Tecumseh's prophecy was coming true right before Weatherford's eyes: forests being stripped of trees to make way for fields, rivers turned brown from runoff silt; all that remained was for the Indians to be turned into slaves. Convinced that the only way to put an end to this was to kill as many of these settlers as possible, Weatherford and his band, known as the Red Sticks (à la Tecumseh, for the bright paint on their war clubs), engineered a war of savage depredation against the whites.

Farmers from all over the territory began fleeing into Mobile, the only significant city on the Gulf Coast at the time, or moving into stockades and blockhouses scattered throughout the area. One of these was Fort Mims, a rude stockade hardly worthy of the name, near the Tensaw River about forty miles north of Mobile, owned by a prosperous landowner and ferry operator, Samuel Mims, and recently garrisoned by 120 militia from Louisiana. In addition, inside were approximately 175 white settlers and their women and children, as well as a lesser number of slaves and friendly Indians.*

Despite several warnings from slaves who reported they had seen hostile Indians in the neighborhood, just before noon on August 30, 1813—and five days before Jackson's disgraceful gunfight with the Bentons—William Weatherford's war party of about 700 braves came screaming out of a ravine a hundred yards from Fort Mims, completely surprising the settlers and the garrison while they were eating their lunch.

The gates to the fort had become stuck in rain-washed sand and clay, and the war party quickly rushed inside. The carnage was deliberate and awful. All the buildings and houses in the fort were set afire by the Indians, and many settlers burned alive. The rest were tomahawked, scalped, and otherwise mutilated, with only a dozen or so managing to escape by running into a swamp. A militia officer who went to the fort three weeks later—when it was finally considered safe to do so—reported to U.S. authorities that after they had driven off buzzards, wolves, and dogs, his detachment buried "247 white men, women and children."

Word of the massacre soon spread to Nashville along with eyewitness accounts of bloodcurdling description: ". . . blood and brains bespattered the whole earth. The children were seized by the legs, and killed by batting their heads against the stockading. The women were scalped

---

* Every source for the Fort Mims massacre gives a different tally for the number of occupants, ranging from 250 to 600. I decided to use Frank Owsley's *The Struggle for the Gulf Borderlands* (University Press of Florida, 1981), simply because it presents the most logical and well-researched account.

and those who were pregnant were opened, while they were alive, and the embryo infants let out of the womb." As the historian Frank Owsley notes, "It was Indian warfare at its worst."

Reports of this atrocity ignited in Americans a collective cry of indignation and demands for retribution. To the authorities it was obvious that the Indians had now declared full-scale war on the United States. No man recognized this more than Major General Andrew Jackson, who commanded the nearest and most powerful military force that could deal with it. When someone in the legislature lamented how unfortunate it was that Jackson—only two weeks into recovery since his near-fatal wounding by the Bentons—would be unable to command, the general roared, "The devil in hell I'm not!" and published an order to his troops: "The health of your general is restored. He will command in person." With that, Jackson climbed out of his sickbed, and on October 7, 1813, with his fractured and still bleeding arm in a sling, he marched his 2,500-man army of frontiersmen out of Nashville, southward to the empire of the Creeks.

Four

Andrew Jackson's brand of warfare, while not as brutal as that of the Red Sticks, was certainly no picnic for the Indians. Whenever he reached a Creek village whose occupants were suspected of participating in the uprising, Jackson burned it to the ground and sent the inhabitants fleeing toward Spanish Florida. If they resisted, he ordered them hunted down and killed. In the process, Jackson had the additional concept of establishing a permanent north-south road through the wilderness from Nashville to Mobile—felling trees, removing stumps, filling, backing, leveling, and bridging—to open the Gulf trade to Tennessee (which, in fact, he did).

Not only that, but when he was finished with the Creeks in Alabama, Jackson had determined to move against the Spanish stronghold at Pensacola to eject them from or neutralize their control over West Florida. Although Spain was ostensibly at peace with the United States, Jackson knew from his many spies that the Spanish were quietly arming and supplying the Creeks and other Indians, inspiring them to cause trouble in the southern regions of the country. And there were worse things, too, far worse, that Jackson did not know at the time.

With Brigadier John Coffee's 1,200-man cavalry as its spearhead, Jackson's army marched southward. There were several major battles, the first fought at the large Creek town of Talluschatchee. There Coffee, a giant of a man who would go on to become Jackson's most trusted lieutenant, was fighting the first military engagement of his life, but proved he had an unerring aptitude for it. He posted his men in two large half-circles, performing an envelopment outside the town. When the Indians spotted several riders sent in as "bait," they all rushed out to give chase, and Coffee's men sprung the trap. Many Creeks were killed, and the rest ran back into the town, where they were relentlessly hunted down by the Tennesseans. "We shot them like dogs," Davy Crockett remembered.

Several dozen braves ran into a large hut guarded at the door by a Creek squaw with a bow and arrow. When she killed a young lieutenant with it, she was in turn shot by his troops and the hut set afire, roasting the Indians alive. One hundred and eighty-six dead Indians were counted when the battle was over, and several dozen women and children taken into custody, including a beautiful boy about three years old who was found terrified and crying in his dead mother's arms. When Coffee's men marched the women and children back to Jackson's camp, the general immediately noticed the boy and inquired of the squaws who among them was going to take care of him. Their reply disgusted the general: "All his relations are dead; kill him too," they said.

Jackson did no such thing, but instead took the little boy into his tent and nursed him with brown sugar water until the child could be sent to Rachel in Nashville. Afterward, the Jacksons named the boy Lincoyer, and he lived with them as beloved as any of their own family until his death from tuberculosis at the age of seventeen.

Next on Jackson's list was the large Creek encampment at Talladega,* where some 1,000 Red Sticks had besieged an old fort inhabited by about 150 friendly Creeks. They had been on the verge of starvation when one of their chiefs, "enveloping himself in the skin of a large hog with head and hoofs attached, left the fort and went about rooting and grunting, gradually working his way through the hostile host until he was beyond reach of their arrows."

By the time this bold hog-man reached Jackson's camp, the Americans, too, were on the edge of starvation, their suppliers having failed them. Jackson nevertheless saddled up almost his entire army and moved on Talladega, which he reached in the early hours of November 9, 1813. They formed ranks at sunrise and moved toward the enemy in

---

* Now site of the Talladega Raceway of NASCAR fame.

an envelopment formation similar to the one Coffee had used previously. In the ensuing battle 239 Indian bodies were left on the field, and others, wounded, undoubtedly died in the woods into which they had run. Jackson had 15 men killed and about 80 wounded.

So far the campaign was going well except for the food situation. The men were down to eating a few biscuits, and "for several days General Jackson and his military family subsisted on tripe, without bread or seasoning." When that ran out, they began dining on acorns, a meal that has become legendary in accounts of Jackson's career. As the story goes, when several officers came to Jackson's headquarters on behalf of their men to complain about the lack of food, the general had laid out before them an elegant table, complete with fine china, linens, and silver water goblets, and he invited them to dine with him. When the astonished men had been seated, Jackson's orderly brought out a large silver platter piled high with acorns, whereupon Jackson solemnly pronounced words to this effect: "Here, gentlemen, you can see before you that we have no crisis. This country is filled with a wonderful bounty of natural food."

Before it got better, it got worse. The Tennessee militia mutinied over the lack of rations and tried to march back toward Nashville; Jackson halted them with his volunteers. Then the volunteers mutinied because their one-year enlistment had run out, and Jackson stopped them with his militia. But clearly the situation had become intolerable, and as the new year of 1814 began Jackson was compelled to cease operations and recruit an entire new army, which he did, bringing in some 2,000 men, supplemented now by a U.S. Army regiment of regulars that included a young lieutenant named Sam Houston, subsequently known as the Father of Texas.

After retiring to winter quarters, Jackson at last was able to iron out the ration and supply foul-ups and ready himself for the spring campaign, in which he aimed at striking a final, decisive blow to destroy William Weatherford and his Red Sticks. The opportunity came in March 1814 at an obscure loop on the Tallapoosa River called Horseshoe Bend.

The Indians considered Horseshoe Bend sacred ground. The bend itself was an oblong peninsula formed by the serpentine river and consisting of about a hundred acres of brush and timber, across the neck of which the Indians had built a formidable breastwork of logs, keeping their canoes at the opposite point in case they had to escape. Eight hundred Red Sticks manned the fortification in which they had fabricated two rows of firing loopholes. It was apparent on both sides that the Red Sticks were hunkered down for a fight to the finish.

On March 27, upon a misty dawn, Jackson had the bend surrounded, while friendly Indian scouts attached to Coffee's cavalry swam the river and took most of the Red Sticks' unguarded canoes. The general had placed 1,000 of his soldiers on the banks opposite the Horseshoe to prevent the Red Sticks from swimming to safety, while along the narrow neck he formed up another 1,000 for the assault on the breastwork itself. About ten a.m., his army's small six-pounder cannon roared into action, slamming balls into the Indian breastwork, but they merely buried themselves in the soft pine planks. Creek riflemen retaliated, but so far no one much had been hurt. Then, when Jackson observed the Indians trying to remove their women and children across the river, out of harm's way, he halted fire.

So it went until about half past noon, when there was no more reason for delay. Then the drummers of the 39th Infantry Regiment of U.S. Army regulars began to beat out the long roll—the signal to charge. Jackson's 1,000 infantry rushed the Indian lines, with the 39th Regiment leading the way. The first man to get atop it was Major Lemuel Montgomery, who was immediately killed by a shot to the head.* Big Sam Houston was one of the next to claw his way up the

---

* Could he have been a brother or other relative of my great-great-great-grandfather Major Elijah Montgomery? It is possible. Both had biblical Christian names, both were regular army officers serving at the same time. But it cannot be known without further genealogical investigation of the Virginia Montgomery family. In any case, Lemuel Putnam Montgomery became the hero of the Battle of Horseshoe Bend, and two years later, in 1816, Montgomery County, Alabama, in which the state capitol is located, was named after him.

rampart and, brandishing his sword, was seen to jump down into the swarm of Indian defenders, slashing away.

For the next three hours the battle raged fierce and desperate, breaking down into dozens of separate fights throughout the hundred-acre peninsula; with rifles, bayonets, swords, knives, spears, clubs, bows and arrows, tomahawks, rocks, fists, and teeth the Indians and soldiers went at it. About three p.m. it began to rain, and Jackson sent an offer urging the Red Sticks to surrender. Instead, they shot the messenger, and the battle continued with renewed fury. Houston was carried from the field, shot twice through the shoulder and with "a ghastly wound in his thigh" from a barbed arrow. He was not expected to live. Some of the Indians tried to escape by plunging into the river, but rifle fire from both banks soon turned the Tallapoosa red with blood.

Late in the afternoon the fighting became desultory as the soldiers came together against isolated pockets of resistance. "Not an Indian asked for quarter, nor would accept it if offered." Finally, when it became too dark to see, the fighting ceased, and next morning's sun rose over a frightful tableau. Five hundred and fifty-seven Indian bodies were strewn over the little bend in the river; at least another 200 had "found a grave at the bottom of the river," while it was estimated that another 100 or so died of their wounds in the forest.

The back of the Red Stick confederacy was broken.

After weighting down his own 49 dead and sinking them into the river to keep them from being scalped by any returning Indians, Jackson by midday on March 28 had his army—including 157 wounded—on the five-day northward march back to their encampment. His only regret was that William Weatherford was not found among the Indian dead and would have to be hunted down—or so he thought.

Jackson had established his base at Fort Toulouse, ironically the original French outpost at the fork of the Coosa and Tallapoosa that Weatherford's great-great-great-grandfather had built a hunded years earlier. It was rehabilitated and renamed Fort Jackson, and there the remaining Creek chiefs began coming to Jackson to surrender—

fourteen of them in all. After securing promises of their good behavior, he pardoned them and set them free.

Then one day a tall, light-skinned Indian with a newly killed deer slung over his saddle rode into the American camp and asked directions to Jackson's tent. When it was pointed out, the Indian spurred his horse in that direction, where, at the flap of the tent, he encountered Chief Big Warrior, one of the friendly Indians who had been fighting at Jackson's side.

"Ah!" Big Warrior exclaimed. "Bill Weatherford, have we got you at last?"

Weatherford began damning his antagonist as a traitor, and threatening to shoot him, when Jackson suddenly burst out of the tent.

"How dare you ride up to my tent after having murdered the women and children at Fort Mims!" the general shouted.

According to witnesses, Weatherford replied with the following soliloquy, as if from some staged modern-day Indian pageant:

"General Jackson, I am not afraid of you. I fear no man, for I am a Creek warrior. I have nothing to request on behalf of myself. You can kill me if you desire. But I come to beg you to send for the women and children of the war party, who are now starving in the woods. Their fields and [corn] cribs have been destroyed by your people, who have driven them into the woods without an ear of corn. I am now done fighting. The Red Sticks are nearly all killed. If I could fight you any longer, I would most heartily do so. Send for the women and children. They never did you any harm. But kill me, if the white people want it done."

The great crowd of officers and men who by now had gathered around the tent began to shout in chorus: "Kill him! Kill him! Kill him!" But Jackson hushed them up, declaring, "Any man who would kill as brave a man as this would rob the dead."

The general invited Weatherford to dismount and come into his tent for an interview, which he did, dragging the deer along as a gift. It is said that Jackson talked of forming a lasting peace with the Indians and that Weatherford agreed, telling the general, "Once I could animate my warriors to battle; but I cannot animate the dead," and similar sentiments, until the conversation finally ended, with Weatherford free to go. Afterward, Weatherford returned to his plantation at Little River, north of Mobile, where he resumed the white man's ways and dress and lived the remainder of his long life amid his many slaves, raising cotton and livestock and telling stories from the days of the Red Sticks. For his part, Jackson, as Weatherford had requested, called in the Indian women and children from the woods and, as the spring of 1814 turned to summer, maintained more than five thousand Creeks against starvation by feeding them from U.S. Army stores.

When news of the victory over the Creeks was received in Washington, Jackson—despite misgivings in the War Department—was commissioned a major general of regular troops in the United States Army, a significant leap for a former general of state militia or even of volunteers. He must have wondered, though, general of what, since his Tennesseans were all sent home to be mustered out, and in his whole department he could call on no more than three understrength regiments of regulars.

Nevertheless, there was important work to be done. Washington had decided that Jackson should negotiate a peace treaty with the Creeks that would not only spell out their prospective relationship with the federal government and delineate their future territory, but also provide for "reparations" for the cost of the war. Naturally the reparations would have to be concessions of land in what the Indians presently considered their territory. Since the Indians didn't have much to bring to the bargaining table, the general, in the August 1814 Treaty of Fort Jackson, was able to persuade the chiefs to cede to the United States for settlement some 150,000 square miles of land—twenty-three million acres—nearly three-quarters of the state of Alabama. When word of the treaty terms spread through the North, some people decried it as excessive and unfair, but Jackson's reasoning was that American settlers were going to move there anyway, like it or not, and that it was best to separate them and the Indians from close proximity.*

Then there was the subject of Spanish West Florida, which had been chafing at Jackson for more than two years. Many of the unrepentant Red Sticks had fled to Florida under the protection of the Spanish authorities, who gave them arms and military supplies. Jackson was certain no good would come of that. He fretted about it all spring and summer, but since the United States was technically at peace with Spain, he could think of no good reason to oust the Spaniards from Florida without causing an international incident. Though Jackson didn't know it yet, a reason had already been provided by events five thousand miles away.

Following his retreat from Moscow in the bitter winter of 1813, Napoleon Bonaparte saw his European empire beginning to crumble. His armies were defeated time and again by an allied coalition of Great Britain and most of the other countries of Europe. At the same time Jackson was slaughtering the Creeks at Horseshoe Bend, Paris was captured and Napoleon sent into exile, thus freeing tens of thousands of soldiers of the British empire to deal with the Americans.

Accordingly, by the summer of 1814 some 40,000 British troops had been shipped to the American theater as well as additional numbers of British warships. The Americans, though, could by now themselves muster nearly 45,000 men in uniform, but these were spread all over the land, and no one could know where a British force would strike.

They found out soon enough when a British army from Canada occupied Maine and took control of its public property, while at the same time an armada sailed into the Chesapeake with the intention of taking Washington and Baltimore. News of the British arrival caused alarm in both cities, since everyone recalled the depredations a year

---

* Sixteen years later, in 1830, as president of the United States, Jackson signed the Indian Removal Act, in which *all* Indians who had not fully assimilated into American society (and some who had) were removed west of the Mississippi.

earlier when a British force had attacked Hampton, Virginia. In that sorry episode, according to a British officer who was there, "every horror was committed with impunity, rape, murder, pillage, and not a man was punished!"* Thus, the frightened citizens of Washington and Baltimore wondered, if the British had done that to sleepy little Hampton, what would they do to *them*?

On August 24, 1814, the British landed in southern Maryland and marched on the nation's capital with 4,500 veterans, many of them veterans of the Napoleonic campaigns, who simply steamrolled over the green 7,000-man American militia that Secretary of War Armstong had hastily assembled.† Under the command of Major General Robert Ross and Admiral Alexander Cochrane, the redcoats entered Washington that same evening and set fire to all the public buildings, including the Capitol, the White House, and the Library of Congress. Spared only was the U.S. Patent Office, presumably on the theory that valuable things might be taken from it instead.

The librarian of Congress had quickly grabbed the Declaration of Independence, the U.S. Constitution, the papers of George Washington, and other sacred documents and put them in carts to be taken into the Virginia countryside and, it was hoped, out of danger. (The next time this occurred was on December 8, 1941, the day after the Japanese attack on Pearl Harbor, when all important and irreplaceable documents were shipped off in railroad trains to the U.S. gold reserve safes at Fort Knox, Kentucky.)

Administration officials, including President Madison, fled into the countryside, but not before the president's saucy little wife, Dolley, saved a portrait of George Washington and other historic keepsakes. So hasty was their exit that a full dinner table in the White House dining room, set with china, silver, and crystal, was left with a still-warm meal

* The British first blamed this on conscripted French troops forced to fight under the Union Jack, then on Irishmen similarly situated, but the fact remains that British officers allowed it to happen.

† Again, the number of enemy troops is disputed by historians. Some say 2,500, others 3,000. I stick with Dr. Hickey's estimate because it seems most informed.

served on its plates—enjoyed with irony and mirth by British soldiers just before they burned the place down, or so it was said. The inability to defend even its capital city became the conclusive disaster for American arms.

With Washington laid in ashes, and much plunder removed, the British next turned on Baltimore, which they attacked on September 12, after landing about fourteen miles below the city. There, however, things began to go wrong. The Baltimoreans had assembled a militia army estimated at 10,000 to 20,000 men and built up a strong line of earthworks. To the dismay of the British troops, along the route of march General Ross was killed by an American sniper, and no amount of bombarding by His Majesty's imperial navy could bring Fort McHenry—key to the city—to surrender.* When "dawn's early light" revealed that Fort McHenry was still standing and that the Americans were firmly entrenched in their lines, Admiral Cochrane sourly called off the attack and sailed out of the bay, but not before his men plundered private property, razed churches, and even looted graveyards, prompting a congressman to exclaim that their conduct "would have disgraced cannibals!"

The British operations against Washington and Baltimore were never intended to actually occupy those cities, but rather were intended as a diversion to remove American attention from New Orleans, a port with a population of about 25,000—by far the largest and most important city west of the Appalachians. Nevertheless, the attacks were humiliating for the citizenry, who could not understand how their soldiers had let such things happen. A young minister passing through gloomily described "the traces of devastation and death . . . visible in the half-covered graves along the highway between Baltimore and

---

* On one of the bombarding ships was a young American lawyer named Francis Scott Key, who had come aboard to negotiate the release of a civilian prisoner and been taken captive himself for the duration of the battle. There he witnessed the new Congreve rockets blasting away at the old brick fort all night. This inspired him to pen the lines to "The Star-Spangled Banner," which he set to the tune of an old British drinking song. It became the nation's official national anthem by an act of Congress in 1931.

Washington. The blackened walls of the Capitol at Washington, and the destruction in every part of the city, presented an awful picture of the horrors of war."

Precisely what the British intentions were regarding Louisiana will probably never be known, but some of the facts and questions follow. The British government never considered Napoleon the legitimate ruler of France, and so whatever transactions he made while in power— including selling the lands of the Louisiana Purchase to the United States in 1803—were deemed null and void. That having been said, the British claimed to be anxious to conclude the war and entered into peace negotiations with the Madison administration at the very time that Cochrane's fleet was sailing west to sack and burn the American capital. The American and British peace commissioners got down to business at Ghent, a town in western Belgium, but negotiations quickly stalled just about the time the British foreign secretary made his threat about burning the cities of the East Coast, capturing New Orleans, and turning the United States into an island upon which the Americans would be prisoners. Shortly afterward, however, the British prime minister, Lord Liverpool, wrote his foreign secretary to the effect that Britain should "not continue the war for the purpose of obtaining or securing any acquisition of territory."

The American peace commission wasn't so sure, however, as one of its members wrote: "It is impossible to tell what is the real intentn. of the British Govt. on the question of Peace or War. They probably mean to be govd. by events." In fact, the American suspicions were not unjustified; England then was on the verge of becoming the greatest imperialist power on earth, and her foreign policy tended to be shifty and opportunistic. Who is to say that if, as expected, the British army crushed the New Orleans militia as they had the militia at Washington, and took the city, they would not then declare the Louisiana Purchase void and plant the Union Jack in that priceless territory, comprising all of the American land west of the Mississippi—an area larger than the United States itself prior to the purchase. That certainly seems to have been the object, for Cochrane's orders stated explicitly that he was not to be governed by any events arising from the peace commission then sitting at Ghent. Historian and Jackson biographer Robert V. Remini believes the British plan was "to occupy a large stretch of important and valuable territory . . . that could be demanded as the price of peace." In other words, once New Orleans was conquered, British terms for ending the war would include the Americans ceding the Louisiana Purchase territory over to them.

In any event, no sooner had Cochrane's ships departed the Chesapeake than he received orders from the Admiralty to proceed with the 4,000-man army southward to the Caribbean, and once there to rendevous at Jamaica with an even larger fleet embarking from Portsmouth and from Bordeaux, containing an army of the Duke of Wellington's veterans of the Peninsular campaign. At the time they wrote the orders, Imperial Army headquarters in London had assumed that General Ross would command this combined force; while dismayed to learn of his death, in his stead they hurried off Lieutenant General Sir Edward Pakenham, Wellington's brother-in-law, to catch up with the armada, already at sea, and lead it against New Orleans.

Wellington himself had just been tapped to take overall charge of the American war, but he remained pessimistic. "I don't promise myself much success there," he told the prime minister. Still in Europe trying to tidy up affairs after his defeat of the French, Wellington also tried to persuade the British to tone down the proposed peace terms with the United States, and, as we shall see, disapproved of the operation to take New Orleans.

Unquestionably, both nations were growing weary of war. The British had at first embraced the American conflict with fire-breathing newspaper editorials and much shouting and foot-stamping in Parliament, but they soon became appalled at the prospect of renewed taxes to finance it, especially because of the costliness of the recent wars against Napoleon. In America, where the war had never been popular in the first place, by now things were far, far worse.

For one thing, the economy was almost in paralysis; the U.S. Treasury was bankrupt and the government had defaulted on the national debt. Pay for the army was months in arrears and desertions were rising.* The financial situation had gotten so bad that there wasn't even enough money to pay for firewood to heat the newly built cadets' quarters at West Point, and the students had taken to stealing rails from nearby farmers' fences, causing an uproar in the area. America's once-prosperous trade in agricultural products became almost nonexistent because of the British blockade. There was some blockade-running, of course, but the skyrocketing cost of maritime insurance made this problematic. All the bountiful American cash crops—cotton, tobacco, sugar, grains for flour—had become worthless to plant. Corn farmers had begun feeding their crops to cows and pigs.

When Congress convened in September, it was understandably shocked at the ruins of what had been the shining capital city. Some members even demanded moving the capital elsewhere—back to Philadelphia or up to New York. And *everybody*, Federalist and Democratic Republican alike, was furious at Madison, who now was lampooned on both sides of the Atlantic. Administration officials began to resign, including Secretary of War Armstrong, who was blamed for the Washington disaster. In his place was put Secretary of State James Monroe, who concluded that it would take at least 100,000 regular soldiers to win the war at some point in an uncertain future—and this with not a cent in the Treasury to pay them.

Especially troublesome was the situation in New England, which had opposed the war from the outset and now, predictably, was perhaps the hardest hit. Its vital shipping industry was at a standstill, with both ships and cargoes rotting at the wharves. Unemployment had soared to the point that many citizens were forced to resort to public relief or even beggary. So fervent was the disaffection that many New Englanders defied the embargo against trading with the enemy and began an open

* Executions for desertion had gone from 3 in 1812 to 146 in 1814. As Donald Hickey points out, this posed a dilemma: "Executing those who were caught might serve as a deterrent to others . . . but this undermined the recruiting service."

commerce in livestock and other goods across the Canadian border. The circumstances became so inflammatory that in the early autumn of 1814 the New England state legislatures (minus, of course, what is now Maine, which had been occupied by the British) voted to convene at Hartford, Connecticut, to discuss a formal secession from the Union.*

Not even during the darkest days of the Revolution was there more doomsaying, hand-wringing, and despair across the land. Citizens began to wonder if their country really was second-rate; certainly there was little to be proud of at present. Then came word that a large British fleet and its accompanying army were on their way to the practically defenseless Gulf Coast—to do who knew what? The disheartenment wasn't limited to just New England; there was talk of upheaval, disaffection, even disunion across the country—in the taverns, newspapers, legislatures, churches, parlors, and streets and even in the Congress.

On August 22, Jackson established his headquarters at Mobile. Though word of the British attacks on Washington and Baltimore would not reach him for some time, Old Hickory in any case felt he had sufficient cause to march into Spanish Florida, which he considered to be in cahoots with England.

This put an unfortunate kink in his plan to reunite with Rachel, whom he hadn't seen for most of the year. It had been his intention that Rachel, bringing Andrew Jr., join him in Mobile, where the family could enjoy the hospitality of that quaint French-Spanish city by the bay. After arranging for a new carriage and "a good pair of horses" for the trip, Jackson proceeded to instruct his wife in the proper comportment for her newfound status: "You must recollect that you are now a Major Generals lady in the service of the U.S. and as such you must appear elegant and plain, not extravagant, but in such state as Strangers expect to see you."

---

* This might have altered a lot of history down the road, for if the vote had been taken for sesession, there was little the federal government—given its present crisis—could have done to prevent it. And what effect would such a crucial precedent have created forty-seven years later, when the Southern states voted to secede from the Union?

Shortly after his arrival in Mobile, however, Jackson's spies told him that a British squadron had arrived at the port city of Pensacola on the Gulf of Mexico, about forty miles east. With not so much as a by-your-leave, the British commander, Colonel Edward Nicholls, escorted by a force of redcoats, had marched up to the quarters of the Spanish governor and informed him that the British would be using the city as a base of operations against the Americans. With an unctuous acquiescence from the Spanish *comandante,* the British raised their flag to equal height with that of the Spanish colors, and Colonel Nicholls got down to business. He installed his troops in several large Spanish fortifications and began recruiting an army of disaffected Indians—many of them leftovers from the Red Stick War—promising to reverse the Treaty of Fort Jackson and restore their lands, as well as, more materially, promising them firewater.* They were to be armed with a shipload of twenty thousand weapons sent by Admiral Cochrane, then to speed southward for his rendezvous and the anticipated attack on New Orleans.

On August 29, Nicholls issued a windy "proclamation" and ordered it distributed to the "Natives of Louisiana" (by which he meant Frenchmen and Spaniards and their offspring, who comprised the majority of that state's white population). This document called for them to "assist in liberating from a faithless, imbecile government [meaning the Madison administration] your paternal soil." In case they chose to disagree, Nicholls went on to threaten them: "I am at the head of a large body of Indians, well armed, disciplined and commanded by British officers [and] a good train of artillery [as well as] numerous British and Spanish squadrons of ships and vessels of war," and then concluded, "The American usurpation in this country must be abolished."

That was enough for Jackson. After sending off a letter to the Spanish *comandante* at Pensacola, demanding to know the meaning of British

* It was reported to Jackson by his spies that battalions of Indians had been seen dressed in British red coats, marching up and down the streets of Pensacola, being drilled by British sergeants in the manual-of-arms.

troops in his district, and another to Governor Blount to hurry Tennessee troops down to Mobile—as well as one more canceling Rachel's visit—Jackson set about reinforcing the shabbily built Fort Bowyer, the first British objective at the mouth of Mobile Bay and the key to the city. Having done so, he then began to calculate operations against Pensacola to rid that whole territory of both the British *and* the Spanish. Although he'd requested permission to do this back in June, Jackson had received no answer from the War Department, but now he was determined to charge ahead, permission granted or not. If war with Spain was the result, so be it—events were rapidly coming to a head, and Andrew Jackson was prepared to deal with them on his own.

On the night of September 12, Jackson sailed from Mobile to inspect the rehabilitation of Fort Bowyer, about thirty miles south on the gulf. Three hours later his schooner encountered a small sailboat, whose passenger had an urgent message for the general: Fort Bowyer had just come under siege by the British, with four warships bombarding from the sea and a party of 600 Indians and 130 British marines attacking by land. Quickly understanding the peril he was in, Jackson ordered his boat to come about for Mobile, where he dragooned a company of infantry and sent them rushing to the besieged outpost down the bay.

The next morning the relief force sailed back into Mobile Harbor with distressing news: Fort Bowyer had apparently exploded and been lost. The citizens of Mobile spent an anxious day and night, fearing the momentary arrival of the British to capture their city and turn them out of their homes. The following morning brighter word arrived: Fort Bowyer was secure. The giant flash that the relief party assumed was the fort's powder magazine blowing up was actually the British twenty-gun man-of-war *Hermes* being blown to bits in the pass. The other three enemy ships departed, as did the shore raiding party, leaving 162 Indians and Englishmen dead on the beaches and aboard the ships. Fort Bowyer's commander, a Major Lawrence, had gathered his defenders before the battle and—in a play on the famous last words of his namesake on the ill-fated *Chesapeake*—made them repeat their new motto: "Don't give up the fort!"*

With Fort Bowyer secure, Jackson set about organizing his attack on Pensacola, a task he looked forward to with relish, since the Spanish *comandante* had replied to his earlier letter by calling him "impertinent."

Slowly but surely, the troops Jackson had called for from Tennessee began to arrive, among them the reliable General Coffee's 1,800 cavalrymen. On November 2 Jackson marched on Pensacola with an army of 3,000, including 700 regulars. Four days later it stood before the city while a messenger under a white flag walked toward Pensacola to deliver an ultimatum to surrender. He was fired upon, not apparently by the Spaniards but by the truculent, newly arrived British. That night Jackson maneuvered his soldiers so as to encircle the city, and at dawn on November 7, 1814, they stormed the town. There was brief fighting, but soon Jackson was informed that the Spanish *comandante*, "old, infirm and trembling, was stumbling around with a white flag in distracted quest" of him. The surrender was quickly arranged, but not before the British blew up their commandeered garrison at Fort Barrancas, reboarded their ships, and sailed off for parts unknown. What happened to the majority of hostile Indians has never been fully explained, although a number of them were rounded up after they were observed staggering drunkenly around the city, proudly wearing their British red coats without pants.

Leaving a large number of his men to garrison Pensacola, Jackson then countermarched back to Mobile. After leaving even more men to protect that city, he took Coffee and his cavalry and pushed on to New Orleans, where he expected the main battle to break out.

* After the war, Fort Bowyer was enlarged into a powerful fortification known as Fort Morgan. It was here in 1864, during the Battle of Mobile Bay, that Admiral David Farragut was said to have uttered his equally famous words: "Damn the torpedoes, full speed ahead!"

Five

Central to the British design for the capture of Louisiana was an extraordinary scheme devised by Colonel Nicholls to enlist the services of the "pirates of Barataria," who were for the most part not pirates at all but "privateers," operating under "letters of marque" from foreign countries. Under the agreed concessions of maritime law, these official letters, or commissions, allowed the privateers to prey on the merchant shipping of any nation at war with the issuing country without—in the event they were captured—being subject to hanging as pirates, the accepted punishment of the day. Privateering had a long if not always honorable history—Sir Francis Drake, famed navigator of the Elizabethan era, was also a privateer. In certain instances, New England businessmen owned privateering ships, and Jefferson himself approved of their use in place of naval warships. But any time a diverse band of armed men is organized without the strict discipline of military rules and regulations, excesses can occur, and in privateering, especially, they occurred frequently.

In the Gulf of Mexico, a large gathering of these strange and ruthless men had set up operations on Grand Terre Island, Louisiana, which lies about forty miles south of New Orleans as the crow flies, but with the only route to the city lying along the twisted tangle of rivers, bayous, creeks, and canals, it was about a hundred miles and normally took three days or so to get there. The leader of this band was a tall, handsome, magnetic Frenchman named Jean Laffite, who, using his blacksmith shop in New Orleans as a front, came to run a phenomenal business smuggling contraband (illegal goods on which no federal duties had been paid) to the grateful citizens of New Orleans, rich and poor alike, who had been deprived for years by the American embargo and the British blockade. At any given time there were as many as a thousand (some say five times that number) of these "Baratarians" on the island of Grand Terre, constantly coming and going in their armed sloops and schooners-of-war to attack mostly Spanish and sometimes British shipping in the gulf and the Caribbean.

It was to the Baratarians that Colonel Nicholls dispatched his emissaries from HMS *Sophie* to see if they, with their valuable skills, armaments, and priceless knowledge of the area, could be enlisted into the British effort against New Orleans.

On the morning of September 3, 1814, the *Sophie* dropped anchor in the straits between Grand Terre and its next-door neighbor Grand Isle and fired a signal cannon to announce her arrival. Through spyglasses the British observed hundreds of sleepy-eyed, ill-dressed men begin gathering on the sandy beach of Grand Terre, wondering no doubt at this strange new visitor. Presently a small boat was launched from the beach, rowed by four men with a fifth man in the bow. From the *Sophie* a longboat was likewise launched, carrying its captain, Nicholas Lockyer, and a Captain McWilliams of the Royal Marines. The boats met in the channel, and Lockyer, in his best schoolboy French, asked to be taken to Monsieur Laffite; the response from the man in the bow of longboat was that Laffite could be found ashore. Once on the beach, the two British officers were led through the suspicious crowd by the tall man in the bow, along a shaded path, and up the steps of a substantial home with a large wraparound gallery. At that point he genially informed them, "Messieurs, I am Laffite."

Jean Laffite remains among the most enigmatic and persistently romanticized figures in the American historical experience, ranking up there with such legends as Davy Crockett, Daniel Boone, Kit Carson, Wyatt Earp, and Wild Bill Hickok. (Most of these, in the 1950s and '60s, had their exploits turned into popular television serials. Laffite, however, had two major feature movies made of his life—one starring

Fredric March and the other Yul Brynner—both produced by the flamboyant Cecil B. DeMille.) For a man who lived on the edges of society, Laffite would perform for the failing young republic a valuable and patriotic service when he might just as easily have sailed out of danger as a very wealthy man.

Jean Laffite was born at Port-au-Prince in the French colony of San Domingo (now called Haiti), probably about 1782.* His father had been a skilled leatherworker in Spain, France, and Morocco before he settled on Haiti and opened a prosperous leather shop. His mother died "before I could remember her," and he was raised by his maternal grandmother, whose husband, a Jew, had been a pharmacist in Spain before he was murdered during the Inquisition. Laffite's grandmother "never lost an opportunity to tell me about all the tribulations her relatives were subjected to," and—like Jackson's youthful hatred of the British—this became the cornerstone of young Jean's lifelong antipathy toward the Spanish. There were eight children in the Laffite family, of whom Jean was the youngest. Of these, his brothers Pierre, two and a half years older, and Alexandre, a seaman eleven years older, would figure prominently in his life.

After a rigorous education beginning at age six, Jean and Pierre were sent away, by the time they reached their early teens, to advanced schooling on the neighboring islands of Saint Croix and Martinique. Next they went to a military academy on the island of Saint Christopher (Saint Kitts), where they received training in swordsmanship, navigation, and artillery; later they honed their skills in the martial arts of dueling and fencing back in Port-au-Prince.

In the meantime, Alexandre returned occasionally from his adventures as a privateer attacking Spanish ships in the Caribbean and regaled his younger brothers with engaging stories of his exploits, among which was a stint as an artilleryman in the service of Napoleon. A short man with a bull-like build, hooked nose, large alert eyes, and a

---

* Widely varying accounts of Laffite's life have resulted in sometimes harsh disputes, academic and otherwise. For a discussion of the author's information and conclusions, see the Notes on Sources section at the end of this book.

fiery temper, Alexandre had by now assumed the alias "Dominique You," an unusual name, perhaps, but a common practice among privateers who realized that at any given point—in the days before photos and fingerprints—some authority might be looking for them under another.*

So captivated were the two young Laffites by their older brother's tales that nothing would do but for them to follow him to sea, despite their grandmother's fervent protests. A cousin, Renato Beluche, also of French ancestry but a native of New Orleans, apparently helped them get aboard one of the many privateers bearing French letters of marque, where they "learned the trade," so to speak, of this variation on piracy.

For a quick look at how such men operated their everyday business back then, let us turn to an account attributed to Laffite of an unusual encounter between two privateering ships and a Spanish corvette, the *Atrevida*, in the spring of 1801. Spying the Spaniard off the coast of Vera Cruz, Beluche (who, because he was a bit older, was known as Uncle Reyne by the Laffite boys) ordered his vessel to pour on sail and overtake the corvette. When they closed, Beluche's men were bewildered at what they saw. At first it appeared that there were many armed men on deck waiting for them. But soon it became apparent that, in fact, a mutiny was in progress. The *Atrevida* was manned for the most part by a crew of Frenchmen who, having been deported from Mexico by Spanish authorities, had been forced to work their way across the Atlantic as servile crewmen to the Spanish captain.

As the three ships rolled along side by side in the ocean swells, the privateers watched the development of the mutiny. The Spanish officers slowly gained ground against the unarmed Frenchmen—one of whom was shot dead when he called out to the privateers' ships, "*Vive la*

* Here is one of those vexing historical inconsistencies that crop up so frequently in this story. Many historians, including the authority Dr. Remini, state that Dominique was in fact the older brother of Jean and Pierre, but William C. Davis, the Laffites' latest biographer, asserts otherwise, noting that in those days it was common for a man to call someone "brother" without such a relationship existing in fact.

France!" Once the Spanish regained control, according to Laffite, "they ordered the mutineers to be bound and forced to go up on deck, where the officers ordered the chef, the black cook, to hit each on the head with an axe and, afterwards, throw them into the sea.

"Uncle Reyne," recorded Laffite, "was very upset by the massacre of the Frenchmen," and shouted out for the *Atrevida* to surrender. When this produced no response, a shot was fired at her bow, knocking off the bowsprit. Still no surrender, but the Spanish captain was operating under a considerable handicap since he had just executed most of his own gun crews. More cannon shot from the privateersmen finally had the desired effect, and the *Atrevida* was captured. Its captain, however, became surly and refused to show the privateersmen where the gold and other valuables were.

To get this information, the privateers tied him up on deck in the equatorial noonday sun, and when he was still not forthcoming, a magnifying glass was used "to focus more of the sun's heat on him." Not only that, but pistols were repeatedly discharged "close to his ears to create a vibration of his nerves." This did the trick, and the privateers sailed home to Haiti with their prize in tow and their hold full of Spanish gold.* Thus Jean Laffite, like Andrew Jackson, experienced at an early age some terrible sights that left with him a lasting impression that the world was a violent and unforgiving place. In lieu of Jackson's hatred of the British, Laffite developed an abiding hatred of Spain.

At the age of eighteen Jean fell in love with and married Christine Levine, whose parents were Danish Jews, on the island of Saint Croix. Over the next four years she presented Jean with two sons and a daughter, Denise Jennette, but Christine died during the final childbirth. Jean's sister took in Denise, and the two boys were sent to live with Pierre's wife, Françoise Sel, while Jean and Pierre plied their privateering trade. Then further calamity struck.

---

* The Spanish captain, Laffite tells us, was spared his life for the massacre of the Frenchmen, and instead "sequestered in a French colony at forced labor for life."

Led by Toussaint-Louverture, a charismatic former slave, a massive slave rebellion erupted on Haiti that ultimately, in 1802, terminated French rule on the island. The later fighting centered around an attempted annihilation by the slave army of the prosperous colony of free light-skinned blacks—quadroons, octaroons—who themselves kept slaves, and who formed a sort of black upper class on the island. But it quickly spread into a movement to free all 600,000 Haitian slaves and establish an independent black republic. Aided and abetted by the Spanish, Haiti soon became engulfed in a monstrous civil war in which thousands were slaughtered, plantations were burned, and their French owners and families were put to the sword, gallows, or burning stake.*
Napoleon responded by sending a 34,000-man army from France to put the rebellion down, but it was decimated amid a scourge of yellow fever in which more than two-thirds of the soldiers died, including the commander.

The situation on Haiti had become so intolerable by 1804 that the French colonists—as well as most of the free men of color, the mulattoes—were forced to flee, and many of them wound up in New Orleans, with its large French population. This included the Laffites, who evacuated their families and friends to the new American republic.

Many of the wealthier French-Haitian planters found a natural transition for themselves in the rich Mississippi bottomlands south of New Orleans, which they soon discovered were ideal for growing sugarcane. Ever since a plague of caterpillars wiped out their indigo crops half a century earlier, Louisianans had been planting sugarcane, but it had been only recently that they learned how to refine it into granulated sugar. Up until then, the best they could produce was a kind of sweet gummy syrup, which they soon realized could be used to make rum, a development that caused the governor to complain that "the immoderate use of [rum] has stupefied the whole population."

Soon the production of sugar became Louisiana's principal cash

---

* The Haitian revolution has the distinction of being the only successful black slave rebellion in history.

crop; a successful planter could easily make $20,000 to $30,000 a year ($300,000 to $400,000 in today's dollars). Sugar growing was a labor-intensive operation, however, and as more plantations were added more slaves were needed to plant and cut the cane, grind it for boiling, then pack the crystallized sugar into barrels for shipping abroad.*

By this time the riverbanks for miles had become a continuous row of sugar plantations, most of them about eight hundred to a thousand acres, upon which the planters often built sumptuous plantation homes, in addition to keeping their luxurious town houses in the city. All in all, during the first years of the nineteenth century, New Orleans prospered dramatically—not just from sugar but from the upriver trade of furs, grains, flour, cotton, salt, sawn timber, whisky, and other goods, which came down on flatboats from as far away as Ohio and Pennsylvania to be loaded onto ships destined for the far corners of the world.

Good things don't usually last forever, and in the case of New Orleans they certainly didn't—beginning on the first day of January 1808. First there was the aforementioned Embargo Act, passed by Congress to retaliate for the assaults on American shipping by England and France during the Napoleonic Wars. Next was the African Importation Act, which banned the introduction of any more slaves into the United States. With these two measures in place, maritime commerce in New Orleans slowed almost to a standstill, broken only by the time-honored practice of smuggling.

It was amid this setting that the brothers Laffite began their rise to prominence.

When Jean and Pierre arrived in Louisiana from Haiti they did not come as wealthy French planters but as privateersmen—a barely respectable and unquestionably dangerous business—and just in time to learn that the U.S. government had ordered all American ships to

---

* Interestingly, another crop that seemed to thrive in Louisiana was citrus—in particular oranges—which contemporary writers describe as having been grown all over the region in groves of a thousand acres or more. This could not be done today because of frequent freezes.

remain in port indefinitely under the Embargo Act. Accordingly, the Laffites set themselves up in New Orleans with a blacksmith's shop in which, using slave labor, they began fabricating, among other things, the fancy kinds of cast-iron grilles that dress so many New Orleans balconies and windows.*

A mere smithing enterprise, reputable as it was, never quite suited the ambitious Jean Laffite, who by now had grown into a somewhat formidable presence. In his mid-twenties, Laffite was described as a handsome, dark-haired man† about six feet tall with "dark piercing eyes," and a furious vertical crease in his brow—he was "well made," in the parlance of the day—with a physical comportment something like that of a large, powerful cat. He was also recorded as being smart, shrewd, and convivial—if not jovial—and a gambling and drinking man as well. One of the first American chroniclers of the era was Judge Alexander Walker, a New Orleanian whose book *Jackson and New Orleans* was published in 1856, and who thus knew firsthand many of the personages of the Jackson-Laffite era. According to Judge Walker, Laffite "was a man of good address and appearance, of considerable shrewdness, of generous and liberal heart, and adventurous spirit." Laffite spoke English, Spanish, and Italian with a heavy French accent, and was reputed to be something of a ladies' man, though little is known of his romantic life except that he regularly attended the fabulous Quadroon Balls, in which young men of means in New Orleans mingled (and more) with the beautiful light-skinned "free women of color" from the Caribbean islands.

It was said that Jean dressed as a gentleman and had a gentleman's manners to match, but that neither he nor Pierre (and certainly not their older brother Dominique You, who still dressed like a pirate) were

* The Laffite blacksmith shop stands today as a well-known landmark at St. Philip and Bourbon streets in the French Quarter, maintained by the city of New Orleans (that is, if you choose to ignore those who—as in so many areas of fact surrounding the Laffites—claim that the brothers were never in the blacksmithing business at all).

† It has also been said that Laffite sometimes washed his hair with potash and gunpowder, which turned him into a redhead.

actually treated as such in the rarefied society of nineteenth-century New Orleans. Though they were accepted as daytime equals and night-time drinking and gambling partners because of their bearing, wealth, demeanor, and prowess with the dueling sword and pistol, the male upper crust of the city excluded them from their extravagant social events, let alone their parlors to meet their wives and daughters.

Just how the Laffites became involved so quickly and prominently in the massive smuggling enterprise then engulfing New Orleans is a matter of historical controversy. The most plausible explanation comes from New Orleans historian and LSU professor Jane Lucas De Grummond,* who tells us that in the summer of 1805 Jean sailed into the city after a privateering cruise with 12,600 English pounds that he needed to dispose of (without anyone asking a lot of questions). Brother Dominique You (who had been in the city awhile) found the answer in the person of Joseph Sauvinet, a Frenchman who had become one of the principal businessmen of New Orleans. As head of the largest accounting and banking house in the city, Sauvinet had divined the enormous profits to be made from smuggling and just as quickly recognized the value of a man such as Jean Laffite—not to mention the value of his 12,600 British pounds (about $860,000 today).

Sauvinet set up Jean and his brothers in the smuggling business, with instructions on how to avoid U.S. Customs by off-loading their goods and booty downriver below a bend called English Turn, from where it could be transported to Sauvinet's warehouses for resale in New Orleans. According to De Grummond, this "was the beginning of a contraband commercial venture that was to involve nearly everyone in New Orleans."

Using some of their share of the captured English pounds, the Laffites then began acquiring a small fleet of privateers with which, over the next half dozen years, they terrorized Spanish shipping in the Gulf

* Her two books *The Baratarians and the Battle of New Orleans* and *Renato Beluche: Smuggler, Privateer and Patriot, 1780–1860,* published by the Louisiana State University Press, are considered classics of the genre, but there are always those who will disagree.

of Mexico. Under the rules of the French letters of marque, prizes seized were to be taken to French ports, where a court would award the privateers a percentage of money based on the value of the prize itself (minus copious administrative fees and costs). But as the first decade of the nineteenth century wound down, fewer and fewer of these ports were available owing to a long string of French defeats in those island waters, and finally, after Guadeloupe and Martinique fell to the British, there were none left at all.

Naturally this became a pressing problem for the privateers, since the bulk of their haul often consisted of the captured ship itself, and because America was not then at war with Spain (or, for that matter, with France or England), it was illegal to dispose of the craft within the United States. A base of operations, as it were, was required to take these valuable prizes and somehow turn them into cash. The privateers found their base on the remotest part of the Louisiana coast, at a place called Barataria Bay.

There are parts of Barataria today as dark and unsullied as they were two hundred years ago; it is a place somehow set adrift in time. The bay is hemmed in on the Gulf of Mexico by Grand Isle and Grand Terre (the latter is about six miles long and three miles wide), as well as by several smaller barrier islands, but its name is not just a play on that term; rather, it seems to have been aptly named by some prescient early Frenchman after the mythical island of Barataria in Cervantes's *Don Quixote*, which translates, roughly, into "a place of deception."

The bay,* dotted with many small marshy islands, is about twenty miles wide at its widest point near the coast and tapers out northward to a length of about thirty miles. Among its virtues was that it provided a safe haven from the harsh winter northers as well as all but the fiercest summer hurricanes that blow out of the gulf.

---

* It is also known as Lake Barataria, but because of egress into the gulf it is probably more appropriately described as a bay.

For the privateers of those times seeking a secure harbor, it must have been a paradise, a place of breathtaking natural beauty and serenity. Wondrous varieties of oysters, shrimp, crab, and fish teemed in the blue-green waters right up to shore. Ducks, geese, woodcock, snipe, and other waterfowl were in abundant profusion. Deer roamed the surrounding forests, as well as squirrel, rabbits, and turtle (and frogs, for those so inclined) in the marshes. The island upon which the early Baratarians had settled—Grand Terre (named after a similar isle near Guadaloupe)—was elevated enough to provide protection from all but the worst hurricanes and was covered with canopies of Spanish moss–draped live oaks, palms, pines, and, close on the beaches, a low, scrubby, and gnarled pearlike tree that, judging from its defiantly bent appearance in later photographs, must have custom-designed itself against the strong winds that blew in across the gulf.

There are two other reasons Barataria was an ideal place for a smuggling operation. To the north, behind the barrier islands, the bay was isolated by cypress swamps—their tall branches filled with the nests of eagles and waterbirds—and surrounded by a thousand square miles of nearly impassable quagmires and marshes in which resided dangerous alligators and bears, rattlesnakes and water moccasins, as well as the ever-present anopheles mosquito that carried the deadly "yellow jack." All this made Barataria secure enough from prying official eyes, or so the privateers thought. Second, through a serpentine waterway of rivers, lakes, canals, and bayous, Grand Terre was connected directly to New Orleans, so that smuggled goods could be brought unimpeded into the city in blunt-bowed pirogues, the customary means of inland travel then in south Louisiana.

About halfway between Grand Terre and New Orleans is a raised piece of land in the swamps, which, judging from the huge mounds of clam- and oyster shells, was in centuries past used by Indians for ceremonial purposes, including, many believed, ritual sacrifice—owing to the large numbers of human bones also found there. Known as the Temple, it now became utilized by the privateers as a sort of midway sales and auction spot at which as many as five hundred wealthy New Orleanians at a time would arrive by boat on designated days to buy captured slaves and other smuggled goods and merchandise.

The slave trade was central to the Baratarians' economy. Spanish ships carrying Africans were usually easy marks for the heavily armed privateers, and it was not extraordinary for them to have on hand several hundred or more of these miserable people, whom they kept on Grand Terre in slave pens called "barracoons" to await purchase by the ever-expanding number of sugar plantation owners.[*]

Other merchandise was kept in warehouses, and soon there would be more than forty of these on Grand Terre containing the wealth of Spain, Mexico, South America, and the West Indies: fine silks, Moroccan rugs and leather, elaborately carved furniture—beds, chairs, tables—ornate silver flatware, china, crystal, tapestries, lace, clothing, lamps, and kegs of whisky, rum, and wine. Almost everything imaginable that could be seized on the ocean was sold to the acquisitive citizens of New Orleans, for whom these things were unattainable as a result of the Embargo Act and, close on its heels, the British blockade—and at a healthy discount to boot.

As we have seen, Jean Laffite was not an inconsequential man, but, like so much else about him, exactly how he became the leader of the Baratarians remains murky. History records that there were then two types of Baratarians. First was a band of Grand Isle and Grand Terre islanders who for many years had engaged themselves in fairly minor smuggling undertakings in between their usual fishing and hunting activities. Then, after the British conquest of the French-held Caribbean islands, there sailed into Barataria Bay a new sort—the homeless

---

[*] A few historians have damned Laffite and the Baratarians as lowlifes for dealing in the slave trade. That might be so, but if it is, the question arises as to how they would describe all those wealthy, upstanding citizens who owned the sugar and cotton plantations and bought the slaves to work them. Practically everybody in Louisiana who could afford slaves had one or more, including the so-called free men of color.

privateers. Soon the two groups began squabbling, and often fights broke out, some of them deadly.

At the same time the more successful privateers realized they needed an agent, as it were, to represent them in New Orleans, promoting sales of their booty, negotiating prices, arranging auctions, and keeping the law out of their way. Jean Laffite, a privateer himself, came highly recommended, since he also mingled and mixed with the richest and most powerful men in the city. This worked out well for several years; then the two Baratarian factions started feuding again, and it became apparent that what they really needed was a genuine leader. Laffite had experience with both factions—and they with him—so much so that they managed to drop their differences long enough to ask him if he would come down to Grand Terre and become the headman, or *bos*.

Laffite agreed, and among the first of the differences he settled was a dispute between himself and a villainous Italian captain named Vincent Gambie over the latter's attack on an American sailing vessel. A confrontation ensued during which one of Captain Gambie's men, armed with a pistol, moved threateningly toward Laffite, who—without so much as a "Stop or I'll shoot!"—shot him through the heart. Recalling the incident many years later, brother Dominique You stated, "That put the fear of God in them."

The ascendency of the Laffites marked the beginning of a heyday for the Baratarians, which would last several more years. Under Jean's stewardship the privateers captured more than one hundred prizes with all their cargoes, the most valuable of which were slaves taken in the waters around Havana, which had become the center of the trade in the Western Hemisphere. Being in charge of such rough customers was not always easy. In addition to Gambie, there was another fiery Italian captain named Louis Chighizola, known as "Nez Coupe" because he had lost half of his nose in a swordfight.

With the exception of Laffite, who still attired himself as a gentleman, the rest of the Baratarians—and by this time there were probably more than a thousand of them—dressed just like the swashbuckling pirates from the old stories: bright red and black striped blouses, pantaloons, tall boots, and colorful bandanas tied around their heads. Many wore gold earrings, and all carried cutlasses, knives, and pistols.

As business grew, the activities of the Baratarians became more and more outrageous. Flyers were posted in broad daylight on buildings throughout New Orleans announcing the booty auctions, cataloguing the items to be sold. These were attended by the most prominent men in the city, who bought up everything from slaves to pig iron to dresses and jewelry for their wives. Everybody knew smuggling was illegal, but for the Creoles, poor and upper crust alike, it had been a way of life under both the Spanish and the French regimes for as long as anyone could remember. Occasionally, some of the Baratarians ran afoul of the law, yet Laffite's connections included not only powerful members of the state legislature but also the most outstanding lawyer in Louisiana, Edward Livingston.

Under Laffite, Barataria took on a remarkable new look. In addition to the large home he built for himself, other houses of the thatched-palm-roof "cottage" variety began to spring up on Grand Terre as the money poured in. At any given time dozens of ships lay at anchor inshore, and not infrequently Baratarians could be seen strolling defiantly upon the streets of New Orleans in various stages of sobriety. Laffite had ordered the construction of a fort at the west end of Grand Terre and armed it with cannon from plundered ships. After the fall of the French in the Caribbean, Laffite arranged for the privateers to operate quasi-legally under the flag and letters of marque of Cartagena, a large city-state in what is now Colombia that had recently declared independence from Spain and was at war with that country. In addition, Laffite began to squirrel away large stores of arms, gunpowder, flints, and cannonballs at various secret locations in the wilds of Barataria—for use against exactly what is not clear—but these munitions would prove a godsend when the Battle of New Orleans broke out.

Six

Not everyone was pleased with the cozy arrangements between Laffite's Baratarians and the citizens of New Orleans, especially William C. C. Claiborne, the new governor of Louisiana, which had recently been admitted as the eighteenth state of the Union. Claiborne's complaints against the "pirates of Barataria" soon became abundant. First, they were violating U.S. tariff regulations right under his nose—no inconsequential matter either, since, without a federal income tax, the government in Washington depended for most of the nation's revenues on duties collected on imported goods. The fact that the U.S. Treasury was about to go broke did not help things at all.

Then there was the African slave issue. Not only had the importation of slaves become illegal by federal law, but there were apparently further consequences of the Baratarian smuggling of this human cargo that distressed Governor Claiborne. Several years earlier a slave rebellion had erupted on the plantations north of New Orleans; after murdering a number of whites, the slaves marched on the city itself but were finally broken up by militia units. To Southern whites the notion of a slave uprising was their most dreaded fear, and the fact that it was blacks from Haiti who had instigated the earlier rebellion caused the governor and others to conclude that slaves from the Caribbean islands were rebellious by nature and thus not to be trusted—*these* were precisely the kinds of bondsmen the Laffites were importing to Louisiana.

Not only that, but Jean, Pierre, and a couple of dozen Baratarians had recently been apprehended at night by a company of U.S. Army regulars while attempting to smuggle about $4,000 worth of cinnamon into New Orleans. After posting bail, the Laffites skipped town for Grand Terre, from where they taunted the authorities. Claiborne issued a proclamation damning the activities of the Baratarians and specifically naming Jean Laffite as the principal troublemaker. The governor personally offered, "in the name of the state," a $500 reward for the capture and delivery of Jean Laffite.

No one could accuse Laffite of not having a sense of humor—let alone audacity—because he immediately responded by having handbills plastered all over New Orleans promising a $5,000 reward for the capture and delivery to *him* of Governor Claiborne!

Numerous writs of arrest were also brought against the Laffites by federal authorities, but U.S. marshals, fearful for their lives, refused to go into Baratarian territory to serve them, and the court records are filled with marshals' notations about the Laffites: "Not found in New Orleans." Even the U.S. government surveyor declined to practice his business in the Baratarians' lair, writing his boss in Washington, "They are an outlaw set [and] I am fearful they will give me some trouble." In fact, the surveyor went on, the Baratarians had actually arrested several customs agents and sentenced one of them "to ten years at hard labor with a 56-pound weight hung to his leg." As if that wasn't enough, a number of American merchants in New Orleans began to complain to Claiborne that since most of the smugglers' goods were being acquired by their French Creole rivals, their own businesses were suffering.

Try as he would to rid himself of this lawlessness, the governor was continually whipsawed. After an encounter between customs agents and the Baratarians left one agent dead and two others "greviously wounded," Claiborne went to the Louisiana legislature to seek action. The legislators—preponderantly of French extraction—considered the governor's request for money and men to destroy the Baratarian stronghold and "took it under advisement," where, as the New Orleans historian Stanley A. Clisby aptly put it, "it remains to this day."

Time, however, was running out for the Baratarians. In his frustration Governor Claiborne finally appealed directly to President Madison, who ordered the secretary of war and the secretary of the navy to do something. They in turn told Commodore Daniel T. Patterson of the navy and Colonel George T. Ross, commanding the 44th U.S. Infantry, to come up with a plan to rid the country of these "banditi" who were attacking ships on the high seas belonging to "nations not at war with the United States."

Accordingly, the *Carolina*, a schooner-of-war armed with fourteen guns, was moved to New Orleans for the express purpose of breaking up the operations at Grand Terre. The fact that she was still there when the British attack broke out, and the crucial role she played in repelling it, remains one of the delicious ironies in a war filled with irony.

In the meantime, further trouble came the Laffites' way. In the late summer of 1814, just as Jackson was concluding the Treaty of Fort Jackson with the Indians, a federal grand jury in New Orleans indicted Pierre Laffite for aiding and abetting piracy, a hanging offense. Pierre had recently suffered a stroke (which left him somewhat cross-eyed), and he had taken to spending time in the city with his wife and family, which was where the authorities caught up with him. He was thrown into the calaboose—the filthy, lice-ridden, old Spanish jail—without bail and chained to the wall, in case he entertained the notion of escape.

This development weighed heavily on Jean, for he had every reason to be concerned for his brother's health in those conditions. No amount of legal maneuvering by lawyer Edward Livingston could spring Pierre from "the depths of a dungeon," as Laffite described it, and for all Jean knew Pierre's next steps might be to the gallows. These matters were on Jean's mind when he received the delegation from His Britannic Majesty's military services at Grand Terre on that sultry day in early September 1814.

After recovering from the surprise that their tall, swarthy guide was none other than the infamous Laffite himself, the British captains got down to business. Initially, this consisted of handing over to Laffite a packet of documents produced by their superiors that included an advance copy of Colonel Nicholls's "proclamation," which was about to be distributed to the citizens of Louisiana. Next were two documents of the carrot-and-stick variety, signed by Captain W. H. Percy, British senior naval commander in the Gulf of Mexico. On the one hand, Percy threatened to send a fleet to destroy the Baratarians and their stronghold because of their privateering activities against Spanish and British shipping. On the other, if the Baratarians would join with the British, they would receive "lands within His Majesty's colonies in America" and the opportunity to become British subjects with a full pardon for any previous crimes.*

Finally there was a personal note from Colonel Nicholls to Laffite as "Commandant at Barataria," in which the Irishman explained himself by announcing, "I have arrived in the Floridas for the purpose of annoying the only enemy Great Britain has in the world. . . ." What the British wanted, the letter went on to say, was use of all the boats and ships of the Baratarians and the enlistment of the Baratarian gunners and fighters in the invasion of Louisiana. Nicholls also promised Laffite, personally, that he would be made a captain in His Majesty's Royal Navy.

This was quite a bit to digest, but at the same time it seems to have made Jean hungry, too, for as Judge Walker tells us, after glancing over the papers Jean ordered an elaborate feast to be laid out for His Majesty's envoys, consisting of "the best wines of old Spain, the richest fruits of the West Indies, and every variety of fish and game, spread out before them and served on the richest carved silver plate." Apparently a good time was had by all, for when they were done eating, "they all smoked cigars of the finest Cuban flavor."

The drift of the conversation, according to Walker, then came around to the declaration that Laffite and his minions were crucial to guiding the British invasion force up through the swamps, and that once New Orleans was secured the army would move upriver and "act

---

* Even the Baratarians must have thought this strange, since there no longer *were* any of His Majesty's colonies in America.

in concert" with the British forces in Canada, thereby, as Laffite put it, "to shove the Americans into the Atlantic Ocean." The British officers indicated that His Majesty's forces also intended to set free all the slaves they could find and enlist their help in subduing the presumptuous Americans.

The two Englishmen next offered Laffite their pièce de résistance: a bribe of 30,000 British pounds (more than $2 million today) if he could convince his followers to join with the British against the United States. If this seems like a lot of money—and it was—the British would nevertheless have consided it well spent, since it was understood that the Baratarians' knowledge of those tangled, trackless marshes and bayous leading up to New Orleans would be nearly priceless. To attack the city by appearing on its outskirts right out of the swamps would for all purposes amount to a British coup de main in which the money was a pittance compared to the enormous amount of booty they expected to confiscate from New Orleans warehouses after so many years of embargo and blockade.

As Laffite was pondering this generous offer, however, trouble began to brew. Upon seeing the red-coated British marine and blue-jacketed British naval captain, the run-of-the-mill Baratarians suspected that something nasty was afoot. Not a few of them were Americans and, despite their troubles with the law (which they mostly considered a nuisance), they wished no part of a British scheme to conquer America. Accordingly, a disturbance broke out, with the Baratarians demanding to know the meaning of the Britons' presence; some grumbled that His Majesty's emissaries should be hanged as spies.

After considerable remonstration, Laffite managed to get his people calmed down long enough to spirit the Englishmen back to their gig and send them on their way, but, playing for time against the threatened British assault on his stronghold, he told the two envoys he needed "a fortnight" (fourteen days) to compose his men and put his personal affairs in order. After that, according to papers later filed with the U.S. Federal Court in New Orleans, Laffite promised the Englishmen that he and his men would be "entirely at your disposal."

What was going on in Jean Laffite's mind as he watched the British-ers sail happily away is uncertain. He must have considered the bribe, for it would have been far out of character for a man of his makeup to turn down that kind of money without a thought. Then there was the fact of his brother Pierre languishing in the wretched jail, contemplating the hangman's noose—the British having also promised that, upon their victory, Pierre would be set free.

On the other hand, Laffite, though a Frenchman by birth, apparently considered himself something of a patriot where America was concerned. After all, the country had been good to him—at least until recently—as he had amassed a considerable fortune (though in blatant contravention of its laws) by being a smuggler on her shores. Also, under the British offer, he would have had to give up all his ships to take advantage of the promised "lands within His Majesty's colonies in America," and farming was not exactly Laffite's goal in life. The slave-freeing business must have bothered him too; after all, being a slaver himself, Laffite would not likely cotton to any notion of arming slaves.

What exactly he might have thought about all or any of this appears to have had little more moment than a passing shadow, because Laffite promptly sat down with pen and paper and proceeded to double-cross his newfound British friends.

The British—at least Colonel Nicholls and his people—seemed to live in a fool's paradise so far as the makeup of the American people was concerned. First, they had convinced themselves that a vast body of Indians from Florida would join them in the descent upon New Orleans, but they were, of course, disabused of that particular scheme by Andrew Jackson's attack on Pensacola, which sent the Indians scattering into parts unknown. Likewise, they believed that the French and Spanish Louisiana Creoles hated America enough to rise up and join with them to separate from the United States.

More far-fetched was the British conviction—embodied in Nicholls's proclamation of August 29—that even the Anglo-Americans living west of the Appalachians were so disaffected with the government in

Washington that they would gladly acquiesce to a British invasion of their soil. (In a stunning display of geographical misunderstanding, Nicholls had appealed in his proclamation to the "Inhabitants of Kentucky, you have too long borne with grievous impositions . . . ," failing entirely to include the then populous state of Tennessee, as well as the territories of Alabama and Mississippi.) As the historian Wilburt S. Brown aptly pointed out, these British soldier-diplomats "seemed to have become victims of their own propaganda."

No matter what anybody would say about it later, Laffite's letter to the U.S. authorities (even if somewhat tainted by a logically self-serving pardon request) was a bold, loyal, audacious, and public-spirited declaration of patriotism. Addressing himself to his powerful friend Jean Blanque, Laffite revealed the entire British scheme, as well as their smarmy offers and bribes to him, in such a way as to express a clear and present warning of the danger. He also informed Blanque that he was stringing the British along and asked for instructions from the authorities at New Orleans. A huge British fleet containing an entire army was at the moment gathering for an attack on the city, Laffite said, and he asked Blanque to do whatever he would with the information but obviously assumed Blanque would take it to the governor. When he was finished, Laffite put his letter into a packet and sent it by a special courier who reached Jean Blanque in New Orleans in less than a day, a remarkable feat in itself, since the trip from Grand Terre normally took three.

Jean Blanque did exactly what Laffite had expected him to do: he rushed those critial communications to Governor Claiborne. As a wealthy and respected lawyer, banker, and member of the Louisiana legislature (as well as an investor in Laffite's privateering enterprise), Blanque carried considerable weight, especially since Laffite had included all the documents the British had given him, imperial seals and all.

At this point, Jean Laffite, if had he wanted, easily might have sailed over to the British and requested (at least a part of) his bribe, and then sailed away again to places unknown, a rich man. Or he simply could have ordered the Baratarians to load up their ships from the warehouses and done the same thing. That he didn't seems testimony that Laffite must have felt either a certain loyalty to America or perhaps an animus against the British-Spanish cabal, but the fact remains that he did not take the easy way out; he chose sides.

If Laffite thought that the New Orleans authorities were now going to forgive him for smuggling, however, he was mistaken. Not only did they do no such thing, they decided not to believe him. When Blanque delivered Laffite's communiqué to Claiborne, the governor convened the legislature's Committee of Public Safety, which recently had been organized as the present crisis unfolded. This committee consisted, in addition to the governor, of a number of prominent citizens, including the American army and navy commanders, Ross and Patterson, Major General Jacques Villeré, head of the Louisiana militia, and the U.S. Customs collector, among others. Claiborne laid out the letters for the committee to read, then asked: "The council must decide two questions: first, are these letters genuine; second, is it proper for the Governor of Louisiana to enter into any correspondence with Jean Laffite or any of his associates."

Most committee members insisted that the letters must be fakes, forgeries, and that Laffite was a low-down pirate simply trying to get his brother out of jail with a cheap gambit. The one voice that spoke out on Laffite's behalf belonged to General Villeré, who declared that the Baratarians were privateers operating under the Cartagena flag, that they had adopted the United States as their country, and that they must be trusted. If anyone knew the fragility of Louisiana's defense forces, it was Villeré, but he was overruled; just in case, though, it was decided to send a verbal reply with Laffite's messenger telling him not to do anything until the matter could be given further consideration. In any event, Commodore Patterson and Colonel Ross—who were not bound by any decisions of the state government but took their orders direct from Washington—announced they were going ahead with their expedition to oust Laffite and company from Grand Terre.

Meanwhile, Laffite, who had been anxiously on the lookout for the return of his messenger, was both surprised and delighted to see in the messenger's pirogue none other than his brother Pierre, who had magically "escaped" from jail. The magic probably had something to do with bribery, but in any case Pierre was free. Yet, as good news is so often followed by bad, Laffite's spies in New Orleans also returned with the unpleasant wind that Patterson's flotilla and army were assembling at New Orleans to put him out of business. This prompted Laffite to write another letter, this time to Claiborne himself, regarding "the safety of the country," in which Laffite candidly admitted his sin of smuggling but offered his own services and those of the Baratarians "in defense of the country," asking in return a pardon for himself, Pierre, and any other of his men who were indicted or about to be. "I am a stray sheep," he wrote, "wishing to come back into the fold."

Matters then began unfolding very quickly, as they are apt to when war is just over the horizon. At about this time an anonymous letter from a privateer spy in Havana—where Nicholls's flotilla had put in before sailing on to Pensacola—was delivered to Laffite. The spy was apparently a good one, too, because the letter revealed the British plot to enlist thousands of hostile Indians in Florida, as well as the slaves; provided the names and types of British ships, plus a description of troops and artillery; and gave a summary of the entire plan of operations: first attack westward from Pensacola and secure the American fort at the mouth of Mobile Bay, then the conquest of Mobile itself, followed by a march on New Orleans in concert with the two British fleets now headed in that direction. The spy closed with a warning: "You have not a moment to lose; because if they get a footing, it will be very difficult to get clear of them." He went on to describe Colonel Nicholls as "an impatient blustering Irishman, apparently brave and cruel." (The letter proved to be chillingly accurate.)

Laffite immediately rushed this letter to Claiborne by another special courier, and the governor, in turn, not only sent it along to Jackson with the others but had them all published in the newspaper, further adding to the city's growing alarm. Along with the other unfolding evidence of a British invasion, Laffite's communications undoubtedly confirmed Jackson's decision to attack Pensacola, but when he saw Laffite's offer to bring his Baratarians to the defense of New Orleans in exchange for a pardon, Jackson unwisely reverted to doctrinaire pedantry. He denounced the Baratarians as "hellish banditi" and finally got around to issuing a proclamation of his own—directed to the Louisianans—in which he informed the startled Creoles that the "base, perfidious Britons" were "the sworn enemies of all Frenchmen," and that all Creoles should "nobly die in the last ditch" before accepting Nicholls's suggestion to join with the British in the overthrow of American rule in Louisiana. What Jackson failed to understand at this point was that he would soon need all the help he could get, including that of the hellish banditi.

Laffite, for his part, was now waiting for the other shoe to drop; he knew not whose, nor where nor when. His fortnight time limit to join the British invasion had expired, and several of His Majesty's warships now lay off Barataria Bay, possibly to enforce the "stick" part of the naval commander's earlier warning to him—and now the Americans, too, were organizing a force to send against him. What was a pirate to do? Laffite was not a man to wonder for long; he ordered most of the Baratarians to sail away from Grand Terre with whatever of value they could carry, including munitions. He put his older brother Dominique You in charge of the island with about five hundred men, instructing him to fight the British from the fort if they attacked and, if that proved unsuccessful, to burn all the warehouses and ships at anchor. Pierre, who had become ill, was then sent off to a plantation to the west. With all that done, Laffite did the sensible thing and fled with Pierre to a friend's plantation on the so-called German Coast, northwest of the city, to await developments, which were not long in coming.

A contemporary American visiting New Orleans from New York, Philadelphia, or Boston might easily have concluded that he had been deposited in a foreign land—which, for all practical purposes, he had. A brief examination of the New Orleans of the time is useful now, since to understand the forces at work under the impending emergency one would almost have to go back several hundred years to the bewildering days of the Borgias.

The city had been founded in 1718 as a trading post on a crescent switchback curve of the half-mile-wide Mississippi River by the French-man Sieur de Bienville, who had recently established a similar post at the head of Mobile Bay, about 140 miles to the east. In many ways the site was ideal, for it provided an expansive riverfront to accept the downriver canoes, rafts, and boats that brought goods from the rivers that drained the Mississippi Basin all the way to the Great Lakes, with tributaries such as the Ohio, Tennessee, Missouri, Wabash, Arkansas, and dozens of smaller streams leading into the interior. It had access to world markets both from the river, about a hundred twisting southward miles from the Gulf of Mexico, and from Lake Pontchartrain, just a few miles away.

In other important ways, however, the site was far from ideal, pri-marily since it lay about eight feet below the level of the river, which during storms—let alone hurricanes—could (and did) cause serious problems, until the levees were built. The site was also swampy and would have to be drained to make it habitable. Nevertheless, Bienville named the place La Nouvelle Orleans, after the priggish Duke of Orleans, and sailed away—no doubt after wishing his small colony of French settlers good luck—never to return.

For the next half century New Orleans languished as a trading backwater with the dreaded yellow fever and other tropical diseases periodically reducing its population dramatically. Frenchmen being Frenchmen, however, they tried to make it nicer by laying out a formal, symmetrical city of European design, with elegant government build-ings, a cathedral, and a large convent for the Ursuline nuns. Then, in 1763, after losing the Seven Years' War, the French were forced to cede the territory of Louisiana to Spain, which began adding its consider-able national flavors, until 1800, when the Spanish, then under Napo-leon's domination, transferred it back to France. By 1803 Napoleon realized that pressing military affairs on the European continent foreclosed his ability to support, defend, and administer the great territory, and, needing cash, he got the bright idea to sell it to the foolish Americans, who overnight doubled the size of their country for a paltry $15 million.

By this time there was a small but growing Anglo-American presence in New Orleans, but as the War of 1812 broke out, most of its twenty-five thousand citizens were of French, Spanish, or African extraction. Of these last—which comprised the majority of people in the district—about half were so-called free men of color, including the several thousand who had recently arrived from Haiti, or they were slaves.

The blacks, despite their population superiority, could not play much of a role in the political intrigues, since free men of color were not allowed to vote, sit on juries, run for public office, or intermingle publicly with whites. Mostly they became tradesmen—bricklayers, carpenters, lamplighters, tailors, and oftentimes overseers on the burgeoning sugar plantations. Slaves, on the other hand, were treated basically like barnyard animals.

That left the three white groups—the French, the Spanish and their descendants (Creoles), and the Americans—each of which detested the others. The first impression most of the by then self-assumed aristocratic French and Spaniards* had of Americans was of those ragged, ill-mannered, drunken, and profane flatboaters from "Kaintucky" who arrived dressed in animal skins with their cargoes of furs, lumber, and occasionally something more useful, such as corn whisky. Because the current flowed so strongly southward, there was no way the rafts could make it back upriver, so the Kentuckians (and Tennesseans, Illinoisans, and Ohioans—all lumped together as "Kaintucks") often stayed and brawled and drank and whored and made

---

* Despite their pretensions, the majority of the French and Spanish who had settled Louisiana were not descended from aristocrats but were the offspring of traders, soldiers and sailors, or even in many earlier cases deported criminals. Nevertheless, as they gained wealth and position, the Creoles assumed the trappings of the European upper crust and soon began to believe that they were aristocracy themselves.

themselves otherwise obnoxious to the recently refined tastes of the Mediterranean Creoles.*

It has been said of New Orleans that it is so romantic you leave it either crying or drunk, and that was probably just as true in 1814 as it is today. A Sunday stroll around town would have found the levee path along the river thronged with colorful people in their Sunday best: Creoles, Kaintucks, mulattoes, quadroons, and with some Irish, Germans, Italians, and Portuguese thrown into the mix, speaking a variety of tongues, gathering around impromptu musical bands, fighting, flirting, laughing, and cursing, all against the backdrop of the tall masts of sailing ships that crowded the city wharves. The naturalist John J. Audubon described the levee on Sunday as "crowded by people of all sorts as well as colors, the market very abundant, the church bells ringing, the billiard balls knocking, the guns [of hunters] heard all around." At night, several theaters presented (in different languages) the latest plays from Europe. Probably the most eclectic theater in town was the Grand Opera, where performances were sung in numerous languages, including Russian. For those interested in sport there was a racetrack and any number of cockfighting pits.

There were even more exotic entertainments. For $1 (half price for children) one could see large animal fights, pitting a Bengal tiger against a bear, twelve dogs against a large bull, or six bulldogs against a Canadian bear—each event serenaded by a military band.[†] One could, if one wished, attend a voodoo rite conducted by Haitian immigrants, at which some participants were turned into zombies while others drank the warm blood of a live rooster (as a cure for zombiism). And, of

---

* Vincent Nolte, a German-born New Orleans cotton and sugar merchant, wrote in his 1854 book *Fifty Years in Both Hemispheres* of his revulsion, while traveling through Kentucky, at discovering that so many of the backwoodsmen had let the fingernails on their thumbs and forefingers grow long, sharpening them with files. This, Nolte recorded, was for the purpose of "eye gouging," a customary tactic of the time during fights. Nolte professed himself astounded at the number of one-eyed Kentuckians he encountered on his trip.

† According to a handbill for this affair, if the tiger beat the bear, it would then be sent against the last surviving bull, and if the bull happened to win, "several pieces of fire-works will be attached to his back, which will produce a very entertaining amusement."

course, there were the Quadroon Balls, where for an entrance fee of $10 wealthy men could drink, gamble, and make personal arrangements with young "high-yellow" women.

A walk along the unpaved and often muddy streets of New Orleans was rarely without anxiety, especially in certain parts of town. Thanks to the volatile mix of sailors, gamblers, riverboat men, soldiers of fortune, and other dubious characters, the city boasted the nation's highest crime rate, particularly for murder. Even so-called gentlemen went armed with concealed pocket pistols, sword canes, and elaborately carved knives and daggers.

Then there was the dueling, for which New Orleans was infamous. In earlier days the duels had been mostly swordfights in which *honour* was satisfied with the first drawing of blood, but later, when men began using firearms, duels turned into far more deadly affairs. According to the New Orleans writer John Bailey, on a single Sunday morning twenty men paired off to fight back-to-back duels beneath a tree called the Dueling Oak on one of the sugar plantations, and three of them were carried away dead.

By 1814 relations between the French and Spanish Creoles and the Americans had so soured that each group sullenly occupied a different part of town. The Creoles despised the Americans as greedy, dull, and uncouth, and the Americans returned the compliment by branding the Creoles frivolous, foppish, and arrogant. The Creoles were Catholics and the Americans Protestants; the Creoles delicately dipped snuff and sneezed into their lace handkerchiefs, while the Americans chewed and spat tobacco juice on the ground; the American men shook hands, the Creole men kissed one another on the cheeks; and the Creoles conversed in French and Spanish, for which the Americans considered them "foreigners." Because the Creoles enjoyed a voting majority, they controlled the state legislature and city government, and some had even refused to recognize that they were now part of the United States. When William Claiborne, a Virginian by birth, was appointed Louisiana governor by Thomas Jefferson, it led to even more resentment, especially since Claiborne did not speak, and refused to learn, any language but English, which, upon reflection, might not have mattered much since he and the legislature were barely on speaking terms anyway.

As the intelligence of a British invasion of Louisiana unfolded, the problems exacerbated, because Claiborne began to fear that—as the British had implied—Creoles (especially the Spaniards) might not only refuse to help defend the city but actually join the enemy. When Claiborne communicated that unpleasant prospect to Andrew Jackson, it could not have been reassuring news for the general.

The American attack on Barataria arrived at just after daybreak on September 16, 1814, the morning after Jean and Pierre Laffite had fled. The invasion force, organized by Commodore Patterson, consisted of the schooner-of-war *Carolina,* six gunboats, and a number of barges carrying Colonel Ross's men of the 7th Infantry Regiment. Having dropped down the Mississippi, the flotilla entered the gulf through the Southwest Pass and made for Grand Terre.

Ashore, and on the privateers' ships anchored in the harbor, anxious men waited with their cannon at the ready, matches lighted, wondering if the approaching fleet was British or American. Laffite's instructions had been to fight if it was the British but, if American, not to resist. He had felt certain that his offer to help defend the country against the British would be accepted, the requested pardon bestowed, and the Baratarians' stores of prize property respected, but it certainly didn't look that way now. As the ships neared, word rang out that they were American, and so the Baratarians began to scramble for any means of escape—pirogues, rowboats, gigs, anything that would float—and headed west and north toward the trackless marshes.

"I perceived the pirates were abandoning their vessels and were flying in all directions," said Patterson. "I sent in pursuit of them."

Most got away, but about eighty were captured and thrown into the calaboose, including Dominique You and many of the other ship captains. It took Patterson and his men four days to collect all the goods and merchandise in the Baratarian warehouses, which they loaded into the twenty-six captured privateer schooners. Afterward they burned the Baratarians' buildings—forty in all—and sent everything up to New Orleans to be catalogued and filed for themselves as claims in the prize court. It was quite a haul for Patterson and Ross—estimated at more than $600,000, a considerable fortune today—and that was the end of Barataria, though not of the Baratarians.*

* This seizure became the subject of an almost decadelong three-way federal lawsuit. Not only had Patterson and Ross claimed the seized goods as a legitimate prize to be awarded to them and their men, but the United States attorney in New Orleans also claimed them on behalf of the U.S. government to sell as contraband for evaded customs duties. The Laffites themselves filed suit as well, asserting that the goods had been illegally seized since all their ships were accredited under the privateering laws of Cartagena.

Seven

The rendezvous of the British invasion armada was a sight to behold when it converged at Negril Bay, Jamaica, in November 1814. The pride of the navy, more than sixty vessels—from the huge eighty-gun ships of the line such as *Tonnant*, Admiral Cochrane's flagship, to fighting brigs and frigates and armed troop transports, as well as dozens of cargo ships to carry off the millions in goods and merchandise they expected to capture at New Orleans—rested at anchor, each with a large Union Jack snapping in the breeze above the sparkling azure waters and tall promontories of this safe harbor. Aboard a number of the ships was a small army of British civil administrators—judges, Indian agents, colonial secretaries, and their minions—schooled to deliver His Britannic Majesty's intended decrees and edicts to a defeated and cowed Louisiana population. There was even an acting governor, who had brought with him his five "fashionable, marriageable" daughters. This bureaucratic host came complete with a printing press to compose the edicts and decrees, along with an editor and printer.

Also aboard many ships were the wives of British officers, invited to see the show.* At night, on deck, regimental balls and dances were often held to the tunes of musical bands, and colorful lanterns swung from the shrouds and other rigging. It was said that the password and challenge during this period was "beauty and booty," which some authors per-

* It was later widely repeated in print that the wife of Lieutenant General Edward Pakenham had come along, intending to become the duchess of Louisiana, or some such, when her husband secured the victory. But it was not so; Pakenham was a bachelor.

haps rightly have interpreted as "rape and plunder," an allusion to the dark affair at Hampton, Virginia, earlier in the year.

In the convoy, sailing down from the affairs at Washington and Baltimore, was Lieutenant George R. Gleig, a nineteen-year-old Oxford dropout who had been commissioned in the 85th Light Infantry Regiment. Three times wounded with Wellington's army in Spain and France, Gleig kept a detailed journal of his experiences. Despite the death of their leader, General Ross, Gleig recorded that the British soldiers and sailors were filled with optimism during their passage south. As they neared the equator, the men were treated to hazing associated with the traditional initiation into the Order of Neptune.* And on Gleig's ship they also managed to catch a large shark—considered a delicacy, if only because it was fresh food.

When the ships from France and England arrived in Jamaica on November 24 and anchored beside those that had come down from the Chesapeake, it was one of the largest such gatherings yet assembled at sea, including the Spanish Armada. It was said that the entire of Negril Bay seemed taken up; that one could almost step from ship to ship without getting a foot wet. The scene on the beaches had taken on a sort of carnival atmosphere: dozens of small boats coming and going; large ships constantly signaling one another with semaphore flags or "shouting trumpets" (megaphones). Many officers had pitched tents, or marquees, or even built grass-roofed huts on the beach, and the free Jamaicans were selling tropical foodstuffs as well as other things: papayas, star apples, oranges, pineapples, bananas, fresh fish, sea turtles, rum, sugarcane, nuts, coffee, pimientos, wood carvings, dyed kerchiefs, and, inevitably, the services of women.

Aside from the 10,000 sailors and 1,500 marines of the fleet, also aboard the ships were 8,000 British soldiers of the invasion army, with another 2,700 sailing close behind. They were some of the most famous regiments in the army: the 4th (King's Own), 24th (Royal Fusiliers), 95th Rifles (who wore bright green jackets instead of the traditional red

---

* This consisted, among other things, of being painted with kitchen grease and slops and getting dumped into a tub of bilgewater.

coats), 85th Light Infantry, 44th (East Essex), and the 93rd Highlanders, numbering 1,100 men, each of them by regulation over six feet tall, dressed in tartan trousers and wearing Scots' tams on their heads. To cap it off were two cavalry squadrons of the 14th (Duchess of York's) Light Dragoons. Also in the mix were two astonished regiments of Jamaican "colored troops," the 1st and 5th West India.

Still a few days behind at sea were three more regiments: the 70th, the 40th, and the 43rd. For the moment, all these soldiers were under the command of Major General John Keane, the thirty-one-year-old son of a baronet and member of the House of Lords, who—obviously with some help from his powerful father—had entered the army as a captain, at the age of thirteen! Keane knew his command was tempo-rary, since General Ross's true replacement, General Edward Paken-ham, was presently coming across the ocean, but until he arrived Keane was in charge, along with Admiral Cochrane, whom one early historian characterized as "a ruthless and indefatigable Vandal." This was an ill-fated situation for the British army because, being somewhat cowed by the elder admiral's prestige and strong demeanor, Keane acquiesced to Cochrane's intention to land the invasion force in an amphibious oper-ation just below New Orleans, which, in turn, influenced the calamity that followed.

Cochrane had formed his determination after learning of Jackson's victory at Mobile and the capture of Pensacola, which foreclosed that route of approach (as Jackson had earlier observed, that would have been the obvious course "for any true military man"). Although Cochrane had intelligence from a spy in New Orleans that he could easily ascend the Mississippi River in his ships, "with only two small forts to oppose you," he was skeptical. He quickly realized that none of his larger vessels could get over the bar at the river's mouth, a hundred river miles below New Orleans; that navigation on the Mississippi was slippery going upstream; and, in addition, who could tell what forces the Americans might muster against him once they learned that he was trying to get up the river? He also understood, once he got to Jamaica, that the efforts to turn the Baratarians to the British side had failed, putting Barataria Bay out of the picture so far as an easy invasion route to New Orleans went. He doubtless also had been informed through spies of Jackson's public calls for troops from Tennessee and Kentucky, which made it improbable that the invasion force would be facing only a few "undisciplined militia," as the spy had suggested.

Having ruled out other approaches, Cochrane pored over his charts and maps and decided that the most sensible way into New Orleans lay through Lake Borgne, and from there to ascend one of the various bayous that flowed into it just below the city. This would require a herculean effort for almost everyone concerned, since Lake Borgne was shallow and the entire army would have to be rowed in small boats across some sixty miles of treacherous open water. But there was no getting around it from the admiral's point of view, and so while in Jamaica he set about buying or building forty shallow-draft barges to transport the army from the big ships to the point of invasion.

By this time the whole adventure seemed to be turning into a risky proposition, which more prudent men at that point might have abandoned. To achieve victory Cochrane surely must have assumed they would need complete surprise. But what if the bayous were all obstructed? What if he was discovered? After all, it was not easy to hide a 10,000-man army, even in the remote wilds of the Louisiana coast of 1814, and an amphibious landing under fire was (and still is) the most dangerous of all military operations. Yet Cochrane had his orders, which were to invade, conquer, and secure Louisiana and the Mississippi River for the British crown, and he believed he had the most skilled, best-equipped, best-trained, bravest, and most experienced troops in the world.

There was something more: the aforesaid beauty and booty. The notion had to have crossed Cochrane's mind of the fabulous prize money he personally would receive from the sale of the goods piled up in New Orleans warehouses—estimated to be worth some $15 million.*

---

* Many military men of the day, especially admirals, were able to retire as wealthy men with great estates, owing to their shares in captured enemy property. The booty believed to be in New Orleans, however, dwarfed anything previously considered as a prize.

As admiral commanding, Cochrane would get the lion's share, but with that much at stake it must also have been on the minds of all those 20,000-plus soldiers and sailors, too, who would likewise get their cut. And so with only Cochrane and General Keane and their staffs to ponder the formidable obstacles, the men of the fleet and their cargo of soldiers pressed on, seemingly blissfully unaware of the perils.* But these were confident, determined—even arrogant—men, the vanquishers of the mighty Napoleon, immolaters of the American capital. Listen to Lieutenant Gleig's journal entry for November 26, 1814: "In half an hour all the canvas was set, and the ships moved slowly from the anchorage, till, having cleared the headlands, and caught the fair breeze, they bounded over the water with the speed of eagles, and long before dark the coast of Jamaica had disappeared."

Had Gleig and his comrades in arms fully understood the character, courage, and indomitable will of Andrew Jackson and his cobbled-together crew of Tennesseans, Kentuckians, New Orleans lawyers and merchants, "undisciplined militia," U.S. Army regulars, free men of color, and Baratarian "pirates," they might have worried some.

As the Canada geese and migratory ducks began to arrive in the Gulf Coast marshes and the hardwood trees finally flamed into a riot of color, Andrew Jackson was getting fidgety. Despite the pleas of Governor Claiborne and others, he had continued to make his headquarters at Mobile, convinced that "any true military man" would first land the British army there or at Pensacola or some point farther west, then march cross-country to Baton Rouge, above New Orleans, and fall upon the city from the north, rather than try to attack it from the swampy morasses to the south. He was wrong, of course, but could not know it at the time; all he *did* know, in fact, was that there was likely a large British fleet bearing down on him, carrying an army of Wel-

* The now deceased General Ross had been told by the War Office before he'd left England to cooperate with the navy but not to get involved in any action he considered militarily inadvisable from the army point of view. The inexperienced Keane had received no such instructions.

lington's veterans, while he could muster only a couple of undersized regiments of U.S. regulars, militia from Tennessee and, he hoped, Kentucky, as well as an uncertain number of volunteers, conscripts, and raw recruits of dubious loyalty from New Orleans.

To an ordinary man of the time this surely must have been a terrifying prospect, but not to Andrew Jackson, who, as Teddy Roosevelt noted, "had hereditary wrongs to avenge on the British," and he hated them with an implacable fury that was absolutely devoid of fear.

Many of the pleas for Jackson to come to the city and personally take charge were made by his old friend from his first days in Congress, the lawyer Edward Livingston—the same Edward Livingston who presently represented Jean Laffite and his so-called hellish banditi.

Livingston was a curious character, born into the wealthy and famous family of the Hudson River Valley who were among the Founding Fathers. After graduating from Princeton he became, in turn, a lawyer, a congressman, and later mayor of New York City, until, it was claimed, a trusted assistant mishandled city funds, which caused Livingston to go bankrupt and in 1804 leave New York for a fresh start in New Orleans. There he married into a wealthy Creole family, and because he spoke flawless French was accepted at all levels of social and political society.

Livingston was no particular admirer of Governor Claiborne and had recently organized a committee of defense, which vied with the legislature's Committee of Public Safety, chaired by the governor. From this eminent position he argued persuasively and privately with Jackson to include Laffite and the Baratarians in the New Orleans defense force. Livingston's reasoning was well founded; he cited Laffite's written offer to have the Baratarians fight for the United States and the fact that many of the privateers were skilled artillerymen, having served aboard their fighting ships as cannoneers and, if worse came to worst, as cutlass men or pistoleers.

Jackson was as yet unmoved, but he finally responded to the calls from New Orleans on November 22 by saddling up with his staff and journeying over the dingy trails from Mobile in a pouring autumn rain, personally scouting out for himself any possible landing sites for a British invasion. By that time the general had become wracked with severe dysentery, an excruciatingly painful, emaciating—even life-threatening—disease that bore only a scant comparison to its milder cousin diarrhea.* When he arrived in New Orleans nine days later, gaunt and pallid, Jackson could barely stand up, but, cheered on by grateful crowds, he was able to ride into the city in a carriage thoughtfully provided by a wealthy landowner.

To some his appearance might not have inspired confidence: his clothes and boots were filthy from a week on the trail, his face was prematurely wrinkled for his forty-seven years, and his great head of hair had gone gray. He was sallow and appeared frail from the dysentery and from the bullet wound in his shoulder received during the disgraceful gunfight with the Benton brothers. But later that day, when he appeared on the balcony of his headquarters on Royal Street, there was something in his voice and his icy blue eyes that convinced the gathered crowd that the city's salvation had arrived. In contrast to Governor Claiborne, who had tried to maintain leadership but often seemed wishy-washy to his diverse constituency, Jackson emitted an unshakable aura of defiance that few could mistake. From the moment he arrived he was like a rock in the surf of chaos and fear, and his very presence, wrote one newspaper (pilfering a phrase from the Song of Solomon), "was like an army with banners."†

With Livingston translating his words into French for the largely Creole crowd, Jackson "declared that he had come to protect the city, that he would drive the British into the sea or perish in the effort." He

---

* Dysentery is usually contracted by ingesting bacteria-contaminated water or food. There was no cure then but to let it run its course, for better or worse.

† The story is told that before he entered the city proper Jackson was invited to refresh himself and have breakfast at a plantation just outside town. A genteel neighboring Creole lady had been superintending the meal for what she was told was "a great general." Afterward she confronted the plantation owner and told him: "I worked myself almost to death to make your house *comme il faut* and prepared a splendid *déjeuner* and now I find that all my labor is thrown away upon an ugly old Kaintuck flat-boatman, instead of your grand General, with plumes, epaulettes, long sword and moustache!"

told the citizens "to cease all differences and divisions and unite with him . . . to save the city. . . . If you are not for us, you are against us, and will be dealt with accordingly," a dire warning to spies and wafflers. All these words "produced an electric effect," and a cry arose from the streets: "Jackson has come!"

That very day Jackson got down to business. First he needed to supplement his staff to suit the emergency. Edward Livingston became an aide-de-camp and chief proclamation writer. Major Arsene Lacarrière Latour, a local architect, military engineer, and mapmaker, was also called into service to supplement Jackson's own engineer staff officer Howell Tatum. Latour would become indispensable to Jackson because of his knowledge of the area; one year after the war he would write a firsthand account of the battle that has likewise become indispensable to students of the campaign. Other aides would be added in the days to come, including some surprising choices.

Having done this, Jackson and his staff rode over to the Place d'Armes to review his troops. Considering that the British army then descending on Louisiana was variously thought to number from 10,000 to 20,000 regulars, all veterans of the Napoleonic Wars, Jackson didn't seem to have much to work with. New Orleans offered him the following:

A battalion of local businessmen, lawyers, planters, and their sons, numbering 287 men, commanded by Major Jean Baptiste Plauché. They were colorfully uniformed* and high-spirited, but most of the companies had been organized for only about a month, and their fighting capabilities were untested. Likewise there were "two regiments of Louisiana State Militia, badly equipped, some of them armed with fowling pieces, others with muskets, others with rifles, some without arms, all imperfectly disciplined."

Then there was an understrength battalion of 210 free men of color.

---

* These splendidly uniformed companies contributed inadvertently, and in some inconclusive way, to the ultimate British tactics that cost them the battle. Seeing all the various uniforms, the British wrongly concluded that each represented a full regiment of militia, rather than only a company.

It was composed mostly of the displaced Haitians, commanded by Major Jean Daquin, a bakery owner. Until Jackson got into the picture these people had, as usual, been treated badly. Claiborne and others had been reluctant even to arm them, and they were denied most of the rights of white volunteer soldiers. Jackson fixed that with another proclamation, in which he informed the blacks that they would be accorded the same amenities as the white soldiers, including equal standing, equal pay, a $124 enlistment bonus, and 160 acres of land after their term of service was up.[*]

There were the Tennessee volunteers under General Coffee. This motley-looking crew numbered about 1,800, most of whom had fought with Jackson in the Creek War and at Pensacola. They were rough, tough, unshaven, buckskin- or homespun-clad, and generally wild and murderous-looking backwoodsmen—many wearing coonskin caps—who, according to one participant in the battle, carried nothing but their rifles, cartridge boxes, hatchets, knives, and powder horns. "They had no idea of military organization and discipline; they paid attention only to the more important part of their calling, which, according to their notions, was quietly to pick out their man, fix him in their aim, and bring him down." The British would soon bestow upon them a derisive nickname of which the backwoodsmen became justly proud—the "dirty-shirts."

Equally important, though also understrength, were the two regular U.S. Army regiments, the 7th and the 44th, numbering together 796 riflemen. To round things out was a company of 107 mounted Mississippi dragoons under Major Thomas Hinds, as well as a detachment of 18 friendly Choctaw Indians (soon to be enlarged to 62), commanded by Captain Pierre Jugat, who, for their part, would make things plenty disagreeable for the British, as they would soon find out.

---

[*] The fear by influential citizens and politicians of arming and training these men was based on two factors: that it would "place them on a too equal footing" with the whites and, second, that it would create in the city a large group of armed and trained blacks who might possibly turn on their white brethren. The solution to the latter issue was, after the emergency ended, to pay off the free men of color and then run them out of town—preferably out of state.

Jackson could thus muster just under 3,000 men, many of questionable ability. With any luck, the promised 2,400-man force of Kentucky militia under Major General John Thomas, as well as General William Carroll's 2,200 Tennessee volunteers, would arrive in time for the invasion. These upcountry reinforcements were coming by flatboat down the Mississippi, but so far no word had been received as to their whereabouts. Likewise, to arm them, Secretary of War Monroe had scraped up the money to order a shipment of five thousand rifles from the munitions factories at Pittsburgh, but nothing had been heard of this, either.

Having surveyed his army, Jackson now embarked on a weeklong survey of the city's defenses. For a city so far removed from punctual help from the rest of the nation, New Orleans was practically defenseless in purely military terms—or so it seemed at the time—and any notion of defending it presented a problem of staggering difficulties. Neither the federal nor the Louisiana legislature had seen fit to appropriate any funds necessary to build the proper fortifications to protect the city. This appeared to be inviting calamity, but in fact, except for an invasion force marching overland to descend on the city from the north or east— as Jackson expected it to—New Orleans had fairly good natural defenses in the form of all those impassable bogs, marshes, and quagmires that make up the lower Mississippi River Delta. With that in mind, Jackson posted Coffee's mounted infantry north, up at Baton Rouge, to defend against the possibility of an attack developing from there, and then he took his surveying trip.

With the engineer Major Latour as his guide, Jackson and his party visited what he considered the other most likely routes of an invading British army. The geometry of the problem was maddening; there were so many ways an enemy could come. First on his list were, of course, the eastern approaches to New Orleans from Mobile or points westward along the Mississippi Gulf Coast. Chief among these was the Chef Menteur Road, running east-west along the coast, which had been built through impassable swamps. It could be fairly easily defended by a small force by blocking it with trees and other debris, Jackson concluded. He ordered the requisite number of troops and artillery posted, issued them their orders, and moved on.

Next was Bayou St. John, a water approach in which the British army would have to arrive in shallow-draft boats through Lake Borgne, a bay off the gulf that led through a narrow channel into Lake Pontchartrain, guarded by a half-finished fort called the Rigolets. Once into Pontchartrain, however, Bayou St. John branched nearly into the city, guarded only by a decrepit installation from colonial days, Fort St. John. Jackson ordered it strengthened and garrisoned.

The calculus of approaches to the city from the south proved difficult. First, there were any number of bayous, streams, and canals that, left unguarded and unobstructed, could have allowed the British through. Jackson ordered all of these blocked by felled trees, with guards from the state militia posted to watch them. (Lack of diligent enforcement of this order proved to be his greatest mistake.) And of course there was the Mississippi River itself, which might have become a huge highway for the ships of the British navy. As we have seen, though, the trouble with the river route was that the passes out of the gulf to access it were too shallow to permit entry of the big three-decker sixty- to eighty-gun British ships of the line, and even if their smaller men-of-war were able get over the bars, they'd face formidable obstacles, the first of which was Fort St. Philip, about sixty miles downriver from New Orleans. The fort was not in bad condition, but Jackson wisely ordered it strengthened, its wood barracks pulled down to prevent fires in case of bombardment, and a reinforced garrison of trained artillerists stationed inside. Then, on the trip back upriver, he visited Detour d'Anglais—English Turn.

English Turn was an almost two-hundred-degree bend where the river practically doubled back on itself about twenty miles below New Orleans. For sailing ships it was a challenge and often a trial even in peaceful times. As was no doubt pointed out to Jackson by Commodore Patterson, to negotiate the first part of the turn, whatever wind direction was available to get them there would be right in the ship's face, making progress impossible until the wind changed direction, which could be hours, days, even weeks. (And until it did change favorably, the ships had to make for the banks and tie up to trees lest the swift current carry them back downriver.)

The French and Spanish colonists had thoughtfully built a small installation at English Turn, but Jackson ordered more batteries, then two additional batteries across the river, just in case. From these an unfriendly ship could be bombarded in an almost helpless state while waiting for the wind to change. It is not clear where Jackson got the extra artillery to brace up Fort St. Philip and English Turn, but a good bet might be that it came from those armed privateer ships and shore cannon that Patterson had captured in his raid on Laffite's Baratarians.

Having done all this Jackson returned to New Orleans to be greeted with distasteful newspaper headlines complaining of his absence from the city. Jackson paid the criticism not the slightest attention. Nor did he just sit on his hands waiting for the British to arrive; his problems continued to be manifest. All through the ages a defending commander's worst dilemma has been lack of knowledge of where and when the enemy would strike. Even though Jackson enjoyed the advantage of shortened interior lines, he was by necessity forced to disperse many of his troops over every possible venue of attack—leaving himself vulnerable at all of them—until he could divine the true intentions of the British. There wasn't anything he could do about that, though, so he devoted himself to other enterprises.

First he went to the contentious Louisiana legislature and persuaded the state to pay for all the military improvements he'd requested.* He continued to press authorities in Washington, Tennessee, and Kentucky by express courier to discover the whereabouts of the reinforcements and arms he had expected by now. He made efforts to enlist more men from the city and state to defend against the invasion.

Jackson next reacted unwisely to another sticky problem. Members

---

* Not only that, but the usually do-nothing legislature issued a proclamation of its own, urging all plantation owners to send as many slaves as they could spare to work on fortifications.

of the committee of defense, after declaring Jean Laffite's original warnings about the British invasion to be forgeries, now paid a visit to Jackson. Ever since it had developed that Laffite's communications had been proved perfectly genuine, Governor Claiborne as well as Edward Livingston, Laffite's lawyer, had been urging Jackson to accept the Baratarians' offer to join in the defense of New Orleans, but so far Jackson had clung stubbornly to his original sentiments in the negative.

Now the committee of defense, led by the Louisiana legislator and wealthy aristocrat Bernard de Marigny—who had urged accepting Laffite's offer from the beginning—came to Jackson for another try, along with other committee members who had changed their minds. With the danger clearly at hand, Marigny explained, every available man and woman in the fractious city had now become coalesced toward the emergency. Older men were serving as police officers to free younger men for military service. Women were already wrapping bandages as well as making clothes and blankets for the militia and troops not yet arrived. The Ursuline nuns in their convent were readying their hospital.

Marigny's main point was that manpower was still the critical factor, and that while all these fierce and battle-experienced Baratarians were presently in jail or on the run, it only made good sense to enlist their valuable services. Jackson was still having none of it. "The General was unrelenting," Marigny wrote. "He told us these men were being pursued by the United States Civil Officers, that many were in prison . . . that he could do nothing about the matter."

One factor in all of this might have been that Jackson appears to have taken a dislike to Marigny, who was young, handsome, somewhat of a sophisticated playboy about town, and generally acknowledged as the leader of French Creole society in New Orleans. He was also the son-in-law of the old Spanish *comandante* at Pensacola who, a few days after Jackson accepted his surrender, had produced a letter, which Marigny showed to Jackson. In it, the *comandante* showered Jackson with fulsome praise ("I kiss your feet . . .") and so on) and asked his son-in-law to open the doors of his elegant New Orleans home as headquarters for Jackson when he arrived there.

At first Jackson accepted the offer, but apparently he thought better of it afterward. When he got to New Orleans, he curtly declined Marigny's offer of hospitality and instead established his headquarters on Royal Street. Perhaps Jackson was suspicious of the in-law connection between Marigny and the Spanish *comandante* and fingered Marigny as possibily disloyal—maybe even a spy. Who knows? History is silent on the matter, but the relationship between the American general and the patriotic and influential young New Orleans Creole remained chilly throughout the campaign.

Soon events began to overtake the citizens of New Orleans, for on December 12 the British invasion force arrived offshore. Fears that had drifted obscurely regarding His Imperial Majesty's intentions suddenly began to clarify themselves with alarming rapidity.

Laffite, for his part, was still persona non grata in the city and, with an arrest warrant hanging over him, was more or less hiding out at the homes of plantation owners whom he knew and had had dealings with in the smuggling business. According to one story, among them was Elmwood in Tchoupitoulas, above New Orleans, where Laffite had no sooner arrived than "a servant announced the approach of the carriage of another guest." The guest, it turned out, was none other than the beautiful wife of Governor Claiborne.

The horrified mistress of the manor sent away all of her servants "except a trusted one named Henrietta, whom she warned to address Monsieur Laffite as Monsieur Clement." Laffite was much amused by this ruse and entered into it "with all his ease and natural grace." Throughout the afternoon and evening Mrs. Claiborne was charmed and coquettish, never realizing that the man she was flirting with and her husband each had a price on the other's head. When she returned to New Orleans, she "was extravagant in her praise of the most remarkable man she had ever met."

Eight

It was certainly not as if an invasion was unexpected; warnings had been abundant, the most recent arriving on December 8 in an unsigned letter from Pensacola delivered by a friendly Choctaw Indian to Commodore Patterson, the New Orleans naval commander, when he returned to the city from his inspection tour with Jackson. The anonymous writer began, "Dear Sir . . . a very large force of the enemy is off this port, and it is generally understood New Orleans is the object of attack. I am not able to learn how, when or where the attack will be made, but I heard they have vessels of all descriptions, and a large body of troops."

Not only was the source of this communication mysterious, it also seems odd that it was conveyed in such fashion, since Jackson had stationed a U.S. garrison at Pensacola, and surely if there had been a large British fleet offshore someone among them would have seen it and sent the information along in a less surreptitious fashion.

When Patterson showed Jackson the letter, the general was skeptical, wondering if it might not be a ruse to steer him in the wrong direction. Patterson, however, took more stock in it and ordered his squadron of five sloop-rigged gunboats, a dispatch boat, and a tender to redouble their already sharp lookout on the approaches to Lake Borgne, which he had always considered the most likely approach for an amphibious invasion of the city.

This tough and valiant little flotilla represented just about all of Patterson's command. He also had the 85-foot, 230-ton sloop of war *Carolina* mounting fourteen guns and partially manned by sailors from New

England. The much larger ship *Louisiana,* a corvette, mounting sixteen guns, was also under his command, but she remained tied up at the city wharves because Patterson could find no sailors to man her—for the unforgivable reason that the navy offered no bounty for signing on and that pay on merchant vessels was much higher. The gunboats, on the other hand, were fully manned, but no match for any of the large ships of the British navy. The sailors derisively called them "Jeffs," after Thomas Jefferson, who had ordered scores of them built on the theory that they could substitute for a proper world-class navy. They were strictly coastal craft, sloop-rigged, shallow-draft, black-hulled, about 45 feet long and 80 tons, armed with four or five small cannon each, and sailed by a crew of twenty.* The gulf flotilla was commanded by a naval lieutenant with the interesting name of Thomas Ap Catesby Jones, whose assignment was to be Jackson's eyes for the expected invasion.

Reconnoitering off the coast of Mississippi on December 10, two of Jones's gunboats came upon what must have been a breathtaking sight. There in the deep blue waters to the east they beheld in the distance a line of tall white sails, stretching as far as the eye could see. These could only be the British warships, an assumption further investigation soon confirmed. The gunboats shadowed them at a respectful distance for the two full days it took to get the enemy armada assembled and anchored off the north end of the Chandeleur Islands, near the mouth of Lake Borgne. For the larger ships this was as far as they could go, because of the shallowness of the lake, but there were also a number of smaller sloops of war and other armed vessels attached to the fleet, which took station at Ship and Cat islands, closer to the lake, so about all Jones could do was watch and report their movements to Patterson in New Orleans.

Aboard the huge flagship *Tonnant* Admiral Cochrane was growing

---

* Building the gunboats as the mainstay of America's national naval defense had been the brainchild of the Jefferson presidency as a way to save money. Naval historian Teddy Roosevelt damned the reliance on them by the Jefferson and Madison administrations as, variously, "ludicrous, painful folly and stupidity," "bungled," and "humiliating," and Jefferson himself as "the most incapable Executive that ever filled the presidential chair."

impatient to start the invasion. He had sighted the shadowing gunboats and realized the Americans had become aware of his presence, but they would not know precisely where and when his army would strike. In order to keep them in the dark as long as possible, Cochrane knew he would have to dispose of the pesky gunboats that were keeping an eye on him and gave the order, "Clear the lakes," setting into motion a fierce little battle that opened the campaign.

Jones's orders from Patterson had been to defend New Orleans from the Rigolets, the narrow channel from Lake Borgne into Lake Pontchartrain, only a few miles from the city. A small fortification, Fort Petites Coquilles, was still under construction there, but it presently contained a number of artillery pieces. Patterson's idea was that between the fort and the gunboats enough U.S. firepower should be available to drive off a British attempt to enter Lake Pontchartrain.

Patterson never got to find out whether or not that was so. As soon as Cochrane arrived he sicced his small, heavily armed sloops and corvettes on Jones's gunboat flotilla, and no sooner had these medium-draft war craft entered the lake than they promptly ran aground. Jones had by now moved farther up the lake, anchoring off what was little more than a glorified marsh appropriately called Malheureux Island. From there he watched and awaited developments, which proceeded apace. On the afternoon of December 13, the Americans could see through their spyglasses a number of small barges being lowered into the water by the larger ships. At sunrise the next morning they noted that the barges were entering Lake Borgne and rowing toward them in a long line, half a mile wide. There were forty-five in all, occupied by no fewer than 1,500 British sailors and marines, armed with sabers, hatchets, pistols, and muskets. In addition, the bow of each barge mounted a carronade, a small cannon extremely lethal at close range.

Jones took cognizance of his orders and prepared to move farther up the lake to assume his positions at the Rigolets, but here nature foiled him; there was no wind. Not only that, but a strong current flowing out of the lake was actually pushing him *toward* the fierce-looking little barges; all he could do at that point was drop anchor, prepare for the worst, and pray for wind. Of course, Jones couldn't have known the odds exactly, but he surely knew they were not in his favor. His force totaled 182 men against whatever number the barges contained, and even though his five boats were more heavily armed, the forty-five barges were maneuverable, being pulled by oars, while the becalming wind had left his boats dead in the water.

All morning the gunboat crews watched, resigned to their fate, while the line of barges rowed steadily toward them, stretched out closely abreast. At one point midmorning the American sailors became puzzled, and possibly a little relieved, when the line of barges stopped, oars were pulled in, and they dropped anchor. But soon the anchors were weighed and the rowing began again in earnest. It turned out the commander of the barge army had decided to stop and feed his men lunch before the battle began.

As has been aptly pointed out by the historian Wilburt S. Brown, the best move for Jones at that point would probably have been to burn or blow up the gunboats to keep them from falling into British hands, then make for shore in their dinghies—even swim for it, if need be—to fight another day. But Jones figured his orders called for him to stand and fight the enemy, and that if he did not, his name would go down in disgrace. So he ordered his crews to double-shot their guns and prepare to fight to the last extremity. Then he ran up the (anti-)boarding nets, which, as one witness recorded, "left the gunboats looking as if they were draped in giant spider webs."

Just before eleven a.m. on December 14 the battle began. Jones fired first because some of his guns were longer-ranged than the carronades in the bows of the barges. This did damage, but not enough, since he was outnumbered by more than five to one. Still, the Americans cheered when two of the barges were blown to splinters and their occupants dumped or blown into the cold water. Fifteen barges soon detached themselves and began rowing directly toward Jones's gunboat. Moments later the British opened fire, and Jones was among the first struck, with a musket ball in his shoulder. As he was being carried below he turned over command to his second officer, shouting, "Keep up the fight! Keep up the fight!" just as a blast of British grapeshot struck his second down.

The lead barge was occupied by the expedition commander, Captain Nicholas Lockyer—the same Lockyer who several months back had approached Jean Laffite at Grand Terre on behalf of the British. His boat plowed into Jones's, and the British sailors and marines quickly chopped through the boarding nets. A hand-to-hand slaughter commenced. Superior numbers soon told on the Americans, and the boarding crews quickly turned Jones's boat's cannons on the other gunboats, which themselves were being overwhelmed. It took another bloody hour and a half, but in the end the predictable came to pass: 10 Americans were killed, 35 wounded, and most others captured. The British came away with 17 killed and 77 wounded, including Lockyer, plus five American gunboats with all their armaments and several boatloads of prisoners. Andrew Jackson had not only lost his "eyes" on Lake Borgne, he had lost its defense as well, a circumstance that shortly would bring on near disaster.

In the days leading up to the Battle of Lake Borgne Jackson had shown calm immediacy and determined leadership, but never an outright sense of urgency. He had even wanted Rachel to join him in New Orleans and wrote her saying so on the morning of December 15, before going out with staff to reconnoiter the Plain of Gentilly, which he considered a possible invasion route. It was there that a courier found him with word of the defeat and capture of the gunboats the previous day, and this bad news seems to have energized him as never before.

Considering that he was yet so ill from dysentery he could barely stand up, it is remarkable that Jackson became such a whirlwind of activity in the days that followed. His companions noticed that he was becoming thin as a scarecrow, his menu consisting only of a bowl of grits and some toast in the morning and a little rice for dinner and supper. Unless pressed with something else, he would often lie on a couch in his headquarters to save energy, perhaps taking a sip or two of brandy. But with the news of the gunboat calamity and the British invasion now plainly imminent, Jackson sprang into action. He published another proclamation (written by Livingston) in which he told the diverse population to put aside any remaining animosities, and for anyone who didn't harsh measures were in store. He issued a flurry of orders calling up the militia and sending them to man the various forts protecting the city. He sent a battalion of the free men of color and some militia to the Chef Menteur Road with orders to block and defend it. Orders went out to General Coffee at Baton Rouge and General Carroll, by then at Natchez, to hurry their forces to New Orleans—which they did, arriving on December 20—and he dispatched scouts far upriver to see if they could locate the missing 2,300 Kentuckians.

He also sent a dispatch telling Rachel to postpone her trip.

Earlier Jackson had asked the Louisiana legislature to suspend the writ of habeas corpus so that Patterson could impress a number of the unemployed sailors hanging around the waterfront to man the idle *Louisiana,* but this was refused. Now, after learning that the gunboats had been captured and that the British were close by, the legislature went into an absolute panic that one can only envision—what with all their customary gesturing and shouting in various languages. That was enough for Jackson, and he promptly took the ultimate step, on December 16, 1814, of putting the state under martial law. This established a curfew, closed the city coming and going, and permitted impressment of sailors, as well as any other able-bodied males, who were sent into the militia.

The martial law proclamation established Jackson as being in supreme command over everything, and—though he later himself conceded that it was probably unconstitutional—his authority became absolute, including the right to execute civilians as spies. As one writer observed, "The man had met the hour," and it was a good thing, too, because there wasn't a moment to lose; it was understood that the invasion could start at any time, in any place.

As soon as Lake Borgne had been cleared, Cochrane began launching the British army toward an assembly point at the mouth of the Pearl

River, near what is today Bay Saint Louis, Mississippi. Probably at Pensacola, Cochrane took on "certain Spaniards," former officials who once lived in New Orleans when it was a Spanish colony, and who were more than willing to give the British the lay of the land. Also at some point Cochrane's people made contact with a group of Spanish fishermen who worked Lake Borgne, and doubtless plied them with money for information on possible invasion routes. The assembly-point destination for the army was Ile aux Poix, or Pea Island, a boggy piece of marsh ground so desolate and remote it was hoped the landing would go undiscovered. It did, but it put an awful strain on the men.

When the victorious barge force returned to the fleet anchorage after defeating the American gunboats, the navy began loading the army into them for the forty-mile row across the lake. The soldiers were crammed in so tightly (about thirty men, with all their equipment, on a twenty-foot boat, plus rowing crews) that they had no room even to move their legs or adjust position during the grueling ten-hour trip. As if that weren't enough, the weather suddenly turned against them, as it often will in these climes. Contrary to popular opinion, New Orleans at times can be seemingly one of the coldest places on earth—if not by actual thermometer readings, then at least by what modern-day meteorologists adjust for, such as wind-chill factor. Being as it is between a giant swamp and a giant river, there is always much humidity in the air, making even a moderate cold chilling to the bone. When a winter wet front comes in from the west and collides with arctic air pushing down from the north, the weather in New Orleans can become disagreeably cold. If a rare series of these frontal events occurs, it can be brutal, especially to people exposed to the elements, and apparently that is what happened to the British army in its open boats during the voyage into Lake Borgne.

In the daytime there would be drenching rains that soaked the men; then at night the temperature would dip below freezing and their clothing would actually freeze to their skin. Here is Lieutenant Gleig's recollection of Pea Island: "It is scarcely possible to imagine any place more wretched. It was a swamp containing a small space of ground at one end and almost wholly unadorned with trees of any description. The interior was the resort of wild ducks and other water-fowl; and the pools and creeks abounded in dormant alligators."

During the solid week of constant rowboat relays that it took to assemble the whole army at Pea Island, the men lived "upon this miserable desert without tents or huts or any covering to shelter them from the inclemency of the weather. After having been exposed all day to a cold and pelting rain, we landed upon a barren island, incapable of furnishing even fuel enough to supply our fires. Many of the wretched negroes to whom frost and cold were absolutely new," Gleig wrote of the Jamaican freedmen regiments, "fell fast asleep, and perished before morning." And if it was bad for the soldiers, think also of the sailors who had to row them back and forth around the clock without getting out of their boats during the eighty-mile round-trip. Gleig's next observation, however, is almost enough to make his entire narrative suspect from the historian's point of view: "Yet in spite of all this, not a murmur nor a whisper of complaint could be heard throughout the whole expedition."

Even if that statement represents the ultimate in hyperbole, what he goes on to say makes more sense, which is that the reason the men accustomed themselves to the miserable conditions was that "every one looked forward to the future. From the General down to the youngest drum-boy [there was] a confident anticipation . . . of the ample reward in store for them [meaning, of course, their share of the fabulous prize money]; the expectation of so great a recompense to come."

As the army began assembling at Pea Island, British intelligence officers were engrossed in reconnoitering actual landing spots for the invasion. Pea Island was very close to the Mississippi shore, from which it would have been fairly simple to put the army on the easiest route into New Orleans—the Chef Menteur Road across the Plain of Gentilly, which Jackson himself had been surveying just a few days earlier when he learned of the capture of his gunboats. That obviously must have been under consideration, but for some reason Cochrane rejected it. Perhaps it was because the British had learned that the Americans were blocking the Chef Road and didn't want to force a battle on an approach with swamps on both sides. If so, the decision would have been a sound one, since an infantry commander's worst nightmare is to attack on such a narrow front that maneuvering becomes a practical impossibility. It may have been General Keane who rejected the idea on those grounds, but that is doubtful, given his subservience to Admiral Cochrane.

In any case, on December 18, while the army was still being ferried to Pea Island, two British officers had themselves rowed the thirty miles to the opposite side of the lake, to a winter-bleak blackwater river called Bayou Bienvenue. At its entrance they came upon a cluster of palmetto-thatched stilt houses known locally as the Spanish Fishermen's Village. As the name implies, these were the residences of the forty or so Spaniards—with a few Portuguese and Italians thrown in—who worked the rich waters of Lake Borgne, bringing their pirogues full of shrimp, oysters, turtles, crabs, and fish to the seafood markets in New Orleans.

As noted, British officers had earlier approached these Spaniards on the lake—or perhaps it had been the other way around—but now the Spaniards, who resented American control of Louisiana and knew the lake backward and forward, quickly began cooperating with Admiral Cochrane and his people. Thus, with two of the Spanish fishermen as guides, the British scouting party proceeded to investigate the bayou, which was about a hundred yards wide and six feet deep. To their astonishment and delight, they discovered that, unlike all the other water approaches below New Orleans, Bayou Bienvenue had not been blocked as Jackson had ordered. After they had traveled by pirogue about eight miles along the twisting stream, Bayou Bienvenue branched off into Bayou Mazant, and after another four miles it became too shallow for the larger British barges to navigate. Here, where the Villeré Canal entered the bayou, would of necessity be the British jumping-off point.

At first sight, the position must have looked perfectly awful to the reconnaissance officers. It was in the middle of nowhere in a wretched, boggy marsh (then called a "prairie," but known less affectionately as "land of the trembling earth"). That is what Lieutenant Gleig described when he arrived a week later: "The place where we landed was as wild as it is possible to imagine. Nothing could be seen except one huge marsh covered with tall reeds; not a house nor a vestige of human industry," he said (apparently forgetting about Villeré's canal). Through this godforsaken morass, where the dense reeds grew eight feet tall, the soldiers slogged for a long arduous mile, often sinking to their knees in muck, until they reached a dark and forbidding cypress swamp. The swamp was barely possible to navigate except by stumbling through mire between the knobby trees and wading across the many crisscrossing streams. As darkness fell, the British scouting party emerged onto a wide stable plain, covered with the close-chopped stubble from the autumn harvest of sugarcane. At this point they were about a mile from the Mississippi River, which lay due southwest. In the distance they could see a few slaves toiling away. Beyond that was a large orange grove and, beyond that, the elegant Creole-style home of Major General Jacques Villeré, commander of the Louisiana state militia. The Spanish fishermen had thoughtfully provided the two British officers with rough fishermen's clothing; so disguised, the little reconnaissance party moved casually through the fields, past the orange trees drooping with ripe fruit, and toward the tall levee of the river. Once there, according to reports, they climbed the levee, noting the road running beside it into New Orleans, just nine miles north, then climbed down the other side and had themselves a drink of "the cool and sweet water" of the Mississippi River.

The Mississippi is perhaps a half mile wide at this point, and on both sides for twenty miles below the city its banks were lined with more than fifty sugar plantations. These varied in size according to the terrain, but from the Villeré plantation northward toward the city, each farm after the next fronted the river for about half a mile and extended back toward the cypress swamp about a mile, consisting of from six hundred to eight hundred acres. As was to be expected, most were owned by Creoles—Jumonville, Lachapelle, Chalmette, Rodriguez, Lacoste, Guichard, and so forth. With an eye, no doubt, to the vagaries of the river, many owners had built comfortable villas in the Creole style, one- or two-story affairs with tall windows and wide verandas all around. But others, in flagrant disregard of hydrographic reality, constructed expansive three-story mansions facing the river, with broad, crushed-shell avenues leading up to them, framed with rows of moss-draped live oaks. Many had their own canals extending from the levee to the swamp in order to drain the land in case of torrential rains or if the river topped the levee. According to the engineer Latour, if the river actually broke a major gap in the levee (which had happened more than once), the result would be calamitous; the whole area—fields, homes, sugar refineries, swamps, and all—would be flooded and remain under ten to twelve feet of water for up to six months.

Accordingly, on December 18, the two-man scouting party returned to Pea Island and made its report: the bayou was passable, although the landing spot and its distance from high ground left much to be desired for a 10,000-man army to negotiate. Yet it offered a priceless advantage: cover and concealment. If the army arrived quickly and moved swiftly, it could take New Orleans in half a day, before the Americans knew what had happened to them. When this news was conveyed to the fleet, Cochrane and Keane themselves sailed over to Pea Island for an inspection and review of the army. They apparently brought with them some interesting guests—a number of Florida Indian chiefs and some of their families, whose arrival merits mention here.

The Indians might accurately be described as military observers, consisting as they did of the heads of various tribes—mostly those few Choctaws still hostile to the United States—who had been among those that the British had been training in Pensacola until they were so rudely interrupted by Jackson's arrival. After Jackson's attack, they and their tribesmen had scattered into the wilds, but the British, under the enterprising machinations of the ubiquitous Colonel Nicholls, had somehow managed to round them up and persuade them to join the expedition against New Orleans. This was done on the theory that if the Indians could only see the mighty British army in action against the discounted

American militia, they would regain their confidence and rejoin the effort to overthrow the United States all over the Southern region. At first, getting the Indians interested was a tall order; after they had been chased from Fort Bowyer at Mobile, and then watched Jackson run the British ignominiously out of Pensacola, they had quickly formed an impression of "the remorseless energy and ferocity of Sharp Knife," as Andrew Jackson had become known to them, a man they did not particularly wish to tangle with again. "Hence they were timid, cautious and wily."

But Nicholls was not a man to be undone.

Shortly after Jackson had departed Pensacola, Nicholls marched his detachment, dressed to the nines, into the Choctaws' forest villages. "The chiefs greatly admired the gay uniforms, the large cocked hats and nodding plumes, the golden epaulets and highly-finished swords and scabbards," the historian Alexander Walker tells us. But that was only the first act; the second was as old as the white man's relationship with American Indians. "The British plied them with rum, the greatest of the foes of the poor Indian. They got drunk as Choctaws always have done since their knowledge of alcohol," Judge Walker recorded, and under its spell they pledged to aid the British for "as long as the supply of rum was continued." These chiefs, then, sober or drunk, were on hand to see the great victory promised them by the British officers, after which, if they would only assist by rallying their people against the Americans, all their lost lands and tarnished dignity would be restored.

In the meantime, they provided a curious spectacle for the British soldiers, most of whom had never before seen an American Indian. One captain who encountered a number of them described their faces as being "like masks," and they were "perfectly naked, with the exception of a girdle round their loins, with a dirty blanket or the skin of a wild beast slung round their necks . . . the eyes are generally dark with a sullen expression, the nostrils are distended from which hang[s] a metal ring; the upper part of the bridge of the nose scarcely rises above the face, which is tattooed, which gives a truly savage aspect. In the afternoon they decorate themselves by rubbing their cheeks with a sort of red ochre, and intermingling with the hair the bright plumage of various birds."

Of the chiefs themselves, this officer recorded that he did not see them "in their real costume," as the British had given them red "sergeant's jackets," some "covered with gold lace, but were *sans culottes* . . . and resembled those figures descending the broad stairs at the Italian Opera-house into the infernal regions in the ballet of La Fauste."

Cochrane decided to land Keane's army via Bayou Bienvenue and the barges were reassembled at Pea Island. It was calculated that only one-third of the army could be moved at a time, and the first group to go was an 1,800-man detachment led by Colonel William Thornton, to be followed closely by Keane and Cochrane. So with what must have been an absorbing experience on Pea Island now behind them, the troops climbed into the boats for the thirty-mile pull across Lake Borgne.

Nine

Confident as he might have been that his order to block all bayous had been carried out, Jackson, as a further precaution, on December 19 issued orders to Militia General Jacques Villeré to have each of these waterways guarded around the clock. Ironically, responsibility for Bayou Bienvenue fell to none other than General Villeré's son Major Gabriel Villeré, who at that very moment was stationed with a company of militia on his father's plantation near the head of the bayou.

When he received the order, apparently on December 21 if not earlier, Major Villeré dispatched a picket to the mouth of the bayou consisting of "a sergeant, eight white men, and three mulattoes." These men entered the swamps the same day and by evening arrived at the Spanish Fishermen's Village, a mile or so upriver from the actual mouth of the bayou. There they found but one man, who claimed he was sick and who told them that the rest of his fishermen friends were working on the lake. This was true enough, except they weren't out there fishing; the treacherous Spaniards had hired out their boats and services to the British for the crossing.

Probably because of the weather, instead of setting up their outpost in the marshes at the mouth of the bayou, Villeré's picket cravenly opted to station themselves in the shelter of the village's houses, well up the bayou, and it was there, the next night, that the advance party of the British invasion force found them. Villeré's people initially attempted to hide behind one of the huts, but after the first few barges had passed they dashed to the edge of the bayou for a boat in which to escape.

They were seen by the British, however, according to Judge Walker's account, and four of the dozen were captured trying to drag the boat into the bayou.

"Four others were taken on land," Walker wrote. "Of the four remaining, three ran into the cane breaks, thence into the prairie, where they wandered about all day until worn down with fatigue and suffering, they returned to the village, happy to surrender themselves prisoners. One only escaped, and after three days of terrible hardships and constant perils, wandering over trembling prairies, through almost impervious cane breaks, swimming bayous and lagoons and living on reptiles and roots, got safely into the American camp." By that time, though, his warning was a day too late; the Americans already knew.

From that day to this, Major Villeré's violation of the order to block the canal has never been satisfactorily accounted for and, after the battle, resulted in his court-martial on a variety of charges, including treason. The most likely explanation is that since the Villerés used the bayou to get onto Lake Borgne, which was in turn reached through their canal, the young major had arbitrarily convinced himself that it was an unlikely invasion route and that it would be too much trouble later to clear the scores of large trees that would have been felled to block it. If that was so, he at the least would have been guilty of gross negligence and dereliction of duty.

With the reality of the crisis now urgently upon him, Jackson was once again faced with the question of what to do about Jean Laffite and his Baratarians. After Jackson's rejection to the committee of defense of Laffite's offer to help on grounds that the Baratarians "were being pursued by United States Civil Officers, and that many were in prison," Bernard Marigny, and probably Edward Livingston too, had neatly removed this argument by consulting with Federal District Judge Dominick Hall, who told them if they could persuade the Louisiana legislature to pass a resolution suspending prosecution of the Baratarians, he would have them released from jail. That was promptly accomplished; and not only that, but the judge provided Laffite personally with a "safe conduct pass," which allowed him to come out of hiding and into the city. There he was escorted to Jackson's Royal Street headquarters by his friend Major Latour, where a meeting was held.[*]

Though Jackson had sworn to have nothing to do with the obnoxious Baratarians, when he finally met Laffite in person something made him change his mind. Perhaps he had been expecting a desperado, a man in a pirate's suit: bandana, striped shirt, cutlass, and eye patch. Instead he met a man dressed as a gentleman and with the manners and mien of a gentleman. Although Jackson never recorded his impression in his own memoirs, surely this new apprehension of the leader of the "banditi" must have thrown the commanding general off a bit, and on the favorable side, for this time he listened to what Laffite had to say.

Nor did it hurt Laffite's case that Jackson, who already had many of Laffite's cannons (courtesy of Commodore Patterson's raid), had found to his dismay that New Orleans could offer very little in the way of ammunition and gunpowder to fire them, or flints for small arms either, and that none of those essentials appeared at this point to be forthcoming from the government at Washington. Laffite, of course, still had all of these items in abundance, squirreled away at the Temple and other secret caches in the swamps, and again he offered them to Jackson, as well as the services of his trained cannoneers and savvy swamp guides. Considering this offer to be somewhere between "a match made in heaven" and "a pact with the devil," Jackson concluded pragmatically that Laffite and his men could prove useful to the cause; or, as Professor Wilburt Brown aptly puts it, "Angels appear in curious shapes, at times; perhaps this was an answer to a prayer." Thus the "hellish banditi" were enlisted into the U.S. forces and helped to shape the outcome of the most dramatic and decisive battle so far in American history.

The Baratarians were organized into two artillery detachments, one

* Laffite's journal details a rather fanciful account of meeting Jackson on the street instead of at his headquarters, and some historians have accepted this version. It seems to me more likely that he would have gone instead to Jackson's headquarters.

under Dominique You and the other under Renato Beluche, and they were sent to outposts east of the city. Others enlisted to man the idle corvette *Louisiana* and supplement the crew of the *Carolina*, while still others were formed into companies of "marine artillery." Laffite himself was given an unofficial post as aide-de-camp to Jackson, who instructed him to supervise the defenses leading into the city from Barataria Bay. To that end Jackson wrote a note to give to the major commanding in that sector: "Jean Laffite has offered me his services to go down and give every information in his power. You will therefore please to afford him the necessary protection from Insult and Injury and when you have derived the information you wish, furnish him with a passport for his return, dismissing him as soon as possible as I shall want him here."

Cochrane's confidence at making short work of New Orleans had gotten a significant boost when the Spanish fishermen informed him that Jackson's force included no more than 5,000 men in the entire state, poorly armed militia at that, and that those in New Orleans were scattered at various places around the city. That confidence was shaken, however, upon interviewing one of Major Villeré's captured pickets, a Mr. Ducros, son of a wealthy sugar planter, who told him and General Keane that Jackson's army was nearly 20,000 strong— 12,000 to 15,000 armed men in the city and 4,000 more at English Turn. He was further disturbed the next day when two American emissaries, one of them a doctor, rowed out to the British fleet under a flag of truce to try and secure paroles for Lieutenant Jones and his captured sailors. Cochrane instead imprisoned the two aboard ship so they could not disclose his strength and posted people to listen to their conversation behind thin cabin walls. They, too, were overheard to remark on an American army considerably stronger than the one the Spanish fishermen had indicated. This information—or rather *mis*information, if not *dis*information—came to figure prominently in the actions of the British commanders, and not favorably so. For his part,

Cochrane declared publicly that he would be having his Christmas dinner in New Orleans, to which Jackson, when he got wind of it, replied: "That may be so, but I shall be seated at the head of the table."

By the morning of December 23 the British invasion was well under way. The redcoats under Colonel Thornton had come slip-and-stumble through the muck of the marshes and the mire of the cypress swamp onto the fields of the Villeré plantation. Complete surprise had been achieved beyond their wildest dreams. The surprise was so great that at about ten-thirty a.m. Major Villeré, who was sitting on the veranda of his father's plantation house with his brother, Celestine, "who was cleaning a fowling piece," suddenly noticed flashes of red in the orange grove. Upon further inspection these proved to be British soldiers. Villeré immediately dashed for the back door, only to be greeted by a squad of redcoats led by Colonel Thornton himself, a drawn sword in his hand, and "with infinate mortification, the young creole surrendered."

The Villeré brothers were confined to a room with several guards, but, as Judge Walker tells us, "there were no braver men than the Villerés; their heritage was one of dauntless courage and chivalry." Thus, when it seemed the guards were preoccupied, Major Villeré bolted through an open window, leaped a high picket fence "in the presence of some fifty British soldiers, some of whom discharged their arms at him," and ran across the stubble fields into the cypress swamp. The British immediately gave chase, with Thornton's stern admonition "catch him or kill him" ringing in their ears.

We have the following version of what happened next from historian Walker:

"He could distinctly hear the voices of his pursuers rallying one another and pointing out the course he had taken. His re-capture now seemed inevitable, when it occurred to him to climb a large live-oak and conceal himself in its evergreen branches. As he was about to execute this design, his attention was attracted by a low whine or cry at his feet. He looked down and beheld his favorite setter crouched piteously on the ground. What could Villeré do with the poor animal? Her presence near the tree would inevitably betray him . . . the imminent peril in which Jackson and his soldiers would be placed by the surprise of the city—these and other considerations [led him to conclude that] a sacrifice had to be made. The young creole seized a large stick and soon dispatched her. Concealing the dead body, he ascended the tree, where he remained until the British had returned to their camp."

That account sounds fanciful but may not be. Writing in 1856, Walker had known Villeré as an old man whose eyes still brimmed with tears whenever he told that part of the story. In any event, as soon as the coast was clear, Villeré made for the river, where he ran into a neighbor, Colonel Denis De la Ronde, who had also seen the redcoats. A day earlier, De la Ronde had reported to Jackson's headquarters that he'd seen "strange sails" out on Lake Borgne, and Jackson had already sent out his two engineer officers, Majors Tatum and Latour, to investigate. Villeré and De la Ronde found a boat and rowed across the Mississippi to spread the word that the British were coming.

By ten-thirty at least 1,600 redcoats were on the fields of Villeré's plantation, with more arriving all the time. General Keane appeared on the scene and formed the men up, wheeled them right, and marched them past Villeré's house to a point about a mile nearer New Orleans. They halted near the boundary between Villeré's and De la Ronde's plantations, and Keane established his headquarters in Villeré's home. By this time it was noon. The soldiers were spread in a line from the river to the swamp, many talking about the wealth of spoils and "beauty" that lay in the city before them. They were allowed to stack arms and build fires to cook their rations. The day having turned warm, some bathed in the canal, and all got their first look at the mighty Mississippi. They had also taken time to raise the Union Jack in a tree while a band played "God Save the King."

Not everyone was so sanguine. Captain William Surtees, of the 85th Regiment, noted that "considerable discussion now began to take place amongst the knowing ones, as to the merits and demerits of our situation, in point of security. One officer of ours did not hesitate to assert that we were in a most unprotected and dangerous position." Captain John Cooke, of the 43rd, recorded, "The soldiers were lounging about. . . . Those already landed having no retreat, it might have been conjectured that, like one of Caesar's legions, they would have felled trees or made some stronghold in case of exigencies. But no such thing was done." Lieutenant Gleig was even more blunt and pessimistic: "To put the country to the expense of sending thousands of men across the Atlantic for so mad a venture was little short of criminal."

Back in New Orleans, neither Jackson nor anyone else was aware that a British army was gathering just below the city. For this he has been strongly criticized by numerous historians, including the notable Henry Adams, who complained that "the record of American generalship [in the War of 1812] offered many examples of misfortune, but none so complete as this," by which he meant incompetence. No other American general, Adams went on, however inept—and, as we have seen, there were a great many of these—"had allowed a large British army, heralded long in advance, to arrive within seven miles unseen and unsuspected, and without so much as an earthwork, a man, or a gun between them and their object." This censure is somewhat unfair, since Jackson had ordered the Bienvenue and all the other bayous blockaded and guarded against just the sort of thing that was happening right now.* On the other hand, ultimate responsibility for seeing that those orders were carried out belonged to Jackson alone. What he should have done, in retrospect, was require that General Villeré, the major's father, personally inspect all the bayous and *put in writing* when and how each of them had been blockaded and guarded.

Such "examples of misfortune," of course, were not limited to the American army. When the first brigade of British infantrymen was fully on the field, and without apparent opposition, Colonel Thornton, a most daring officer, proposed to Keane that they march immediately

* It is tempting to suggest that Adams's harsh criticism stemmed from a lasting resentment of Jackson for having prevailed over his grandfather John Quincy Adams in the 1828 presidential election.

for New Orleans without waiting for the rest of the army. They could be in the city within a couple of hours. Keane turned him down. Why he did so remains something of a mystery. It could have been that Keane had put credence in the information obtained from the captured picket that Jackson had 12,000 to 15,000 men in New Orleans, as opposed to the Spanish fishermen's rosy picture. At least he couldn't be sure, and perhaps, like General James Longstreet two generations later at the Battle of Gettysburg, he didn't want "to fight a battle with only one boot on."

On the other hand, here in fact was a golden opportunity. Jackson's main fighting force, the brigades of Coffee and Carroll, were encamped a full four miles above New Orleans, completely unaware that anything was amiss. If the British could get an advance force into the city before the Americans reacted, and with more coming all the time, they would be very hard to dislodge. But Keane was a cautious commander. What remains unclear is why he and Cochrane did not develop a plan beforehand for such an immediate attack. It might have been that they felt it was best to get the entire army into the field and there to destroy, European-style, the American resistance once and for all; we shall probably never know. In any event, the British soldiers rested at their leisure all afternoon and into the evening before they discovered that the capture of New Orleans was not going to be a pushover.

At about two p.m. on the twenty-third, things began to happen nearly all at once at Jackson's headquarters, beginning with the desperate clatter of a horse's hoofs down Royal Street. First a man named Rousseau rushed in with the wild and dazzling news that British soldiers were all over Villeré's plantation. No sooner had he spoken these words than Major Villeré and Colonel De la Ronde arrived, breathless and mud-stained, and confirmed the story, which had to be translated for Jackson from the French. At about this time Major Tatum, Jackson's engineer who had been sent out that morning with Major Latour to investigate the report of "strange sails on the lake," also arrived to reconfirm the news.

Jackson was perplexed. Might this not merely be a feint, and the real invasion come elsewhere? Or might it not be part of a two-pronged, or even three-pronged, attack? Of course, he could not be sure, but Jackson was a man of action, not a ditherer. According to Walker, "The general drew up his figure to its full height, and with an eye of fire and an emphatic blow upon the table with his clenched fist, exclaimed in a voice that slipped like a knife through the ribs: 'By the eternal, they shall not sleep on our soil!' "

Then Jackson did what many reasonable men of the day would do under the circumstances. He poured everyone a glass of strong drink before declaring, "Gentlemen, the British are below, we must fight them to-night."

This was unassailably a bold and daring decision, given the uncertainties Jackson faced. If he had jumped the wrong way, the general might have found his army fighting a British force nine miles south of the city while the main enemy attack developed from another location. Yet absent any firm evidence of that distinct possibility, Jackson did what so many failed commanders have been reluctant to do over the ages, which was to "march to the sound of the guns." Walker points out the irony: "Here was a farmer—lawyer—general who had never commanded a regiment of regular soldiers in his life," going up against the renowned veterans of the Napoleonic Wars, led by a professional soldier (Keane) "who had fought under [Generals] Abercrombie, Moore and Wellington." What Jackson realized was that the redcoats on General Villeré's plantation were only the advance guard; therefore time was on his side, but only for the moment, for the rest of the enemy army would soon follow, like the Goths to Rome.

Within minutes the alarm guns had been fired in New Orleans and the cathedral bells rung, spreading the news with electric rapidity throughout the city. Jackson immediately began issuing marching orders, to Coffee, to Carroll, to the free men of color, to the battalions of New Orleans volunteers, the regulars, and the militia: everyone was to assemble in front of the British position on the Plain of Chalmette.

Amid all this activity the general fumed. "I will smash them," he exclaimed. "So help me God!" At one point he noticed a number of women and children in the streets, wailing and crying, and ordered Livingston to "say to the ladies not to be uneasy. No British soldier shall enter the city as an enemy, unless it is over my dead body." To guard against the possibility that this was merely a feint or just one part of a multipronged attack, Jackson left the various militia at their posts north and east of the city, as well as the Baratarian artillerists, who could not have moved their guns down in time anyway. In the lengthening shadows, Jackson's battalions began to arrive, including Captain Jugat's band of Choctaws with their knives and tomahawks.

Meantime, he had consulted with Commodore Patterson, reaching an agreement that the fourteen-gun *Carolina* would quietly drop down in the river's current to a point nearly beside the British position. This was one of the truly inspired ideas of the battle, for to suddenly bring half that ship's artillery in broadside against an unsuspecting British army would certainly wreak havoc. When they were sufficiently bombarded, Patterson was to fire off a red, a white, and a blue rocket, which would be the signal for Jackson to attack. Thus, as darkness closed in, Jackson had assembled a welcoming committee for the invaders, rude in more ways than one, that was to have a lasting impact on the campaign thereafter.

As the sun began to set and purple shadows fell over the stubble cane fields and orange groves on a short Southern winter day, Jackson's army organized itself. At some point Latour arrived to report that he had made a study of the British position through his spyglass and estimated the force at Villeré's as numbering between 1,600 and 1,800, a remarkably accurate assessment. The general sat astride his horse at the gates of Fort St. Charles on what is now Esplanade Avenue, with Laffite, Latour, Livingston, and others beside him. That was the rallying point for the troops, as the various militia, volunteers, and U.S. Army regulars assembled in marching formation. Some of the units—Plauché's volunteer lawyers, bankers, and merchants, for example—had to run all the way into town from their post at Fort St. John. "Ah, here come the brave creoles!" Jackson was said to have remarked to one of his aides.

Then they began to march out of the city about a mile south to the Montreuil plantation, which was fifteen plantations (about ten miles) above where the British had assembled. "As they advanced along the levee," Walker tells us, "hundreds of snowy handkerchiefs were waved towards them and bright eyes from every window and balcony cheered their hearts and warmed their courage."

From Montreuil's, with General Coffee's mounted riflemen leading the way, Jackson marched his men forward in perfect silence to form a line on an old abandoned canal on the Rodriguez plantation, about two miles from the enemy. He set up his field headquarters in the Macarty plantation house. An old Creole planter who had taken an interest in the stars sent Jackson his astronomical telescope, which proved a godsend. From the second-story balcony—or, even better, the third-story dormers—Jackson could view the entire British line with this powerful optical instrument, while the British, having neither such an elevated observation post nor a telescope of their own, did not enjoy a similar advantage.

By four p.m. the bulk of the American army had arrived. First blood was drawn when a mounted reconnaissance party came too close to the British advance pickets: two men were wounded as well as a horse killed. The Americans had moved into position so quietly, however, that the British never suspected an attack in force that night. As a matter of fact, they did not foresee an attack at all, based on their experience with American militia at Washington and elsewhere. "Militia never attack" had become a military axiom for them.

As a further precaution against a multipronged assault, Jackson reluctantly directed Carroll's strong force of freshly arrived Tennesseans to the Plain of Gentilly, where another branch of Bayou Bienvenue emptied. From there Carroll could either defend against an attack or serve as a ready reserve. Luckily for Carroll, on the way down the Mississippi his force had intercepted one of the munitions shipment boats sent from Pittsburgh by the War Department. No one, apparently, had thought to tell the arms manufacturer to ship the weapons with all deliberate speed, and so, to get a better deal, he agreed that the keel-boat captains could stop along the way and buy and sell other cargo, thus delaying their arrival almost indefinitely. In any event, Carroll was delighted to have overtaken the munitions boat, since many of his men had come unarmed, expecting to be equipped at New Orleans. Now Carroll had eleven hundred new muskets, which he used to drill his soldiers on their flatboats as they steered slowly down the Mississippi. He also set his blacksmiths to manufacturing fifty thousand cartridges.

Jackson's use of Carroll's division was cautious and wise, but it also subtracted more than 2,400 men from his infantry. Still, Jackson knew that it is a foolish commander who goes into battle without a strong and ready reserve, either to forestall a losing fight or to take advantage of a success. (A note on troop numbers: each of the various official reports, as well as figures calculated by historians, cite different strength figures for both sides throughout the battle. For instance, Jackson in his official report stated that the British force opposing him on December 23 numbered 3,000. Latour, who also was there and wrote the first history, says there were 4,000 and possibly as many as 5,000. Others say there were fewer than 2,000. Likewise, on the American side, it was estimated by Jackson himself that he had only 1,500 men, but Latour gives the figure at 2,100, citing a unit-by-unit breakdown. It is probably safe to say that the two armies on that night—at least at the beginning—were fairly evenly matched at about 2,000 men each.)

The British had stood on American soil unmolested all day, and now, as darkness fell, they lounged about their campfires cooking supper. "Not content with the salt meat and rum allotted to them by the Commissary, small parties were permitted to go out in pursuit of more desirable delicacies. Spreading themselves over the country they penetrated every house, every dairy and negro cabin, pig-sty and poultry-yard, seized everything that was eatable or drinkable and bore it into camp. The officers were allotted the first choice of these luxuries, which consisted of ham, cheese, poultry, wine, brandy and other delicacies with which the houses of the planters are always abundantly supplied."

The night was chilly and cloudy but not yet cold, and many of the redcoats who had endured the ordeals at Pea Island and the long, uncomfortable row across the lake dropped off to sleep after finishing what they considered sumptuous dinners. Pickets and reconnaissance parties reported no contact with Americans after the dustup with the U.S. cavalry patrol. With the round-the-clock ferrying operation going as planned, most of the British army would be in the field by the next afternoon, and there would be time enough then to deal with the Americans.

At about seven p.m., British soldiers posted near the levee noticed that a large schooner was moving slowly downriver. This ship was unlighted, and they could perceive no movement aboard her in the darkness. Like a ghost ship coming out of the mist, the schooner slowly made its way over to the bank where the British were encamped. Less than a hundred yards from the levee, the splash of an anchor was heard. Many of the soldiers assumed the ship was British, sent to guard their flank on the march into New Orleans the next day. Others thought she was probably a merchantman. They hailed her but received no answer. They fired rifle shots to attract her attention, but the ship remained enigmatic, silent as a tomb. Someone informed the officers, who came out for a look, but no one could surmise the meaning of the mystery ship.

At half past seven she revealed herself.

Those who were still watching reported that they saw large firing matches lit. Suddenly the gunports snapped open and, according to Lieutenant Gleig, a "commanding voice" was distinctly heard to say: "Give them this for the honor of America!" At that, the right side of the ship burst into an orange sheet of flame and "a perfect tornado of grape-shot swept down numbers in the camp."

Manned in part by the experienced Baratarian artillerymen, the seven starboard cannons of the *Carolina* wreaked chaos on the British position. The gun crews aimed at the campfires around which the men were resting, blasting pots, pans, kettles, and men. "The scene beggared all description. No mob could have been in a more utter state of disorganization," one British officer said. The entire field was swept by fire,

Portrait of Andrew Jackson around the time of the Battle of New Orleans. His defeat of the British army won him fame and the U.S. presidency. (COURTESY THE HISTORIC NEW ORLEANS COLLECTION)

This caricature of Jean Laffite is one of many attempts to capture his likeness. There are no authenticated drawings of him during his lifetime, though later portraits were painted from descriptions by those who knew him. Considering his shabby past, Laffite probably did not wish to have his picture made public. (COURTESY THE HISTORIC NEW ORLEANS COLLECTION)

Generals John Coffee and William Carroll, both of Tennessee, were two of Jackson's trusted commanders whose troops held down the critical left side of the American line. (COFFEE, COURTESY THE HERMITAGE; CARROLL, COURTESY THE TENNESSEE HISTORICAL SOCIETY)

General David Morgan of Louisiana, commander of the troops on the west side of the river, suffered loss of face when his men broke and ran as the British attacked on December 8, 1814. (COURTESY THE LOUISIANA STATE MUSEUM)

General Sir Edward Pakenham was killed during the battle and his remains were sent back to England in a cask of rum. Brother-in-law to the Duke of Wellington and a competent commander, he inherited a bad field position and made the worst of it. (COURTESY THE DUKE OF WELLINGTON)

Admiral Alexander Cochrane, commander of the British naval expedition, was thought by many to have organized the attack on New Orleans in order to secure for himself the valuable prize money associated with the capture of the city. (COURTESY NATIONAL MARITIME MUSEUM, GREENWICH, LONDON)

Commodore Daniel Todd Patterson was instrumental in the victory by bringing to bear the fire of his two U.S. Navy ships on the British army—especially during the early days of the battle. (COURTESY CHRYSLER MUSEUM OF ART)

This bird's-eye depiction by Hyacinth Laclotte of the Battle of New Orleans on the day of the final British attack is thought by some to have derived from a sketch by Arsene Lacarrière Latour, Jackson's chief engineer. It shows Jackson's headquarters at the Macarty house on the left; Colonel Rennie's attack on the American right; the main attack of the British on the American center and left in which Generals Pakenham, Keane, and Gibbs fell; and Jackson's reserves behind the lines. (COURTESY THE HISTORIC NEW ORLEANS COLLECTION)

Another version of the battle depicting British colonel Rennie's attack on the far right of the American line. Rennie and several of his subordinates were killed just as they reached the top of the barricade. (COURTESY THE HISTORIC NEW ORLEANS COLLECTION)

A third representation, showing the fury of the fighting on the final day of the battle. (COURTESY THE HISTORIC NEW ORLEANS COLLECTION)

A depiction of the Battle of Lake Borgne rendered several decades after the battle, showing the fierce little British barges attacking the American gunboat flotilla. (COURTESY CHICAGO HISTORICAL SOCIETY)

The Macarty plantation house, where Jackson kept his headquarters from the beginning of the battle. Positioning himself at the little dormer on the third floor, he used a telescope given him by an amateur astronomer to watch British positions and movements more than a mile distant. (FROM AN 1860s WOOD-CUT DRAWING BY HISTORIAN BENSON LOSSING)

One of the many paintings of the Battle of New Orleans that immortalized Andrew Jackson and his scruffy, thrown-together army. Depicted here is the popular but false notion that the Americans fought behind a barricade of cotton bales. (COURTESY THE HISTORIC NEW ORLEANS COLLECTION)

The bold pirate/privateer Dominique You, who manned his guns on the barricade throughout the battle, was thought to be the brother of Jean Laffite. (COURTESY THE HISTORIC NEW ORLEANS COLLECTION)

Another fanciful illustration of the final day of the Battle of New Orleans, this one showing soldiers of the battalion of free men of color, as well as American frontiersmen dressed in buckskin. (COURTESY THE HISTORIC NEW ORLEANS COLLECTION)

Generals Sir Edward Pakenham and Samuel Gibbs, killed on the battle's last furious day, depicted here in a remarkable marble sculpture in the hall of St. Paul's Cathedral in London. There is something quite touching about the faraway gaze in their eyes, as if they were watching the defeated British army pass in review. (COURTESY THE WARBURG INSTITUTE, LONDON)

and the soldiers "ran wildly to and fro" until Colonel Thornton dashed out and ordered the men to take shelter under the levee. "Against this destructive fire we had nothing to oppose," reported Gleig. The *Carolina* kept up its fire for a solid hour, during which "the men lay down at full length, listening in painful silence to the pattering of grape-shot and the shrieks of the wounded in the field . . . who were knocked and tossed about like logs of wood, by the remorseless shot of the schooner."

Back in New Orleans the tension was palpable. While a company of old men stood guard in the deserted streets, women and their daughters gathered at a number of homes to sew bandages and make clothes, especially for Carroll's tattered Tennessee soldiers. The sound of cannon fire from below the city rumbled through the night like distant thunder, while residents could only wonder and wait "with emotions that can be imagined, not described." What with the British army's reprehensible behavior at Hampton, Virginia, still fresh on everyone's mind, it was reported that many of the women had concealed daggers on their persons.

At eight-thirty the cannon fire from the *Carolina* ceased, and from the deck of the ship came the three signal rockets in rapid succession—red, white, and blue—of which Jackson and his commanders well knew the meaning. The British, who did not know, found out soon enough when "a fearful yell rose out of the dark and the heavens were illuminated on all sides by a semi-circular blaze of musketry." According to Lieutenant Gleig, "Now began a battle of which no language were competent to convey any distinct idea; because it was one to which the annals of modern warfare furnished no parallel." For Gleig and many of his brother officers and men—even General Keane himself—this was a flatly true statement. In the European wars to which they were accustomed, battles were not fought at night; instead the armies waited until daytime, when every man could be seen, and victory was usually gained by the army marching in line closest to the enemy and delivering withering volleys, then either holding its ground or marching even closer, causing the other to flee.

That was not Jackson's plan. During the bombardment he had stealthily maneuvered the American army forward to the very edges of the De la Ronde plantation, just opposite the British camp. First Coffee's dismounted infantrymen, guided by Pierre Laffite and Colonel De la Ronde himself, burst into the British line at the far end of the field near the cypress swamp. Their object was to cut off the British line of reinforcement and supply that led from their landing site at the Villeré Canal and Bayou Bienvenue and then roll up the enemy's right flank, pushing it toward the river. Major Thomas Hinds and his Mississippi dragoons remained on Coffee's old line as a reserve and mobile force, since trying to negotiate at night the numerous fences, canals, and ditches that interlaced the plantations would certainly have injured or destroyed many of their horses.

From the British perspective, rarely had men been so abruptly pitchforked into battle than those who were just arriving at the landing at the bayou's terminus. With the entire field erupting in gunfire, these startled, hungry, weary troops who had just endured the grueling daylong row across the lake were herded by their commanders through the gummy marshes and the swamp and plunged straight into the canefield fray.

At the same time, Jackson had ordered forward the two regiments of U.S. regulars as well as the lawyer and merchant volunteers, who pitched into the British in their sheltering position behind the levee. A particularly fierce fight was put up by a British captain named Hallen and his 80-man outpost several hundred yards in front of the main enemy line. Try as the Americans might to evict the British from their position near the levee, they would not budge, and, since Hallen was continually reinforced, the Americans had no choice but to go around them.

From then on what has come to be known as the Night Battle unavoidably began to assume the aspect of a wild melee in which lives were measured in anxious minutes. Scores of vicious little fights erupted in the darkness all over the field of several hundred acres, and it soon became a practical impossibility to keep order—it was "a war of detachments and duels," as one participant put it. To make matters worse, a heavy fog had risen up from the river and swamps and covered the battlefield, mingling with the smoke from the many muskets and guns. Every available weapon was used: rifles, pistols, bayonets, gun butts, knives, hatchets, sabers, fence rails, and fists and strangling hands, accompanied by wild yelling, cursing, and the screaming of the wounded. The Choctaw Indians made good use of their tomahawks. The night was black as pitch, illuminated only by the flashes of gunfire against low-hanging clouds and the fog. "We fought with the savage ferocity of bull-dogs," recalled Lieutenant Gleig, whose best friend was killed by a shot through the head and left lying on a dung heap.

As prisoners were taken, and their units determined, both sides employed the ruse of calling out to the other that they were "friends." A British major named Samuel Mitchell and a number of his people were captured in that way over in Coffee's sector when Mitchell shouted out to some men he could barely see in the dark, "Are you the Ninety-third [the regiment of Highlanders expected to land at any time]?"

"That's right!" came the reply, but when Mitchell walked into the group he "was slapped on the shoulder by Captain John Donelson, Andrew Jackson's nephew," who informed him, "You are my prisoner, Major."

Mitchell was so angry that he refused to hand over his sword until it was taken from him forcibly, and he was led to the rear cursing furiously. Then the same thing happened to Donelson and his men after a British detachment responded to their query of "Who are you?" by shouting, "We are Coffee's men."

The butchery went on for a full six hours, and men on both sides were shot by their own in the darkness and fog. The Americans had two six-pounder cannon moved up, but before they could be put in firing position the British attacked them. Jackson rode up and gave a demonstration of his legendary self-control, "indifferent to the shower of bullets which whistled around him." He called out, "Save the guns, my boys, at every sacrifice!"

Sometime around ten p.m. the 1,100-man regiment of 93rd Highlanders began to arrive on the field, and these strapping six-footers lent much needed weight to the British defense. Around midnight Jackson decided to call off the attack; his men were exhausted, ammunition was running low, and the constant stream of British reinforcements was tipping the balance against him. Between those considerations and the fog, darkness, and gunsmoke, which made command and control almost impossible, Jackson sent messengers to Coffee and Colonel Ross of the 7th Regiment of regulars to fall back, but small pockets of soldiers, unable to disengage, continued to fire at one another for several hours more.

At first, Jackson had determined to renew the attack at dawn, but as more information came in he thought better of it. Now he knew that the 93rd Highlanders had arrived as well as other regiments and artillery. His men were neither trained nor drilled to withstand the methodical massed-fire tactics of European infantry conflicts. Many of them didn't even have bayonets, while the British did. They were, basically, Indian fighters—at least those who had been in any battles at all—and the night battle had been in the nature of an Indian-style fight. That they were willing to continue despite the fact that they had no idea of the campaign's outcome or whether they would live or die is testimony enough to their reconciliation with Jackson's antique sense of honor.

Tomorrow, though, would bring a far stronger force against Jackson's already exhausted men. While he pondered matters in the darkest hours before dawn, Jackson must have been struggling with his own basic instincts. He had always been a fighter, not a defender; when a situation called for action, Jackson inevitably was the aggressor—in the school yard, the courtroom, the dueling field, during the Creek War, against the Spanish at Pensacola—but here reason called for something contrary to those impulses that drove his complex soul. The mental processes that formed Jackson's decision are not known; nor is it known whether or not he consulted his commanders. About an hour before dawn he gave the order to retire the army away from the British, back five or six plantations up toward New Orleans. He would return to his field headquarters on the Rodriguez Canal and there, with his astronomical telescope with which to watch the enemy, reorganize, fortify, and await developments. He wrote a simple dispatch to Secretary of War Monroe: "As the safety of the city will depend on the fate of this army, it must not be incautiously exposed." In retrospect, this was his wisest decision of the entire campaign.

When streaks of daylight lit the swamps and stubble fields, the killing ground presented a horrific apparition to Lieutenant Gleig. "In wandering over the field the most shocking and disgusting sights everywhere presented themselves [and] wounds more disfiguring or more horrible I certainly never witnessed. A man shot through the head or heart, lies as if he were in deep slumber . . . but many had met their death from bayonet wounds, sabre cuts or heavy blows from the butt-ends of muskets and the consequence was that not only were the wounds themselves exceedingly frightful, but the very countenances of the dead exhibited the most savage and ghastly expressions. Friends and foes lay together in small groups of five or six—nor was it difficult to tell the very hand by which some of them had fallen. Nay, such had been the deadly closeness of the strife that, in one or two places, an English and American soldier might be seen with the bayonet of each fastened in the other's body."

After searching for some time, Gleig finally located the body of his dead companion, a Captain Grey, who "had been shot through the temples by a rifle bullet so small as scarcely left any traces. Lifting him upon a cart I had him carried down to head-quarters house, now converted into a hospital, and having dug a grave for him at the bottom of the garden, I laid him out there as a soldier should be laid, arrayed not in a shroud, but in his uniform. Even the privates I brought with me to assist in his funeral mingled their tears with mine."

Gleig then visited the hospital, where "every room was crowded with wretches mangled and apparently in the most excruciating agonies. Prayers, groans and, I grieve to add [being himself the son of a clergyman], the most horrid exclamations smote upon the ear wherever I turned. Some lay upon the straw with eyes half closed and limbs motionless; some endeavoured to start up, shrieking with pain, while the wandering eye and incoherent speech of others indicated the loss of reason, and usually foretold the approach of death. There was one among the rest whose appearance was too horrible ever to be forgotten. He had been shot through the windpipe and the breath making its way between the skin and the flesh had dilated him to a size absolutely terrific. His head and face were particularly shocking. Every feature was enlarged beyond what can well be imagined; whilst his eyes were so completely hidden by the cheeks and forehead as to destroy all resemblance to a human countenance."

In one room Gleig came across a number of officers, all of whom he knew. "One had been shot in the head and lay gasping and insensible; another had received a musket-ball in the belly, which had pierced through and lodged in the backbone. [He] was in the most dreadful agony, screaming out and gnawing the covering under which he lay."

British casualties amounted to 276 officers and men, of which 46 had been killed, and 64 were taken prisoner. Jackson had 213 casualties, of which 24 were killed, and 74 were taken prisoner, including a number of "the most respectable citizens of New Orleans," who had formed the rifle company of Captain Thomas Beale. This company had blundered into a large detachment of the newly arriving 93rd Highlanders. Among those made prisoners were the former mayor of New Orleans, the president of the Bank of Louisiana, a number of lawyers, and the port customs collector.*

Despite Jackson's insolent, bloodthirsty, and ultimately unsuccessful attack, the British remained in their positions, hallooing to one another about how they had whipped the Americans and sent them flying, though none among them could again claim they had gone unmo-

---

* These men were hustled off down the bayou in boats and held aboard the ship of the line *Royal Oak*. They were treated roughly until the *Royal Oak*'s captain discovered that one of their number had served as a groomsman in his wedding in New York before the war. "In consequence of this recognition, the captain of the *Royal Oak* caused a very elegant dinner to be prepared for the prisoners which was attended by all the ship's officers of the *Royal Oak* and several other ships."

lested. They had, in fact, been thoroughly molested, and, at least so far, Jackson's assertion "By the Eternal, they shall not sleep on our soil" was nearer to the truth than not. The fact was, the British veterans so accustomed to massive daylight clashes in which long orderly lines of infantry formally marched against enemies, heralded by drums and bugles and regimental flags flying, had been shaken by being jumped at night, Indian-style, by an enemy they considered to be woefully inferior. The British commanders, for their part, were shocked as well by the ferocity of the assault. Colonel Thornton, who had watched U.S. militia run away at Washington and elsewhere, observed darkly, "This boldly attacking us in our camp is a new feature in American warfare."

Ten

Morning presented no better aspect for the British army. Leaving aside Lieutenant Gleig's abominable stroll across the battlefield, the wretched dawn brought a new rain of hell from the *Carolina*, which by now had moved to the opposite bank of the river, well out of musket range, to continue unleashing her broadsides. Far from a mere harassing fire, it killed and maimed without warning, putting every redcoat's nerves on edge. Worse for Keane's army, by midmorning *Carolina* was joined by the much larger and more powerful sixteen-big-gun *Louisiana*—manned primarily by Jean Laffite's expert Baratarian cannoneers—which anchored about a mile upstream and also began to blast the British positions. Captain Surtees recorded that one shot hit a corporal and went right through him: "He gave himself a sort of shake, and fell lifeless upon the earth." Surtees himself nearly became a victim. "We had scarcely left a little wooden hut behind which we had taken our abode . . . when Bang! comes an eighteen pound shot right through the house, just at the very spot where we had a minute or two before been sitting."

The day was gloomy, yeasty, and gray, the ground was damp, and the air was chilly. It was Christmas Eve. The conditions the British found themselves in were appalling. Those digging holes to protect themselves from the fire of the *Carolina* found that after they'd dug two feet or so into the ground, water filled the holes up.

General Keane faced a dilemma, and he wasn't at all happy about it. The ferocity of Jackson's night attack had unnerved him. He knew the Americans had gone, but where? He had no powerful telescope like

Jackson, nor a tall house to observe from, and because of a bend in the river he could not even see if Jackson had formed a line, which Keane fully expected the Americans to do. When he ordered scouts out for reconnaissance, they got only so far and then were sent flying by a large troop of Hinds's Mississippi dragoons, who had been left by Jackson to watch for them. The night action had cost Keane nearly half a regiment, and the remainder of his army was still being rowed over on the dreadful trip from Pea Island. American warships were constantly shelling his men. By the time the army could assemble and take the field, it would be too late in the afternoon to mount an attack against the Americans. Worse, his troops seemed unsettled and grumbling, five thousand long miles from home on Christmas Eve.

About the only thing Keane seemed able to do at the moment was send for heavier artillery to try and drive the American ships from his flank. And yet he would have to wait for the guns to be rowed across the lake, like everything else, and then dragged and manhandled through the awful marshes and swamps before he could launch his attack. Still, he could not wait too long, for there was no ready supply of food in his present location, other than what his men had brought with them or what could be raided from the two or three local plantations, certainly not enough to feed 8,000. The original idea had been for the British army to be dining in New Orleans within a day or so, but clearly the scheme was not playing out as planned, or, as Lieutenant Gleig put it, "all things had turned out diametrically opposite to what had been anticipated."

The only other thing Keane seemed to have found time to do was to complain of the ingratitude of the Louisiana Creoles who, he now realized, had just attacked him with the same ardor as had their American brethren. A few days earlier British spies or agents in New Orleans had hired slaves to nail up a new proclamation throughout the city and upon the fences of surrounding plantations; printed in French and Spanish by the official printing press aboard the fleet, it was signed by Keane and Admiral Cochrane: "Louisianians! [meaning Creoles or native French and Spanish] Remain quiet in your houses. *Your slaves shall be preserved to you,* and your property respected. We make war only against Americans." But any notion that these people were going to defect and join him—or at least do nothing to hinder him—was now dashed to shards, another of Keane's and Cochrane's gross political miscalculations.

A number of slaves belonging to the plantations that the British were occupying did defect, however, though they probably had little choice. In any case, they were immediately set to work performing menial tasks such as hauling water and provisions and digging latrines. "These negroes," recorded a British officer, "were all attired in a strange looking and rudely fashioned dress; it was composed of a coarse French blanket, or horse-cloth, with loose sleeves and a hood. Their shoes were made of bullock's hide, undressed [raw] and with the hair on the outside."

This same officer recorded that he was "accosted by a young negro, of great intelligence, [who] in excellent French implored me to order a collar of spikes with which his neck was encompassed to be taken off." When the officer asked why he had been placed in such a diabolical device, the slave told him that as soon as he had heard the British were coming he tried to run away and join them, but his owner had caught him and this was his punishment. The collar, said the officer, "was contrived to prevent the wearer from using any other but an upright position," so he had not been able to lie down for nearly a week.

"This ingenious symbol of the land of liberty I took immediate measures to have removed at our farrier's forge, and no sooner was the poor devil released from it than he threw himself on the earth and placed one of my feet on his head, and said that he would very much like to serve me," the officer wrote. "He said that he had been accustomed to the care of horses; could speak French, Spanish and a little English, would be faithful and honest, wishing no other reward but meat and drink." He got the job.

Andrew Jackson, too, had to decide what to do next as he surveyed his situation from his observation post. The only way the British were going to get into New Orleans from where they presently sat was to march across the plantation fields. The part of the field on which they now were situated was about a mile wide, running from the river to the cypress swamp. But because of the bend in the river, the width of the plantations soon began to taper down funnel-like toward Jackson's current position, so that an enemy formation in the attack soon would be compressed into just over half that front; thus, between the river and the swamp there would be little room for them to maneuver. Jackson, "an old Tennessee backwoodsman," apparently had studied his military tactics books.

Right in front of Jackson's position was the abandoned drainage ditch called the Rodriguez Canal. It was presently dry and grassy-bottomed, but Jackson saw the possibilities of a good defensive position. He was, however, inclined to launch another attack against the British—and had even ordered Carroll's 2,600-man division down to participate—but his scouts told him the enemy had strongly reinforced throughout the night and more redcoats were pouring ashore, probably, by now, some 6,000 of them. Edward Livingston suggested that Jackson see Major Henri St. Geme, of the Louisiana dragoons, who a decade or so earlier—while Louisiana was still French—had ridden the fields around New Orleans with the famed French military tactician Jean Moreau, one of Napoleon's marshals, during which they discussed how best to protect New Orleans. It was likely with a delicious sense of irony that the Frenchman St. Geme told Jackson that Moreau had pointed out this selfsame Rodriguez Canal as the best spot to defend against an attack from below the city on that side of the river.

That settled it for Jackson, but there remained herculean work to be done. The canal line had to be heavily fortified immediately if the Americans, with their smaller army and mostly untried soldiers, were to stand a full-scale infantry assault by the superior and professional forces of the British. They certainly couldn't withstand it in the open fields.

Accordingly, men were rushed back to New Orleans and to surrounding plantations to gather up as many shovels, spades, hoes, axes, sledges, nails and hammers, horses, oxen, and wagons as could be found. Hundreds of slaves were brought in to help with the work, but a silly disagreement soon arose among some as to whether the Americans and Creoles should work alongside the slaves, since digging was considered "Negro work."

Jackson quickly settled the question and, with one rank sleeping on their arms while another dug and filled, all participated under direct orders, working like dervishes under the general's iron-fisted supervision.

At the same time, Jackson told Latour to get a detachment and break the levee both in front of the British position and behind it. Whosoever's idea this was, it was a canny and wicked one. At that time of year the river ran low, but it was still presently a foot or so above the level of the land and would inundate the entire plain between with the same amount of water; whoever attacked would have to wade through it.

Jackson's design was to widen the canal to at least ten feet, piling up the spoil dirt on the far side to create a fortification. Boards and planks from fences, barns, and houses were ripped out and pounded vertically to create a berm; thus the half-mile-long breastwork started to take shape beginning at the levee on the river and running to the cypress swamp. At a foot and a half the diggers struck water in the ditch but kept on digging until there was at least two feet of water in the canal. It was soon discovered that the thrown-up mud was sliding back into the canal, and, since artillery had already been sent for, some provision had to be made for stable platforms for the big guns to rest upon in order to be accurately fired. Latour suggested using cotton bales to strengthen these artillery redoubts, and Jackson agreed, but this, too, caused a minor friction.

Vincent Nolte, a German merchant in New Orleans, was now in the line as a volunteer rifleman. He recalled years later that at the time cotton could be acquired in the city for seven to eight cents a pound. Jackson had learned that only a mile or so behind their position was a merchant ship tied up to the levee containing a large number of cotton bales, and he immediately dispatched men to go and get them. When the wagons began to return, Nolte immediately recognized from the revenue stamps that it was *his own cotton,* which he had contracted to ship to Havana just before the emergency.

The rub came because Nolte's crop was the rare "long-staple" cotton, with nearly twice the value of the regular seedy variety that most planters produced, and his 245 bales now being manhandled into the muddy fortification were worth, in today's dollars, nearly $100,000. This caused Nolte, ever the businessman, to become "vexed at the idea of their taking cotton of the best sort," and he took his complaint directly to Livingston, Jackson's military secretary. "Well, Mr. Nolte," Livingston replied curtly, "if this is your cotton, you, at least, will not think it a hardship to defend it."

At one point while walking the lines of the fortification with Livingston, Jean Laffite saw something that might have caused a shiver of fear to flow over him. At the far end of the line, where it entered the cypress swamp, the rampart abruptly ended. Laffite remarked to Livingston that in his opinion this was dangerous. Everywhere else, he said, the army could fight from behind a rampart, but here the British were afforded an opportunity to get behind the American position. Then there would be an open-field, broad-daylight fight of just the sort Jackson was seeking to avoid.*

Whether they both went to Jackson with this notion or whether it was Livingston alone who carried back Laffite's assessment is a matter of dispute, but in any case Jackson immediately agreed with it and ordered that the rampart be extended and manned so far back into the swamp that no one could get around it. This was done in spite of the immense discomfort of the Tennesseans of Coffee and Carroll, who, to defend the position, often had to stand knee-deep and even waist-deep in winter swamp water.

---

* Here is another of the nagging historical discrepancies that seem to defy resolution. Several historians, including Remini, Jackson's authoritative biographer, say it was Jean Laffite who warned Jackson about extending the line, but Laffite's latest biographer, William C. Davis, reports that it was Pierre.

Laffite's advice might have been the best suggestion Jackson received during the entire battle, because breaching the American position at just this spot was exactly what the British had had in mind.

All Christmas Eve and Christmas Day the men labored to build and strengthen Jackson's soon-to-be-famous parapet. It was an incredible effort, and when it was at last finished two weeks later it would consist of a fortification more than half a mile long, fronted by planks, behind which would lay a berm seven or eight feet high and about the same width thick, bristling with eight batteries of artillery placed at intervals, firing from defilade (i.e., from above), and in between them would be placed all of the infantry that could be crammed into the line. Not only that, but in front of it, in the canal, they had dug out a ten-foot-wide moat with two feet of water in it. If the British planned to drive them from this position, they had best be bringing their lunch, since they would first have to slog through nearly two miles of knee-deep December-icy water, fetch themselves across a ten-foot moat, then scale an eight-foot embankment, all in the face of murderous cannon and rifle fire. Jackson also ordered a tall flagstaff to be planted near the center of the line and the biggest star-spangled banner they could find hoisted upon it, so that—for better or worse, if nothing else—those Englishmen would see the American flag flying during most of their slog toward them. But that was all in the future; for now the fortification was only beginning to take shape, and Jackson pushed the men relentlessly.

The battlefield remained relatively quiet for the rest of Christmas Eve and Christmas Day. Keane was still waiting for the artillery from the fleet with which to silence the *Carolina* (or, in Captain John Henry Cooke's words, "to blow her out of the water") as well as the last remnants of his army, which did not get into the field until Christmas morning. When it finally did arrive, it came with a surprise for Keane in the form of General Sir Edward Pakenham, who immediately relieved him of his duties and took charge. This change of command had a very good effect on the troops, who had not only been shaken by the American night attack but also were becoming demoralized by the devastating blasts from the *Carolina* and Keane's failure to march them out of its range of fire and into New Orleans for their booty and beauty.

Sir Edward was an officer of some distinction; he had never held the command of a major army but had led regiments and a division. As a second son without hope of inheriting the family estate, he had joined the army at the age of sixteen and quickly rose through the ranks of the officer corps. In 1803, in a battle against Napoleon's forces on the island of Saint Lucia, he was badly wounded in the neck, which caused his head to cock to one side, until, two years later, again fighting Napoleon's army on the nearby island of Martinique, he received another bullet to the neck that, ironically, corrected the droop. Afterward he fought in the Peninsular campaign, in which he distinguished himself at the Battle of Salamanca.

As mentioned, his sister was married to the Duke of Wellington and, after Salamanca, he was put on Wellington's staff, where the Iron Duke assessed him thusly: "Pakenham may not be the brightest genius, but my partiality for him does not lead me astray when I tell you he is one of the best we have."

It has been pointed out that Pakenham's arrival was delayed by as much as a week or more by the captain of his transport ship, who insisted on shortening sail every night—presumably to guard against some possible mid-ocean collision—and that if Pakenham had somehow joined the fleet before the landing, his forceful personality (as well as his close connection to the formidable Wellington) might have swayed the imperious Cochrane from attempting such a daring and dangerous scheme as was in place now. That may well have been so, but it did not happen, so Pakenham was left to take charge of the situation he inherited.

There is no dispute that when the thirty-six-year-old Pakenham arrived at the Villeré plantation on Christmas morning he was displeased; he was "furious," in fact, and, as Cooke tells us, "at once gave vent to his feelings, declaring that troops were never found in so strange a position." From a practical point of view, Cochrane's plan was outlandish. Here Pakenham was with his army bottled up between a river and a swamp, and his train of supply (and route of escape, if necessary) possible only by small boats that had to row fourteen miles up a bayou and then sixty miles across a huge lake during all the vicissitudes of wintertime. Nevertheless, he came to agree with Keane that the *Carolina* must be dealt with before marching against the Americans, lest the troops be exposed to artillery bombardment in the open fields all the way to Jackson's line. This might have been a proper military attitude to take except for one thing: every minute the British delayed in attacking the Americans gave Jackson exactly those same minutes to strengthen his line, and Jackson used them well.

Lieutenant Gleig records that the men cheered when it was announced that Pakenham would be taking over, but also that Christmas Day was definitely not up to standards. He and some fellow officers had decided to pool their provisions and give a little feast, but "so melancholy a Christmas dinner I do not recollect at any time to have been present." They had few plates and utensils, and had to try to eat under the constant bombardment from the *Carolina*. "Whilst we were sitting at a table a loud shriek was heard after one of these explosions, and on running out we found that a shot had taken effect in the body of an unfortunate soldier. Though fairly cut in two at the lower part of the belly, the poor wretch lived for nearly an hour, gasping for breath and giving signs even of pain."

In war, one must always assume the other side has a plan as well, and such was the case with the British on the day after Christmas 1814. Right after dark, the artillery that Keane had ordered for the destruction of the *Carolina* finally arrived—two nine-pounders, four six-pounder field guns, two five-and-a-half-inch howitzers, and a mortar. Before dawn on December 27 a field furnace was set up behind the levee to heat up shot as the guns were manhandled through the marshes, swamps, and fields and finally installed in a battery that had been scooped out along the levee crest. Now it was the Americans' turn to be "annoyed," as the expression of the day went. When the sun had risen enough to present a field of fire, the British battery opened up on *Carolina* at point-blank range.

The second British salvo did the trick. It was a glowing hot shot shoveled into a cannon barrel from the field furnace that burst into *Carolina*'s innards at an inaccessible place beneath her steering cables, and the fire it started quickly became inextinguishable. With one man killed and six wounded, *Carolina*'s crew managed to get two of her cannon ashore before she blew up in a fantastic roar of smoke and flame from the powder magazines. James Parton, one of Jackson's early biographers, tells us, "The explosion was terrific. It shook the earth for miles around; it threw a shower of burning fragments over the *Louisiana* a mile distant." It sent a shock of terror through thousands of women up in New Orleans; it gave a momentary discouragement to the American troops. For the British it was a moment of grand exultation, "as if they had removed the only obstacle to their victorious advance." One British diarist recorded that "among the crowd of spectators collected to witness the attack on the schooner were the Indian Chiefs, who appeared deeply interested in the proceedings." With Laffite's Baratarian gunners pulling at the oars of the ship's boats, the *Louisiana* was able to avoid similar treatment by moving upriver. They anchored her right across from Jackson's ditch, in perfect position to enfilade his front if the British attacked.

Loss of the *Carolina* wasn't disastrous for the Americans, but it became an omen of vexatious things to come. Now that Pakenham had disposed of this floating artillery platform on his left flank, he was able to organize his assault on the American defensive position, which still wasn't finished, since they were continuing to throw up dirt and bring up artillery pieces. By now the British had managed to send out enough scouts to get at least a rough notion of what lay in store for them—namely, Jackson's line—although they were unable to get close enough to tell just how much artillery it brought to bear, or precisely what defensive safeguards it contained. Pakenham then decided not upon a full-scale assault but, instead, a "reconnaissance in force," or the Great Reconnaissance, as it came to be known.

Pakenham's plan was to send the army in its entirety against the American position with the notion of discovering just how much opposition he was facing, and with the secondary expectation of "scaring the Americans out of their wits." In other words, the overall design was not to risk an all-or-nothing battle at this point, but to hope in the first place to find out what scheme of defense Jackson had devised and, at the same time, with the British redcoats marching smartly and deliberately toward the American positions, to frighten them into running away as they had at Washington and other places on the East Coast. If that happened, of course, they could simply march into New Orleans.

An added accommodation for Pakenham arrived as a present from Mother Nature. The Mississippi suddenly began to run lower than usual, so that the cuts Latour had made in the levee no longer inundated the sugar plantation fields, and the water that had covered the plain between the American and British positions quickly ran off via the canals and into the bayous. The ground conditions certainly weren't ideal, since the soil had turned to muck, but at least the British wouldn't have to slog through two miles of river water.

Meanwhile, as Pakenham organized his army for the assault, the Americans were doing some night work of a variety the British weren't familiar with. After dark the Choctaws (now numbering sixty-two in all) with their tomahawk hatchets and the "dirty-shirt" Tennesseans with their long rifles and hunting knives would creep out of the lines and move stealthily toward the advance British pickets, killing as many as they could. The tactic was considered "unchivalrous" by the British, whose pickets usually enjoyed relative amity with their opposites during the European wars. Lieutenant Gleig condemned it as "an ungenerous return to barbarity," though he and others conceded that the Americans were fighting for their own soil.

That night, soon after dark, while the blackened timbers from the blown-up *Carolina* were yet floating in the Mississippi, the British army moved forward en masse in two divisions, with ten pieces of artillery and several batteries of the new Congreve rockets. On the left, led by General Keane, were the 85th, 93rd, and 95th regiments and the 5th West Indians. On the right, commanded by Major General Sir Samuel Gibbs, who had arrived with Pakenham, were the 4th, 21st, and 44th regiments and the 1st West Indians. They drove in the American pickets on the Bienvenue and Chalmette plantations just six hundred yards in front of Jackson's line and hunkered down—but not peacefully, as the Choctaws and dirty-shirts with their knives and hatchets kept up their fiendish nightly activity.

For a better understanding of why the British were angry, disturbed, and frightened by this unorthodox style of warfare, listen to Major Latour's account of one such episode: "An old inhabitant of Tennessee obtained leave from his officers to go on what they called a *hunting party.* He stole through ditches and underwood, till he got near a British sentinel, whom he immediately killed; and having seized his arms and accouterments, he laid them at some distance from that place, and went to post himself in a different direction. When it was time to relieve the sentinel, the corporal of the guard finding him dead, posted another in the same place, where the guard had hardly left him, when the Tennessean shot him down, and having conveyed his arms and accouterments to the spot where he left those of the man he killed before, he again went to lie in wait in another place. The corporal, in his next round, had again to relieve a dead sentinel, and the man who took his place soon shared the fate of the two others; the Tennessean taking the same care to secure his arms and accouterments, and then posting himself in another place. At last the corporal, amazed to see that in one night three sentinels had been killed at one post, determined to expose no more men in so dangerous a spot. Our Tennessean, seeing this, returned to camp with the spoils of the slain, and received the felicitations of his comrades."

Jackson understood that an attack was coming and decided to meet it head-on. This was no easy decision considering that his people were outnumbered by about three to two in infantry and two to one in artillery, and that his line wasn't yet completed and presently contained only five artillery pieces. Although he did have the guns of the *Louisiana* to support him, a lesser man might have postponed the inevitable and retreated to a place closer to the city and hoped for the best. But not Jackson; it wasn't in his nature. As Matthew Arnold once wrote, "Only two things are needed, the power of the man and the power of the moment," and now, on a wintry morning in south Louisiana, apparently both had arrived.

Jackson was determined not to be bested by an army of usurping Englishmen invading American soil. He trusted implicitly his two Tennessee commanders, Coffee and Carroll, and had well-placed faith in the courage and loyalty of their men, with whom he had fought the Creek War. Likewise, despite persistent rumors of their unreliability, he had come to trust the Creole fighters of Louisiana under their somewhat gaudy and affected French-speaking officers.

Lastly, Jackson had come to look upon the once distasteful Baratarians of Jean Laffite as a godsend; their gunnery on the *Carolina* and *Louisiana* had been impeccable in "annoying" the British and thus far forestalling an attack. He now relied upon them enough that he sent a courier to Fort St. John ordering Dominique You and his cutthroat artillerists to come at once to the barricade. That the British would attack at Fort St. John was now logically incompatible with what Jackson was seeing. The Baratarians responded resolutely, promptly, and on the run, with Dominique You leading the way, squat, smiling his perpetual grin, his neck thick as a tortoise, and smoking a cigar. They arrived ready for a fight about dawn on December 28, and just in time for the show.

Eleven

Lieutenant General Sir Edward Pakenham's attack began shortly after sunrise on December 28. His advance troops ran the American pickets out of the buildings they were occupying on the Chalmette and Bienvenue plantations, right in front of Jackson's line, which had been filled with combustibles that were then fired upon and destroyed by American artillery to keep them from being used as shelter by the British. But that was not before at least one British officer got inside the elegant Bienvenue mansion; he later described in salacious detail the boudoir of the mistress of the manor, down to and including the books she read and the items of clothing she wore.

Pakenham had brought forward most of the artillery pieces he had used to destroy the *Carolina* with the intention of using them on, first, the *Louisiana* and, next, Jackson's infantry line, but this did not work out. Gunfire from the *Louisiana* not only raked the flank of the British advance but, along with cannon fire from the five guns now in Jackson's batteries along the Rodriguez Canal (which had become his formidable moat), ultimately silenced the British guns, which were then abandoned by Cochrane's naval artillerymen. The interesting thing is that the renowned skills of the British artillery service were so quickly and thoroughly defeated by the dirty-shirts, Baratarian privateers, Louisiana militia, and a handful of U.S. Army regulars who had been denounced by the British army as nothing more than a "rabble."

It had turned out to be one of those lovely Deep South winter mornings; the temperature was mild, almost balmy, and the skies sunny in contrast to the damp fogs, frost, and freezing rains that had character-ized the past several weeks. It was recorded that as dawn broke, the racket of thousands of ricebirds roosting in the cypress trees filled the air with a cacophonous screech of bird music.

It took the better part of an hour to get the entire British army assembled, but when it came into view it must have been both a magnif-icent and a disturbing sight to the American dirty-shirts. With drum-mer boys beating out an unnerving cadence, there soon appeared thousands of redcoats in two columns, eighty men abreast, filling up most of the front, one column marching along the levee road toward Jackson's right and the other marching across the fields toward Jack-son's left. Pakenham's plan was not an all-out, do-or-die assault, but to discover if there was any weakness in the American position and, if so, to proceed to attack and exploit it. It was, of course, floated in some quarters that the very *sight* of a British army marching against them would frighten the Americans out of their lines and send them flying back toward the city.

"They thought, no doubt to intimidate us by their boldness," wrote Latour, "hoping that the sight of a heavy column marching against our lines, would strike such terror as to make us abandon them. They did not know with what adversaries they would have to contend, nor that they were destined to atone for their arrogance with streams of blood."

As the British formation neared Jackson's line, several redcoat batter-ies opened fire and showered the Americans with their new secret weapon, the Congreve rocket, to which Key had alluded in his "Star-Spangled Banner." The rockets hissed and weaved and sputtered and threw out showers of sparks and flame like giant bottle rockets and then exploded with a bang of shrapnel, but they were wildly inaccurate. Jackson went riding down the lines, dismissing the rockets as "children's toys," although they wounded several men, including a marine major who also had his horse killed by one.

"The British had great expectation from the effect of this weapon, against an enemy who had never seen it before," Latour noted. "They hoped that its very noise would strike terror into us; but we soon grew accustomed to it."

Latour's appraisal was on the money. The psychology of battle is very fragile, as the British were well aware, and surprise plays a great part in it. Men trained to know what to expect from an enemy are far less likely to give up the field than those who are confronted by strange new weapons or sudden, unexpected attacks.

This was Pakenham's first view of the American position, and he wanted to have a good look at it; accordingly, he ordered both Gibbs's and Keane's columns halted and sent one of his engineer lieutenants up into a tree with a spyglass. The engineer informed Pakenham that the entire American fortification was fronted by a ditch that was filled with water to a depth unknown, and that it extended from the river all the way back to the seemingly impassable cypress swamp. In other words, Jackson was athwart the only path the British could use to get into New Orleans from their present position, and they would have to either destroy him or retreat and find some other way. It was a disagreeable situation for a commander to be in because it left no options— either you played the hand you were dealt or you folded.

Pakenham told his chief of artillery, Colonel Alexander Dickson, to bring up his guns to see what good that would do, but when Dickson went back to the river levee where he'd left them, he found that they had been destroyed by fire from the *Louisiana*. Meantime, Pakenham ordered Gibbs and Keane to resume their march against the American positions.

Right in the middle of all this an aide arrived from New Orleans, six miles distant, with information he thought Andrew Jackson should have. News of the British arrival had set in motion the work of busybody theorists bent on raising disturbing issues that best not be thought of at all.

When the messenger rode up to the general, who was sitting on his horse watching the British advance, he informed him that there was talk in the legislature at that very moment of surrendering the city. This was because Jackson had darkly hinted that if the British ever did get into position to seize New Orleans, he might first burn it to the ground, just to spite their "booty and beauty" aspirations. This was no idle threat, as Jackson was to recall later, and the memory of how the Russians a few years earlier had set fire to Moscow to keep Napoleon from profiting from it was fresh in everyone's minds. Naturally, Jackson's notion was alarming to many of the merchants and others with substantial holdings in the city (many of whom themselves were members of the legislature).

Jackson returned the messenger to find Governor Claiborne and instruct him that if there was any more such talk in the legislature he would "blow it up"—whatever that meant. When this startling order reached the governor, he immediately sent armed men to close down the legislature, which caused a lasting uproar all its own.

When the British columns came within artillery range, Jackson's gunners let them have it. So did the *Louisiana,* a single shell from which, according to Latour, "killed fifteen men." The American ship fired more than eight hundred rounds that day from the seven starboard-side cannons she could bring to bear, finally causing the British to disperse their column formation and spread out and take cover in ditches and indentations in the cane fields.

Seeing this, General Carroll, on the far left near the cypress swamp, sent one of his colonels with a 200-man battalion about a hundred yards out in front of the line to outflank the British. But the colonel became confused and went the wrong way; he was killed along with half a dozen of his men before the maneuver was called off. They fought until midafternoon, with American rifle fire—especially from the Tennesseans' long rifles—and Jackson's artillery taking their toll. Finally, Pakenham had seen enough; he called off the assault and took his army back out of range of the American guns.

"That the Americans are excellent marksmen, as well with artillery as with rifles, we have had frequent cause to acknowledge; but, perhaps on no occasion did they assert their claim to the title of good artillery-men more effectually than the present," noted Lieutenant Gleig, who added that he felt lucky to have escaped with his life.

Much of what Gleig related probably was the work of Jean Laffite's Baratarian gunners. Historian Jane Lucas De Grummond tells us that Laffite himself had installed them in the batteries containing two of the largest and most powerful guns in the line, the twenty-four-pounders, which Jackson had ordered dragged down from New Orleans a day or so earlier. If so, Laffite had thus deliberately placed himself in a per-ilous position, since if he was captured by the British he would surely have been hanged for his double-cross of Captain Lockyer, if not on simple piracy charges.

One gun was commanded by Dominique You and the other by the Laffites' cousin Renato Beluche. This made perfect sense because, aside from the navy men, these seagoing artillerists and their crews were the most experienced gunners available. In his campaign against the Creeks (which also constituted his entire military experience), Jackson himself had commanded nothing larger than a single small six-pounder field gun that would compare as a peashooter to these big can-nons, which could blast the British with heavy shot and shell at a distance of almost a mile.

As the British began to retire, the dirty-shirts hooted and jeered at them from atop their rampart. There is one story that Dominique You took particular note of a tall Scotsman from the 93rd striding defiantly to the rear. He set his gun crew on his cannon to action, and within half a minute the match was applied to the powder hole and the charge exploded; a twenty-four-pound ball flew out, tearing the head off the Highlander and sending it "spinning like a football down the field."

Pakenham's withdrawal at this stage may have appeared wise by mil-itary standards. He had reconnoitered the American position and established in his mind its strong and weak points. He also may have simply snatched defeat out of the jaws of victory, because what he did not seem to comprehend was that Jackson's men had been, and would be, working like beavers day and night to bolster their position. The arresting thing about it is not that they attacked but that they quit when victory might have been at hand, because the fortification Pakenham would eventually face would be far stronger than the one he had seen that day.

It is useful here to say a word about the weapons used during the battle. The British infantry was mostly armed with muskets, manufactured in English foundries to strict government specifications. Much study had gone into the design, with considerations as to their weight, accuracy, durability, rate of fire, maintenance, and similar factors. Muskets were smoothbore weapons, with an effective range of about a hundred yards, and an experienced redcoat could fire about two or three aimed shots a minute. This was substantial if you consider that with Pakenham's entire army firing all at once (which it would not be), shooting at that rate could send toward an enemy about twenty-five thousand balls per minute or, put another way, they could deliver four hundred aimed shots every second—certainly a "hail of lead" if ever there was one.

The two regiments of American regulars were armed with a similar weapon, while the volunteer Louisianans brought almost anything and everything, from bear rifles to fowling pieces, which could be deadly in their own ways, depending upon the skill of the user. Jackson's Tennessee dirty-shirts, however, had mostly brought with them their own long rifles, which under most military circumstances would have been a thoroughly unsuitable weapon. But given the conditions at the New Orleans battle, they were just about perfect. These rifles—so called because the interior of the barrel, or bore, had been "rifled," or grooved—could kill a man at three hundred yards, more than triple the range of the British musket.

These "Kentucky rifles," as they were incorrectly known, had been designed as all-purpose personal hunting guns, or as Indian fighting tools, and were individually hand-crafted "to suit the customer" in small independent forges mostly in the state of Pennsylvania. Many of them had elaborate engravings in silver and gold and hand-carved stocks and fore ends. They were only about half the caliber (muzzle diameter) of the British musket, but their ball would kill just as readily, and from a lot farther away.

While most of the British soldiers had been trained in the use of firearms by the army, the Tennessee and Kentucky frontiersmen had learned from their fathers, grandfathers, or on their own, ever since they were old enough to hold the piece and shoot it, and they were almost invariably deadly shots. William A. Meuse, in his excellent pamphlet *The Weapons of the Battle of New Orleans*, published in 1965 on the 150th anniversary of the battle, points out that it was common practice in those days for hunters to shoot just beneath a squirrel sitting way up in a tree, since if you hit it squarely the ball would blow the squirrel to pieces. But hitting just below caused splinters from the branch to do the creature in. They called this method "barking."

Cannon were of either iron or bronze and, like the rifles and muskets, were muzzle-loaded. As previously noted, most of these guns were denoted by the weight of the ball they threw: six-pounder, twelve-pounder, eighteen-pounder, twenty-four-pounder, thirty-two-pounder. Most of these were served by a crew of five, and no fewer than twenty-five different commands were required to be executed before each shot could be fired. Still, a crack gun crew could get off as many as four rounds per minute.

Field artillery was moved about on a carriage with large wheels designed to be horse-drawn and travel along with an army. Fortification guns were usually carriaged on "trucks," small-wheeled conveyances that were designed to be moved short distances inside an embrasure in a fort. Naval guns also sat on the small-wheeled trucks and, like fortification guns, were very difficult to move long distances in a field, especially the large ones, because they weighed thousands of pounds and their little wood wheels were designed to roll on wooden decks or bricks, not on soft ground.

The big guns had an accurate range of more than a thousand yards and could be loaded with a solid iron ball, called a *shot*, the weight of which was the gun's designation. These were terribly damaging against enemy artillery or fortifications or troop formations if they were made to ricochet across a battlefield. The muzzle velocity of these guns was slow, so gunners could actually see the black ball arc up in the air, and the opposing side often could see it come bouncing over the ground. It looked so slow that sometimes, as a lark, inexperienced soldiers would stick out their feet to try and stop it, which usually resulted in a torn-off foot.

A *shell* was a hollow ball filled with gunpowder that exploded on a timed fuse and threw deadly shrapnel in all directions. For closer-in work there was *canister,* a canlike container filed with iron musket balls that spread out in a large fan like a shotgun and could kill a dozen or more of the enemy with a single blast. Variations on canister fire were *grapeshot,* with balls the size of grapes and looking like a cluster of them. *Chain shot,* as the name implies, consisted of simply ramming a big iron chain down the barrel and flinging it at an approaching enemy line or column, mowing down or decapitating whoever was unlucky enough to be in the width of the chain. Also available, in a pinch, was what Jackson's men called *landinage,* plain old scrap iron—nails, metal washers, screws, or what have you—put into a bag and sent flying toward an advancing enemy. Meuse points out that this last "had much the same effect as canister, though it was not quite as gentlemanly in its concept."

Pakenham now understood that it wasn't going to be easy to eject the Americans from their line, so he decided to blow them out of it. After a council of war with Cochrane, Gibbs, and Keane, it was agreed that thirty big cannons from the fleet would be brought up to silence the five pieces of American artillery that Pakenham had counted during his reconnaissance as well as the *Louisiana.*

Since bringing up the fleet guns was going to take several days, Pakenham sought in the meanwhile to annoy the Americans with a series of night raids and reconnaissance operations through the cypress swamp, but Captain Jugat's Choctaws, of whom it was said that "they could maneuver on logs like alligators," were lying in wait and made short work of those people. The practice was quickly discontinued.

Then, in a stunning display of hypocrisy, Pakenham sent by flag of truce a protest requesting that Jackson stop the nightly "assassinations" of British sentries by the dirty-shirts. Jackson coolly replied that he was "repelling an invasion of his country" and was not at all concerned with gentlemanly warfare.

Pakenham's delay had another effect that he had not counted on. Jackson used the time to dramatically strengthen his line. Working night and day like a disturbed colony of ants, the American soldiers and slaves dragged up cannon from other fortifications, for it was now assumed it would not be needed elsewhere, but here instead. They also continued to work on building up Jackson's rampart, which at that point was only about waist high in most places and predominantly mud. It would need to dry out in order to make it more formidable.

As a "just in case," Jackson began fortifying two other strong lines right behind his own—the first one about two miles back, called Line Dupre, and a second one a mile behind that called Line Montreuil, both named for the plantations they rested upon. This left no doubt that Jackson intended to fight it out to the finish.

During these days, "there was no rest for General Jackson," according to one of his early biographers, "and what is more remarkable, he seemed to need none." Still sick and still feeding himself from a few cups of cooked rice, which he ate in the saddle when he was not at his telescope studying the enemy, Jackson was usually out riding his lines exhorting his men to their tasks. After sundown he would pen encouraging messages to his far-flung outposts, such as, "Our troops have covered themselves with glory; it is a noble example and worthy to be followed by all."

In the midst of all this, the riverfront scene was graced with an unusual spectacle. Around the big bend from the north, belching smoke and a shower of sparks, came the newfangled steamboat *Enterprise*, which tied up at the levee. It aroused a great deal of excitement in the city, which had seen only one of the craft before, in 1812, when a boat built by the Roosevelt family arrived with the promise of great things to come.

Indeed, the steamboat would become the future of New Orleans in later years, able to ascend the river against the current as well as descend it, but with the outbreak of war its production was severely reduced. The steamboat's inventor, Robert Fulton, had gone into partnership with a Hudson River Valley neighbor of the Roosevelts, the wealthy Robert Livingston, who was the brother of Andrew Jackson's aide Edward Livingston. Fulton and Robert Livingston had managed to secure from Congress a concession for operating steamboats on the Mississippi that amounted to an absolute monopoly, and it was to break this monopoly that the *Enterprise* had brazenly arrived, captained by a young officer named Henry Miller Shreve.

When Edward Livingston heard the news, he acted to have the *Enterprise* seized for illegal operation, but Jackson stopped him. The general sent for Shreve and told him that inasmuch as New Orleans was under martial law, Shreve should assume that he and his crew and steamboat fell under that category, and so should "hold him self in readiness" for any instructions. Shreve agreed, but was soon besieged with requests from citizens that he put women and children aboard the boat and steam them north out of the danger zone. This he did, but only after a dangerous contretemps with Jackson, who could have had him shot for disobeying orders. In the end Jackson came to depend heavily on Shreve.

Jackson sent Shreve upriver to look for the missing munitions boats, and dangerously downriver, past the British positions, to deliver reinforcing guns, powder, and personnel to Fort St. Philip. This Jackson deemed necessary after he received word that Cochrane had launched an expeditionary force of warships up the Mississippi, presumably to cooperate with whatever Pakenham's next move would be. They had already captured the Balize, a small fort at the river's mouth, and after nearly a week of excruciating twisting, turning, and beating upriver they were approaching Fort St. Philip. When Jackson asked the captain if he could get the munitions and supplies down to the fort, Shreve told him he could with twenty-four hours to do it. He used the time to situate cotton bales all over the port side of the *Enterprise*, which would be exposed to gunfire from the British. Fortunately, a fog rolled in the night of Shreve's run and he was not noticed. Coming back, the British were so surprised by his appearance that by the time they got to their guns he was out of range. It was the first use of a steamboat in war operations.

When the *Enterprise* was finally safe at her dock in New Orleans, Captain Shreve volunteered to Jackson as an artilleryman and was assigned to Captain Humphrey's Battery No. 1. Shreve's good and valuable work during the battle was partly responsible for his getting the Fulton-Livingston steamboat monopoly broken, and in later years he became so successful a river man that the city of Shreveport was named after him.

At the same time, after conferring with Commodore Patterson, Jackson decided to position a sizable battery on the opposite (right bank) side of the river to enfilade the British flank, should they decide to make further attacks. This they set up in an old brick kiln, with two long twenty-four-pounders, which most likely had been blown ashore when the *Carolina* exploded. Over the next week he added five more guns to that side of the river. In addition, he ordered General David Morgan, who commanded the 500-man Louisiana state militia, to cross over from his encampment at English Turn to the right bank of the river and begin building fortifications in case the British tried a landing there (which was precisely what would come to Pakenham's mind). To help accomplish this, Jackson sent over his engineer Latour and Jean Laffite, who knew the territory.

Meantime, in New England things had progressed for the worse. Two weeks earlier a convention had opened in Hartford, Connecticut, whose purpose was described by the one-word headline in the Hartford *Courant:* "SECESSION!"

Hit hardest, first with Jefferson's embargo and now by the British blockade, the New Englanders were determined to end what they derisively called "Mr. Madison's War," even at the risk of splitting the Union. Sympathy with England was openly expressed, with such luminaries as George Cabot of Boston branding the war "unjust" and "morally wrong." It was reported that some New Englanders had even tried to free British prisoners-of-war from an American prison ship.

Newspapers, especially in Boston, were rabidly antiwar and pro-secession.

When news of all this reached Jackson, he proposed a handy solution: "I would hang them all," he said.

It took until New Year's Eve to haul up the big British naval guns. It had been a stupendous task, dragging these iron monsters through the greasy swamps and bogs and then across the muddy cane fields. The night was foggy and the Americans could not see what the British were up to, but they could hear all sorts of banging and hammering and other loud noises, racketing out of the gloom a few hundred yards in front. The British artillerymen and sailors, 500 of them, worked through the night and day, as they had ever since the order was given to bring up the guns.

They had no heavy-lifting tripods, such as are used in the field to hoist artillery (aboard ship, the heavy lifting was done by the yardarms), and so all movement of these six-thousand-pound guns was accomplished by hand. Then there was the problem of how to protect the batteries once the guns were in place. Since digging only a few inches produced water, excavation was not the answer. Someone came up with a solution of using some of the sugar barrels or hogsheads that had been piling up on the plantations ever since the embargo and the blockade.*

These were laboriously hauled or rolled on their sides to the batteries and stacked in such a way as to afford some protection to the gun crews—at least that's what was hoped. Finally all the banging and racketing ceased. The British army then moved forward as quietly as possible to a position about five hundred yards from the American line and just behind the artillery batteries. By Pakenham's order, the artillery bombardment that was to crush the Americans was to begin at first light, but first light brought an impenetrable fog of the kind seen only in those reaches of coastal Louisiana. As they waited for it to lift, the

---

* General Brown believes that the sugar was emptied out and the barrels were then filled with earth but does not cite a source for this statement. Many others think that the barrels remained filled with sugar, which seems most likely.

British were startled to hear the tunes of several musical bands wafting out of the fog. They were playing gay martial music: "La Marseillaise," "Yankee Doodle," and "Chant du Départ." The British waited, thus serenaded for several hours, until ten a.m., when the mist began to clear and the artillery gunners started to light their firing matches.

Twelve

When a midmorning breeze suddenly blew the fog off the cane fields an astounding spectacle unveiled itself to the British army. One officer compared the lifting of the fog to "a change of scene at a theater." In fact, what they were now beholding, strangely enough, was a great American military parade.

It was New Year's Day 1815, and despite indications that the redcoats had been up to something with all that banging and hammering, Jackson had decided that some kind of celebration was in order and decreed that a grand military review be held in the open cane fields just behind the American lines. Citizens of New Orleans, ladies and children mostly, came down in their carriages to watch.

Soldiers brushed the mud and dirt off their uniforms and wiped their shoes and hats to give the best possible impression. Marching bands began by entertaining the crowd with all kinds of tunes* as the approximately 4,000-man American army formed up in regiments and companies to parade past its commander, who was putting the last touches on his finest dress uniform at his headquarters in the Macarty plantation house.

Then all hell broke loose.

The British artillery was grouped in six batteries, including one for rockets, and at ten a.m. they began blasting away as one, with "unex-

---

* "The Star-Spangled Banner," composed only a few months earlier, was not yet known west of the Mississippi.

ampled celerity." Singled out for particular attention was the Macarty house itself, which was wrecked by more than one hundred cannonballs during the first ten minutes. Miraculously, neither Jackson nor any of his staff was injured. Covered with plaster dust, they quickly rushed out to form up the army for battle.

It must have been a wild scene. Lieutenant Gleig describes how "mounted officers were riding backwards and forwards through the ranks, bands were playing and colors floated in the air. In a word, all seemed jollity and gala." Then the British batteries opened up. "The ranks were broken, the different corps dispersing, fled in all directions while the utmost terror and disorder appeared to prevail. Nothing but confused crowds could be observed. *Oh,*" he lamented, "*that we had charged at that instant!*"

His lament was all too true, because it did not take the Americans long to collect themselves and get back behind their fortifications, which were in fact the safest place on the field. During the first ten minutes or so of confusion, if the British had swiftly attacked they might well have succeeded, having caught the Americans so off their guard. Those were not Pakenham's orders, however, because he had not anticipated fog, nor its sudden lifting to reveal the American army out of its lines and on parade, and it seems to have caught him off his guard as well. His plan was to knock out the American artillery batteries with counterbattery fire of his own and then send his splendid veterans over the ditch to deal with these American upstarts. If the British artillerists had been supplied with shell (antipersonnel) as opposed to shot (antifortification) ammunition, they might well have caused a great deal of loss of life, but that was not the case.

In the American lines Jackson went with his staff from battery to battery, despite the hail of iron. First he came to Captain Enoch Humphrey's battery, where the old artilleryman stood, "dressed in his usual plain attire, smoking that eternal cigar, coolly leveling his guns and directing his men."

"Ah," Jackson exclaimed, according to historian Walker, "all is right. Humphrey is at his post and will return their compliments presently."

Just then Robert Butler, Jackson's adjutant, rushed up to the battery, covered from head to toe with white plaster dust from the Macarty house.

"Why, Colonel Butler," Jackson roared. "Is that you? I thought you were killed."

"No, General; only knocked over," Butler replied.

Meanwhile, Captain Humphrey was sighting in on the British batteries, "structures of a narrow front and slight elevation, lying low and dim upon the field." Adjusting a twelve-pounder with exactness, he quietly gave the word, "Let her off."

For the next hour and a half an artillery duel "so loud and rapid shook the delta as had never before been heard in the western world." So wrote historian James Parton, and he was probably correct, assuming that he was referring to the western part of the United States. "Imagine," he went on, "fifty pieces of cannon,* of large caliber, each discharged from once to thrice a minute, often a simultaneous discharge of half a dozen pieces, an average of two discharges every second; while plain and river were so densely covered with smoke that the gunners aimed their guns from recollection chiefly and knew scarcely any thing of the effect of the fire."

According to the German merchant Vincent Nolte, the main British battery, which was situated just to the right of a road that ran through the center of sugarcane fields, "directed its fire against the battery of the pirates Dominique You and Beluche." Once, as Dominique was examining the enemy through a glass, "a cannon shot wounded his arm; he caused it to be bound up, saying, 'I will pay them for that!' and resumed his glass. He then directed a twenty-four-pounder, gave the order to fire, and the ball knocked an English gun carriage to pieces and killed six or seven men."

* Parton was somewhat off in his estimate of fifty artillery pieces. The British had twenty-four guns total, while Jackson's line contained sixteen, for a total of forty guns—still an impressive and volatile number that rattled windows in New Orleans, six or so miles away.

Not long afterward a British shot hit one of Dominique's guns and knocked it off its carriage. While it was being repaired, someone asked him about his wound. "Only some scratch, by gar," he growled, as he ordered his other cannon loaded with chain shot that "crippled the largest British gun and killed or wounded six men." Surtees, the British quartermaster, remembered that the Baratarians had delivered the most deadly fire of all. Referring to the big thirty-two-pound gun of Beluche, he said, "It always struck the battery at first bound. Any of the other guns seemed like child's play to the unceasing and destructive fire from this heavy piece of ordnance. I could distinctly see that they were sailors that worked it—one of whom, a large mulatto with a red shirt, always sponged her out after firing."

Particularly disturbing for Surtees was the actual appearance of the object of his destruction. "I could distinctly perceive the ball from this gun every time it was fired," he wrote, "it appearing like a small black spot in the midst of the column of white smoke, which gradually grew larger in appearance as it approached us. Seeing which way the ball was coming, I told the men when to lie down; and on one occasion was the shave so close, that it actually carried away one of the men's pack as he lay on the ground."

Captain Benson Hill, near the British center, came upon a number of West Indians cringing in a transverse drainage ditch within gunshot range. He told them to go back to their lines.

"No sir, Boss," one of them replied. "No more Jamaica. No more white man's orders. We die here."

The terror of war, of course, was not limited to the British soldiers. Vincent Nolte watched as one of the American militiamen bent over to light a cigar at the same time a ball passed over his head and decapitated the man standing next to him.

The British artillery had struck several of Jackson's guns, but they were repaired while the others laid down a devastating fire that, within less than an hour, dismounted five British guns and so damaged eight others that they could not be aimed properly. The sugar hogsheads proved a disaster as embrasures. They blew totally apart when hit by a cannon shot and sent sugar flying everywhere, clogging guns and extinguishing firing matches.

Once more a party of British, again led by the intrepid Colonel Robert Rennie, tried to flank Jackson's left by going through the cypress swamp, but they were met and repulsed by Jugat's Choctaws and Coffee's Tennesseans. Latour later wrote that "Wellington's heroes discovered that they were ill-qualified to contend with us in woods where they must fight knee-deep in water."

By noon the British fire had noticeably slackened; two-thirds of their guns had been put out of action, and Pakenham ordered a withdrawal. This could not be accomplished, however, because Jackson's guns were still firing, and so the redcoats had to lie miserably in their damp ditches until nightfall, while what was left of their artillery tried to dispute the Americans' decided superiority. "We retired not only baffled and disappointed, but in some degree disheartened and discontented," remembered Lieutenant Gleig. "We knew that with small arms the Americans were foemen worthy of our steel, but we did not expect them—mostly militia as they were—to get the best of an artillery combat, pure and simple."

Just as the sugar barrels had proved unsuitable to the British for combat protection, so the cotton bales turned out to be worthless to the Americans. British gunfire knocked them all over the place and even set them afire, obscuring the battlefield. Jackson ordered them removed. It was found that much of the British fire had gone high and landed behind the line, while shot and shell that actually hit the rampart simply sank into its mud. The Americans had lost 11 men killed and 23 wounded. Jackson issued everybody two ounces of whisky and posted an order of congratulations.

British casualties were more than 100, with nearly half that number killed. Pakenham was in a quandary. He had now failed twice to dislodge the Americans from their line, and there was seemingly no way around it. The only other option was to withdraw back to Lake Borgne or to the fleet and try to find some other place to resume the attack, but this was unacceptable as too much had gone into the enterprise to abandon it now. Besides, the British army was a proud army, an arrogant army perhaps, especially in the wake of their conquests of Napoleon's forces in Europe. They were considered by many—and considered themselves—the most polished killing machine on the face of the earth, and perhaps that was true. In any event, they intended to stay and find out.

It was reported that Admiral Cochrane attempted to shame Pakenham into assaulting the Americans by telling him that, if he and his army had no taste for it, his own sailors would attack and rout Jackson and that Pakenham's soldiers could bring the sailors' baggage up afterward. This story has been repeated by many historians, but, as General Brown points out, it probably has no basis in fact, not only because there is no mention of it in any British document or by a diarist but also because it would have been very out of character for Cochrane to say such an impertinent thing to a lieutenant general of the army who was also the brother-in-law of the legendary Duke of Wellington.

In any case, Pakenham made a fateful decision. He had just learned that a strong 2,000-man brigade of reinforcements under Major General John Lambert had arrived in the Mississippi Sound and had joined the fleet. It would take a few days to transfer them to his army, but after that had been done, Pakenham determined to go at the Americans all out. It would require about a week to prepare.

First, the British would need scaling ladders to climb up Jackson's rampart, which by now was eight feet high and growing. They would also need fascines—tightly wrapped bundles of sticks (in this case, sugarcane stalks)—which they would throw into the ditch in front of the fortification so that the soldiers could use them to cross over.

Pakenham next conceived as part of the plan a landing on the west, or right, bank in order to silence the American artillery batteries there and to either bring over artillery of his own or use captured American guns to enfilade Jackson's line—as Jackson had done to him—and drive him from his position. This force would be commanded by Colonel William Thornton and would consist of about 1,400 men. To accomplish this, Cochrane proposed what soon developed into a herculean enterprise: since approximately fifty large pulling boats (each boat holding twenty-eight soldiers, plus rowing crew) would have to be brought from the fleet to Lake Borgne and then up Bayou Bienvenue, why not lengthen and deepen the Villeré Canal and simply float them all the way across the fields to the river?

This was easier said than done. Like the Rodriguez Canal along Jackson's line, the Villeré Canal was just above the water table, and as soon as the redcoats and sailors began digging it out they were consumed by muck. They worked in shifts, twenty-four hours a day, and it was said that the two Jamaican regiments "were almost worked to death on the project." Pakenham was skeptical of the plan and wanted to use rollers to ferry the boats across the cane fields, but the navy was afraid that rollers would stove in their bottoms, and so work on the canal continued apace.

For the British, things were becoming desperate, especially in the matter of rations. To feed an army in the field of from 8,000 to 10,000 men requires a tremendous supply effort. This large British army had been on the Mississippi for nine days and had by now eaten up all the stored provisions on the several plantation lands they occupied, as well as having killed and eaten all the cattle, swine, goats, and poultry. Food from the fleet had to be rowed in daily across nearly eighty miles of often rough water, and, to make matters worse, the fleet ration stores themselves were running out. It had been planned that by now the British army would have taken New Orleans and be dining off the largesse of the considerable food cellars of that city. Americans who killed or captured British soldiers reported that in their knapsacks they were carrying cooked horseflesh—it had gotten that bad.

British accounts recall that the soldiers picked all the ripe oranges from the groves (December is picking time for citrus in the South) and boiled them in large cauldrons found on the plantations, into which much sugar—also found in profusion on these plantations—was poured, resulting in tart sugar-coated orange peels, a delectable kind of sweet-and-sour candy that at least helped ease the men through their various travails.

Likewise, there was an ammunition problem, since every cannonball and shell as well as powder and cartridges had to be transported with the by now worn-out sailors who rowed day and night to keep the supply going. Part of the reason the artillery attack had failed was lack of ammunition, and now every reinforcement soldier or sailor who left the fleet for the battleground was required to carry on his person at least one heavy cannonball or shell. In today's military this would be called an "offensive load," with the meaning leaning toward the vulgar.

With New Orleans just a few miles in the rear, Jackson had no such rations problem, and Laffite's supply of munitions from his secret stashes seemed to be endless. Still Jackson was fearful, and with good reason. He was outnumbered by about two to one by seasoned British professionals, as opposed to his mostly untrained militia; his position on the Rodriguez Canal was the only thing standing between the British and New Orleans. It was plain to Jackson and the others that so long as the British remained, they could expect a major attack; they simply did not know when or how it would fall. It was said that Jackson, ill and frail as he was, did not sleep at all during this trying period, except to nap on a couch in the now-wrecked Macarty house, which was barely habitable.

Finally, on January 3, word came that the long-anticipated, sorely needed 2,368-man brigade of Kentucky militia was in the area, still on the river but expected first thing the next morning. The bad news was that fewer than about 10 percent of them were well armed, and less than a third had any arms at all! This came as a shock to Jackson, who roared, "I don't believe it! I have never known a Kentuckian who did not always have on his person a rifle, a pack of cards, and a bottle of whisky!" But it was true. The Kentuckians had been told that arms and other military equipment awaited them at New Orleans.

Jackson renewed his scouting upriver for the missing munitions boat (and, by the way, to arrest its captain and bring him to New Orleans in chains), but it was to no avail—the boat would not arrive for another two weeks. In frustration, he sent his aides to scour New Orleans for any piece of firearm whatsoever, but the best they could find was a cache of antiquated Spanish muskets that had been squirreled away by the city government in case of a slave revolt. Most of these weapons were rusty and probably better used as clubs than as firing pieces.

Almost as bad for the Kentuckians was the condition of their clothing. Most of them were in rags after their two-month-long journey downriver, and the weather had turned freezing cold again. The sight of them marching through the streets of New Orleans so tattered and torn, and often clutching at the rents in their clothes to cover themselves from immodesty, actually brought tears to the eyes of many of the women of the city, who immediately began a campaign to fashion blankets, draperies, and bed linens into clothing for these unfortunate creatures. The Louisiana legislature appropriated $6,000, and Louisiana citizens—including many of the men in Jackson's camp—contributed another $10,000; in less than a week the ladies of New Orleans, according to Major Latour, had produced "twelve hundred blanket cloaks, two hundred seventy-five waistcoats, eleven hundred twenty-seven pairs of pantaloons, eight hundred shirts, four hundred and ten pairs of shoes, and a great number of mattresses."

Jackson was concerned, as he had been ever since he arrived in New Orleans, that the British might come at him from different directions, and it was a logical fear, given the wide variety of approaches into the city. He knew he had defeated Pakenham's army twice now, and the question on his mind was: Would the British general try it again, or would he try to find some other way, farther up the bayou perhaps, to attack Jackson from the rear?

Accordingly, he summoned his old friend Colonel Reuben Kemper*

---

* Kemper was a cousin to Confederate major general James L. Kemper, a hero of Lee's Army of Northern Virginia, and later a governor of that state.

and told him to take a detachment to reconnoiter the British positions on the bayou and see if there were any signs that the enemy was about to leave. Kemper was the ideal officer for the job, as well as a man after Jackson's own heart. According to historian Walker, he was an inveterate English- and Spaniard-hater, who had once been kidnapped by the Spanish authorities in New Orleans for complaining about their imperialist outrages.

Kemper and his two brothers somehow escaped their supposed fate of a lifetime in chains in the gold mines of Spanish Cuba, and for their revenge, when they later ran into one of their kidnappers, they "inflicted upon his naked back one hundred lashes, then one hundred more for their brother Nathan who was absent, cut off his ears with a dull knife, and then let him loose. These gory trophies were long preserved in a bottle of spirits and hung up in one of the Kempers' parlors."

It took Kemper a full twenty-four hours, stealing through canal to bayou to swamp, until he reached a position overlooking the British beachhead at Bayou Bienvenue. If the enemy intended to leave, Kemper reported, he certainly did not show any signs of it. The British had fortified their positions and put out pickets, and even burned away the eight-foot-high reed grass of the prairies, apparently to prevent the Americans from sneaking through it and attacking from the rear. The boats Kemper saw arriving were being off-loaded with men and military equipment.

What Jackson quickly deduced from this information was that the British were planning to attack him again on his front. On Friday, January 6, he received another important piece of intelligence.

One of the sailing masters who had escaped the carnage during the Battle of Lake Borgne had observed a small British supply boat headed across the lake toward Bayou Bienvenue, and he dashed out with three armed boats and captured her. From her crew, now prisoners, it was learned that the British were widening and deepening the Villeré Canal from the bayou to the Mississippi. When Jackson imparted this news to Commodore Patterson, the naval officer went down to a point on the right bank of the river just opposite the British encampment and for several hours studied it through his spyglass. When he reported back to Jackson, it was to say that in his opinion the enemy was planning to use the Villeré Canal to launch an invasion of the west bank of the river. Jackson immediately understood the peril, because if the British were successful and captured Patterson's guns, these arms could be turned to bombard the rear of his lines with disastrous effect.

The Kentucky brigade commander, General John Thomas, had fallen too ill on the trip downriver to assume his duties; Brigadier General John Adair, his subordinate, would have to take his place. Actually, this might have been a good thing. Adair was an extremely knowledgeable and competent fighter, with the added benefit that he was good friends with Jackson, who trusted him implicitly. One of the first things Jackson asked Adair was for his opinion of the American fortifications.

It was Saturday, January 7, 1815, and Jackson had spent most of the afternoon at his telescope high in his little aerie in the Macarty house. He could observe that the British in their encampment were as busy as a swarm of bees. Some appeared to be making scaling ladders, and he saw a great number of redcoats clustered about an immense object, apparently in the act of moving it, but whether it was a boat or piece of artillery he could not tell. One thing Jackson did sense, however, was that the following morning the British were going to come at him on both sides of the river. "Oh, there's no doubt of it," he said. "They mean business; they will attack at daybreak."

Jackson ordered General Adair to send across the river as reinforcements 400 of his Kentuckians, who must first march up to New Orleans to collect whatever weapons had been made available to them, then cross the river by boat, and then march back down the six or eight miles to the lines established by General Morgan and the Louisiana militia.

They did not get off until nearly seven p.m., and when they reached the city it was found that there were only weapons enough for half of them—and those the mostly rusted and antiquated Spanish muskets. So about half of the Kentuckians crossed the river to join Morgan's defense and the others returned to Jackson's lines. Jackson tried to consider everything he had done to prepare, and late in the afternoon he asked Adair to tour the line with him.

They started at the river, where construction was still incomplete on the little redoubt out in front of Jackson's line. Jackson had been skeptical of the idea to start with, not happy about leaving an outpost where it could be overrun just in front of his position and its three cannon possibly turned and used against him. But his engineers had persuaded Old Hickory that the redoubt was needed to enfilade the enemy flank, shooting straight down the length of the ditch if the British should get that far. It was manned by a company of regulars of the 44th and supported directly behind Jackson's line by Captain Beale's company of New Orleans lawyers, bankers, and merchants.

This time, though, when Jackson came upon the small gunpost he studied it for a moment, then shook his head and complained to Adair, "That will give us trouble!"

Moving down the line they reached Battery No. 1, on the levee road. This consisted of two brass twelve-pounders and a howitzer and was commanded by the cigar-chomping Captain Humphrey of the 44th. Any British column attempting to attack up the levee road would have to face a hail of iron from these considerable guns.

Less than one hundred yards down the rampart, walking past the 430 regulars of the 7th Infantry, they came to Battery No. 2, a twenty-four-pounder served by the crew of the *Carolina*. And fifty yards beyond this was Battery No. 3, "the famous battery of the privateers," containing two twenty-four-pounders.

Just twenty yards farther, walking past part of Major Plauché's battalion—289 men strong—was Battery No. 4, with the big thirty-two-pounder, manned by more of the *Carolina*'s crew.

Moving on to Battery No. 5, nearly two hundred yards down the rampart, they passed by the lines of Major Pierre Lacoste's 180 free men of color and Major Jean Daquin's 150 free men of color. Here, near the center, Jackson had ordered erected a tall flagstaff flying a large red, white, and blue Stars and Stripes, "visible to both armies and to the countryside all around, on both sides of the river." Battery No. 5 consisted of two six-pounders, served by army regulars.

As they moved from Battery No. 5 to No. 6, just thirty-six yards apart, they passed by the 240 men of the 44th. Battery No. 6 contained one brass twelve-pounder served by a company of Frenchmen under General Garrigues Flaujac, a French royalist and one of the handful of Louisiana legislators who actually fought at the front.

Nearly two hundred yards farther on was Battery No. 7, with a long brass eighteen-pounder and a six-pounder under two lieutenants. Sixty yards beyond was Battery No. 8, consisting only of a small brass carronade commanded by an artillery corporal with General Carroll's soldiers. Here the swamp began, but the rampart, such as it was at this point, continued nearly a half mile into the morass, where Coffee's and Carroll's men "were compelled, for many days and nights, to live the lives of amphibious creatures—even sleeping in the mud."

Precisely what General Adair thought of the fortifications Jackson had erected is not recorded, but he surely must have been impressed. Running for more than a mile and a half from the river to the swamp, the rampart in many places was eight feet high and in some places twenty feet thick at the top, where the artillery batteries were situated. The gun platforms were solid and commanded an impressive view of the battlefield. The moat or ditch in front was an imposing obstacle. What was even more impressive was the fact that two weeks before this line did not exist, and during those two frantic weeks it had rained half the time and three days of it were spent actually fighting the British. That it was here, now, and of such obviously formidable strength, is remarkable testimony to American ingenuity and perseverance under Jackson.

"Well," Jackson asked Adair, "what do you think of our situation? Can we defend these works or not?" That Jackson posed such a question of a brigadier general of militia is evidence enough of his esteem.

"There is one way, and one way only," Adair replied without a blink. "We must have a strong corps of reserve to meet the enemy's main attack, wherever it may be. No *single* part of the lines is strong enough to resist the united force of the enemy. But," he continued, "with a strong column held in our rear, ready to advance upon any threatened point, we can beat them."

It was sage advice, and Jackson took it, just as he had listened to Jean Laffite's recommendation that they extend the line well into the swamp to prevent being outflanked. Iron-handed Jackson might have been, but iron-headed he was not.

With the arrival of the Kentuckians, Jackson now had about 8,800 men. Five thousand of them were in the main line behind the canal, and the bulk of these, Carroll's and Coffee's, were at the far left, where the canal ran into the swamp. Since Jackson did not have enough artillery to fully protect that part of the line, he apparently loaded it up with riflemen. In reserve behind the canal line he sent about 1,500 of Adair's Kentucky brigade, though only a third of them were armed. Across the river, he had about 1,000 men, Kentuckians and Louisiana militia. The rest were posted at other locations in the area.

On January 6, two days before the battle, Dudley Avery, a young physician serving as a volunteer with a regiment of militia, wrote to his wife, whom he had sent to safety in Baton Rouge:

> Dear Mary Ann,
>
> I have just time to say to you that I am well, and employed in my profession as a volunteer in the regt of Drafted Milita. How long I shall remain I cannot tell, I have not seen Saml. for two or three days and where he is I do not know. The enemy are everyday in sight[,] say about one mile distant. New Year's day they gave us a very handsome salute. They began about nine o'clock and kept up a most tremendous cannonade and rocket firing all day till after sundown and it was returned with interest. . . . I was that day with Doct. Lee, on the east side of the river. The shott [*sic*] seemed to come in showers. We have picked up more than 200 of their shott. They had to remove from their

batteries and have not occupied them since. We are everyday exchanging more or less shott. Our pickets are always
skirmishing. I expect something decisive will be done
shortly. More when I know more. Yours Affectionally,

Dudley Avery*

Pakenham did not know exactly how many men Jackson had in his
army, but he assumed there were more than his own 10,000. Aside from
the 1,400 men he was sending across the river under Colonel Thornton,
Pakenham intended to attack the canal line with 5,500 infantry, supported by artillery and rockets. The remaining 2,000-man infantry
brigade under the newly arrived General John Lambert—the 7th
Fusiliers and the 43rd Foot—would be in reserve, ready to exploit any
breakthrough.

The plan was that 2,600 infantry under General Gibbs would attack
Jackson's far left, near the swamp, where there were fewer cannon,
while an equal number under General Keane would attack near the
center. This decision had been reached by Pakenham after he'd
ascended a pine tree with a spyglass and thoroughly studied the American position. He saw that the rampart was not as high or wide on Jackson's left, an observation he had also made during the reconnaissance
attack on December 28. As if to cement his judgment, a Spanish
informer, one Señor Galvez, "made [his] way out of the American cor-
don on the night of [January] 6th and informed General Pakenham
most positively that the whole left of the works was held by militia
imperfectly organized, not regularly armed *and totally unprovided with
bayonets!*"

Depending on developments, Keane would either move left to support Gibbs, should he be successful, or move right and attack near the

* Dudley Avery was the great-great-great-grandfather of the present generation of the
McIlhenny family, owners and operators of the McIlhenny Company, which, since 1868,
has manufactured Tabasco sauce at Avery Island, Louisiana. (Letter courtesy of Avery
Island, Inc. archives)

river, if Thornton's assault across the river was triumphant and the American guns were taken and turned on Jackson's lines from behind. Meanwhile, a force of several hundred redcoats under Colonel Rennie was to move down the levee road and capture the little redoubt that Jackson had predicted "will give us trouble." It was a complicated plan, requiring much coordination, and during the heat and confusion of battle, even in the best of times, things rarely go exactly as planned.

On the night of January 7 Pakenham sent an aide to Lieutenant Colonel Thomas Mullins of the 44th Regiment. His would be the first regiment in line next morning, and his crucial task was to carry the fascines and heavy ten-foot scaling ladders to the ditch. This equipment, which had been constructed by the engineers, would be found at a forward redoubt about five hundred yards from the American lines. Pakenham had told his aide to make sure Mullins understood his instructions.

"Nothing could be clearer," Mullins had replied, and the aide returned satisfied that the colonel knew his orders. After he had gone, however, Mullins turned to his adjutant and moaned, "My regiment has been ordered to execution. Their dead bodies are to be used as a bridge for the rest of the army to march over." Clearly, here was an officer who did not wish to be in charge of the leading regiment of the assault.

Meanwhile, Pakenham was inspecting the deepening of the Villeré Canal in preparation for bringing the boats across for Thornton's assault on the west bank. He still did not like what he saw. A dam had been built near where the cut in the levee was to be, in order to hold the water in the canal, since the river was low and would otherwise run out into the river when the final cut was made. Pakenham asked the engineer if he was certain the dam would hold and suggested building a second one, just in case. The engineer assured him that the present dam was all that was needed.*

* This officer was probably Lieutenant Colonel John Fox Burgoyne, illegitimate son of General John "Gentleman Johnny" Burgoyne, who had disgraced himself during the American Revolution by surrendering Saratoga, New York, in 1777.

As luck would have it, the engineer was wrong, and as soon as the final cut in the levee was made at about nine p.m.—the intended time of Thornton's departure—the dam burst and most of the water drained out of the canal. Thus the boats had to be hauled nearly a mile through the mud of the canal by sailors and anyone else who could be dragooned to help. But it took all night, and even then none of the larger boats could be moved through the canal. By dawn it was decided that Thornton would have to go on with what he had, and so, instead of 1,400 British infantry arriving on the west bank well before daylight, he now could bring only about 500, crammed into the few small boats available.

Unfortunately, no one had bothered to wake Pakenham and tell him of this misfortune, and he was understandably "greatly agitated" when he found out about it. According to Captain Smith, "the general complained, 'The dam, as you heard me say it would, gave way, and Thornton's people will be of no use whatever to the general attack.' " He may or may not have believed this entirely, because right up until the time of the attack Pakenham kept listening for the sounds of Thornton's movements across the river. In any event, the failure to wake Pakenham and alert him to the situation had dire effects. If he'd had time to think about it, he might have sent as many of Thornton's men as possible across the river in the boats then available and had them come back for more; he might have called off the attack before all the men had moved forward and waited for all of Thornton's regiment to get established on the west bank. As it was, he did neither.

In the meantime, artillerymen and engineers had been busy all night setting up batteries about seven hundred yards from Jackson's line. At about four a.m., on January 8, 1815, the army was moved forward quietly for attack at first light. Many marched in high spirits, confident that they would be away from this miserable plain and feasting in New Orleans by nightfall. Others, who had heard the same promise before, felt differently.

Thirteen

There were many things to unsettle Jackson's peace of mind that night, not the least of which was the situation on the west bank of the river. What exactly the British intended to do there he did not yet know, but he believed that by dispatching the 400 Kentucky reinforcements he had done all he could. In fact, he hadn't; he had treated the west bank almost as an afterthought, though that is somewhat understandable, since the bulk of the British army was directly before him. If Jackson had known precisely what the situation was on the west bank, it might have given him much more pause.

It will be remembered that a week earlier he had ordered the 600 inexperienced militia under General David B. Morgan, then posted at English Turn, to cross the river and set up a defense of the west bank. To facilitate this, Jackson sent engineer Latour to assist Morgan in establishing a line similar to his own. Morgan was a forty-two-year-old Massachusetts Yankee who had arrived in New Orleans a decade earlier and become a politician. He was a slightly pudgy man whose most popular likeness shows him dressed in buckskins like a backwoodsman, instead of as the Louisiana legislator he was.

Unfortunately, Morgan did not seem to appreciate the skill of military engineering. When Latour began laying out a line up near the plantation of "fat old Doctor Flood," Morgan rejected it as being too far away from Patterson's marine batteries, which were trained across the river to catch the British in flank if they should try another attack. He might have had something there, considering that if the British were to cross to the west bank in force, Patterson would have to rely on Morgan for protection, as he had none of his own.

The problem was that the site selected by Morgan for his redoubt was nearly two thousand yards long, more than a mile—and almost twice as long as Jackson's fortification, which contained 5,000 men, compared with the measly 800 that Morgan could now muster, including the newly arrived Kentuckians. Morgan had begun work on his line only four days earlier. He employed the labor of some 500 slaves, but in that short a period they could do little more than throw up a shallow, mile-long earthwork behind the ditch they had dug for the dirt. There were twelve American guns on the west bank, but only three of them in Morgan's line; the rest belonged to Commodore Patterson's batteries facing east across the river.

After studying the British preparations from the west bank for several hours on the evening of January 7, Patterson had seen enough. He had watched boat after boat move through the cut in the levee and heard the cheers of the sailors and redcoats as they entered the river. What Patterson concluded from this was that he and Morgan were going to be attacked the next morning and apparently with the bulk of Pakenham's troops. It would make perfect sense that, instead of assaulting Jackson's strong line, they were going to bring their main force across the Mississippi, roll over the small body of Americans there, and enter New Orleans from the west bank of the river. Patterson supposed that once the enemy had landed, and put his cross-river batteries out of action, the British could simply row the empty boats upriver and have them waiting for their infantry when they arrived, to carry them across the river into an undefended city.

Patterson did not at all like the looks of Morgan's line—never had, actually—and it became evident, even to this navy man, that more soldiers were urgently needed. Accordingly, after conferring with Morgan, late that night he sent a messenger to Jackson.

Jackson and his staff had been sleeping on blankets on the downstairs floor of the Macarty house, fully dressed, we are told, although they had "removed their sword belts." When the messenger arrived Jackson asked, "Who's there?" and was given Patterson's message.

"Hurry back," he replied, "and tell General Morgan he is mistaken. The main attack will come on this side [of the river], and I have no men to spare. He must maintain his position at all hazards."

According to Jackson's watch it was past one a.m. He told his resting aides, "Gentlemen, we have slept enough. Rise. The enemy will be on us in a few minutes. I must go and see Coffee."

During the next several hours, to the rattle of drums, Jackson's men were herded into their positions along the embrasure. They were lined up four deep, one man to shoot and then return to the rear of the line to reload, while the second man stepped up and did the same, and so on, to ensure a continuous front of fire. The artillery pieces were readied for action; powder bags and fuses were brought up; cannonballs were set out, as well as canister, grape, and chain shot; boxes of nails, musket balls, and rusty scrap iron were placed close at hand.

In the dark, for one last time, Jackson inspected his entire fortification, walking down the length of the line to Coffee's position at the far end of the cypress swamp. From Battery No. 1 he passed by his battalion of New Orleans businessmen. Reaching Battery No. 2 he gave encouraging words to the regulars of the 7th Infantry Regiment. Halfway between Batteries No. 2 and No. 3, his party was nearly overpowered by the aroma of strong coffee, which, according to adjutant Butler, "was black as tar and could be smelled twenty yards away." It was emanating from the camp of Captain Dominique You, where several of the Baratarians were huddled around a large tin-coated drip pot, ladling boiling water over coffee grounds and frying cornbread, beignets, and bacon.

"That smells like better coffee than we can get," Jackson remarked. "Where did you get such fine coffee? Maybe you smuggled it in?"

"Mebbe so, *Zeneral*," chuckled the irrepressible privateer. He told his men to pour a cup for the commander, and as Jackson proceeded toward Battery No. 4, near the big American flagstaff, he was overheard to say, "I wish I had fifty guns on this line, with five hundred such devils as those fellows behind them."

As Jackson passed by the men, he spoke to a number of them personally, especially those he knew from Tennessee. The mood was neither frigid nor light. As to the emotions a man feels on confronting an enemy, one whom he will actually *see* at any moment, there is no known expression in the English language; his mind can only work through an abstract collage of uncertain thoughts. This morning the men stood or squatted, honing knives, cleaning weapons, talking in low tones, smoking, writing letters by firelight, or dreaming restlessly of violence. It lay ineradicably at the bottom of their minds that within hours they could be killed or mutilated. Nevertheless, they were ready to hold their ground.

On Jackson went, saluting the battalions of the free men of color and spreading encouragement and confidence to the 44th's regulars and the Tennesseans of Generals Carroll and Coffee. Echoing Colonel William Prescott's famous order at the Battle of Bunker Hill, Jackson told them, "Don't shoot, boys, until you see the whites of their eyes."

Over in the British lines simultaneous preparations were being made. Captain Cooke records that there was an uncommon atmosphere of gaiety and boisterousness among the soldiers, who had been told that at last they were going into New Orleans. Walking through the camp with a companion, Cooke observed a "looseness and bawling in the sugar-cane bivouac which we had never seen or heard before within sight of an enemy and on the eve of an attack. We agreed that there was a screw loose somewhere."

Cooke lamented, "I do not remember ever looking for the first signs of daybreak with more intense anxiety than on this eventful morning. It augured not of victory; an evil foreboding crossed my mind, and I meditated in solemn reflection. All was tranquil as the grave, and no camp fires glimmered from either friends or foes." The earlier laughter, one suspects, was mostly braggadocio, mirthless as the cold, bland smile of the Sphinx.

Likewise, quartermaster Surtees felt that no good would come of the enterprise: "I own I did not at all feel satisfied with what I had seen and heard, and retired to rest with a considerable degree of despondency on my mind. . . . I almost felt confident of its failure."

Pakenham was vexed by the failure caused by the breaking of the dam in the boat canal. It threatened to upset an important part of his plan: the overcoming and seizure of the American guns on the west bank in order to turn them upon the rear of the American positions. When the dam collapsed and the soggy mud began sinking back into the canal, hundreds of soldiers and sailors were set to work to drag the boats through the muck. The plan had been for Thornton's people to have crossed by midnight and to have been formed up and in good marching order on the west bank by four a.m. at the latest, so as to capture the American weapons and direct them against Jackson's lines in concert with the main British assault. Now Sir Edward could only fret and wonder and hope.

As dawn approached, only about twenty of the forty-two boats that had been brought from the fleet could be hauled down the canal and launched into the Mississippi River, but it was finally decided to go ahead with these and hope for the best. With muffled oars, Thornton's party at last shoved off just before dawn but was soon caught in the swift main current and carried several miles below the place they had planned to make shore, thus setting them back even farther. Lieutenant Gleig explains, "Day had already broke, while they were yet four miles from the [American] batteries, which ought to have been taken hours ago."

A signal had been prearranged for the start of the main attack at first light: a rocket was to be fired from the British positions in front of Jackson on both the left and the right. At this, Thornton's people across the river would begin firing at Jackson's line with the captured American guns and, at the same time, the British columns would immediately march forward. But as dawn approached there had been none of the telltale sounds of battle echoing from the west bank, and Pakenham had to assume that, at best, Thornton's attack would yet be forthcoming, only probably not in time to coincide with his own—certainly an ominous development.

Pakenham rode to the levee and listened anxiously for the sounds of Thornton's battle across the river. He then turned to an aide and declared, "I will await my plans no longer," and spurred his horse forward toward Jackson's line, where his army waited silently for its orders. First he went to Keane, who was posted nearer the levee. Now he made a fatal decision.

Realizing that Thornton's force was now unlikely to silence Patterson's nine heavy guns on the west bank, and wishing to spare Keane's brigade from the worst of Patterson's enfilading fire, Pakenham told Keane that when the attack began he was to march his men in a right oblique, a diagonal move, toward General Gibbs, which would carry them nearer to the center, toward the cypress swamp and farther away from Patterson's guns. And then he rode off to Gibbs's column, the main one.

Here fate's sleight of hand, which can deal out ironies in spades, dealt a big one that day. When Pakenham found Gibbs, who was to lead the main assault, he received startling news—Colonel Mullins's 44th Regiment, which was supposed to bring forward the scaling ladders and fascines, had failed to do so. This "extraordinary blunder" was most alarming. Gibbs had ordered the regiment and Mullins back for the equipment, but with the approach of daybreak every second must count if they were to achieve any surprise at all, and that counted for everything.

Pakenham ordered one of his own aides, Major Sir John Tylden, to rush forward and discern the situation with the ladders and fascines. Other commanding officers were staring at their timepieces and, at the first faint rosy glows of dawn, wondering what the holdup was. Over in the 93rd Highland Regiment, its commander, Colonel Robert Dale, seemed "grave and depressed" when he was informed by the regimental physician that there had been trouble getting Thornton's men across the river. Instead of answering the doctor, Dale, with the detached air of a condemned man, handed him his watch and a letter, saying, "Give these to my wife; I shall die at the head of my regiment."

While awaiting news of the scaling equipment, Pakenham's aide Major Sir Harry Smith suggested to him that, given the situation with the boats and now this misfortune with the scaling ladders, the attack might best be postponed. Pakenham was having none of it. "I have twice deferred the attack. We are strong in numbers comparatively. It will cost more men, and the assault must be made." Smith, however, again cautioned delay. "While we were talking," Smith said, "the streaks of daylight began to appear, although the morning was dull, close and heavy, the clouds almost touching the ground: Pakenham shook his head. 'It is now too late,' he said."

Tylden returned shortly and reported that Mullins's Irishmen had finally found the heavy gear and were moving in a "most irregular and unsoldier-like manner, with the fascines and ladders," but he concluded that by now they "must have arrived at their situation in column." In fact, nothing could have been further from the truth; the Irishmen were still struggling with the scaling equipment when Pakenham turned to Smith and said, "Smith, order the rocket to be fired." Captain Cooke of the 43rd Light Infantry, which was in reserve that morning, later deemed it "the Fatal, *the ever-fatal rocket,*" and, as it turned out, he was certainly right.

Cooke's regiment was posted on the left, near the river, and when the rocket went off with its great *whoosh,* no one knew what it meant. The projectile whizzed all around the sky, Cooke reported, "backwards and forwards in such a zig-zag way that we all looked up like so many philosophers, to see if it was coming down upon our heads." As Latour remembered it, he was standing with Jackson near the center of the line when the rocket went up. "That is the signal for their advance, I believe," the general said. The rocket finally landed in the Mississippi and, after a moment of silence, suddenly there came a huge cannonade from the British lines on Jackson's left, near the cypress swamp.

The thick fog had begun to lift coincident with the rise of dawn, and Jackson's artillery replied in kind. "The Americans opened upon us from right to left," remembered Lieutenant Gleig, "a fire of musketry, grape, round-shot, and canister, which I have certainly never witnessed any more murderous." Within seconds, according to Captain Cooke, "were the cannonballs tearing up the ground, criss-crossing each other [especially those from Patterson's battery across the river] and bounding along like so many cricket-balls."

When Gibbs's column was still more than three hundred yards away, General Adair tapped one of his Kentucky marksmen from behind.

"See that officer on the gray horse?" he said, pointing to a British major who was riding alongside the leading column. "Snuff his candle!"

The Kentuckian took careful aim, squeezed the trigger, and Major Whitaker toppled from his horse, dead. A British quartermaster, E. N. Borroughs, had seen this from his perch on the balcony of the De la Ronde plantation house and marveled that "at a distance of nearly three hundred yards . . . the bullet passed through his head, out at the right temple and went on." Historian Robert Remini notes: "The final great action in the Battle of New Orleans, which had been anticipated for over a month, had finally begun."

The air was rabid with death and gun smoke, an inferno of cannon and rifle fire belching flame, lead, and red-hot iron; the great *boom* of the big guns and *zing* of musket balls; the strange, mournful music of the battlefield set against the most unearthly sounds of all, the *whoosh* of the British rockets and the shrieks and groans of the wounded and dying. It was Sunday morning, January 8, 1815, and all this noise began racketing back to New Orleans. The Sabbath church bells had already begun to toll, and the bewildered and apprehensive women with their children clutching at their skirts went inside to pray to God that their men could hold back the British.

When the mist had nearly cleared and the first rays of sun broke over the Chalmette plantation that morning, the dirty-shirt Americans beheld a sight that must have been breathtaking. Taking up most of the half-mile-long sugarcane fields before them was the red-coated British army, coming on in columns, each several hundred yards long, to the beat of drums and blare of bugles. With their higher-ranking officers prancing about on horses taken from local plantations, it must have been a stirring spectacle.

These were emotion-packed minutes: if the British broke the American line Jackson faced dismal consequences, since his two rearward lines were not nearly so strong and a retreating army never fights as fiercely as one that has not been beaten where it stands.

Despite the heavy fire from the Americans, the British came on relentlessly. Unlike the Americans—who were fighting together for the first time and, in most cases, were fighting *at all* for the first time—the British army was made up of trained professional soldiers, and was all tradition. History passes along many descriptions of men making a charge or ground assault against an enemy position. Contemporary accounts usually describe them as marching with their heads down, as if they were moving into a strong wind or a rainstorm, or in some cases at a crouch, so as to expose as little of themselves as possible. But when the British marched, they *marched*, ramrod straight, in tight formation and drawn up tall, daring the enemy to do his damnedest.

The dramatic rattle of the British drums was aimed at establishing a marching cadence, but the drums also had another purpose: to unsettle and strike fear in the enemy, sounding that steady *rat-a-tat, rat-a-tat, rat-a-tat* as the red-coated columns drew nearer and nearer, defying shot and shell and rifle fire.

In the American lines the apprehension was powerful and electrifying. All the boasting and hallooing was now just alluring nonsense in the face of this majestic British juggernaut. Conscious of their own inferiority in dress, in training, in experience, the Americans by now must have become at least dimly aware that here, today, they were the keepers of the national destiny; that if they fled, they would let down their nation and their flag. For some it was more personal: the Creoles had families in New Orleans, and the British army's desecrations against civilians were well publicized.

For each of these Americans, privately and characteristically, their single overarching determination boiled down—as it has always boiled down, ever since men have organized to fight one another with rocks, clubs, or guns—to the understanding that they were not going to cut and run, for the simple, honest fear of not wanting to disgrace themselves in front of their comrades.

Fourteen

On the British right the skirmishers of the 95th Regiment waded across the ditch in front of Jackson's line and, since no fascines or scaling ladders had yet arrived, began desperately trying to carve steps into the rampart with their bayonets. The leading companies of the 44th stopped, directly against their orders, which were to carry the American position at bayonet point, and began to shoot at the Americans, but when they were answered by a ruinous volley from Carroll's Tennesseans and Adair's Kentuckians, they ran away, setting into motion a chain of events that would soon shudder through the entire British army.

"Instantly the whole American line, from the swamp to a point near its center, was ablaze," said British quartermaster Borroughs from his vantage point on De la Ronde's balcony. "In less time than one can write it, the 44th Foot was literally swept from the face of the earth. In the wreck and confusion that ensued within five minutes the regiment seemed to vanish from sight—except the half of it that lay stricken on the ground. Every mounted officer was down at the first fire. No such execution by small arms has ever been seen or heard of."

Following Pakenham's revised orders, Keane had begun his diagonal march across the field toward the point where Jackson's rampart intersected with the cypress swamp. Unfortunately, Pakenham had forgotten to tell Colonel Sir Alexander Dickson, his chief of artillery, of the change in plans, and thus, as Keane's brigade started to march in front of Dickson's guns, he had no choice but to cease firing for fear of hitting his own troops. Arriving first on the scene at the head of Keane's brigade was the proud, tall 93rd Regiment of Scotsmen, wearing plaid tartan trousers and playing "Monymusk" on their bagpipes. They, too, were expecting to find the ditch filled with fascines and the scaling ladders against the rampart, but in this they, too, were disappointed. When the members of Mullins's 44th, who were dragging up the scaling equipment, saw the regiment's leading companies coming back toward them in flight, they dropped the ladders and fascines in the field and joined the others in a rush for the rear.

The commander of the 93rd, Colonel Dale, who had earlier given the regimental surgeon his watch and a letter to his wife, ordered his men to halt so he could appraise the situation. At that point he was fatally shot, just as he had predicted. General Gibbs came rushing through the smoke and noise and gloom hollering for Colonel Mullins and threatening to "hang him from the highest tree in that swamp" for forgetting the scaling gear. But Mullins was nowhere to be found.

Over on the left by the levee, three companies of infantry under Colonel Rennie stormed the redoubt in front of the rampart that Jackson had declared "will give us trouble." The Americans who were manning it were outnumbered, but a good deal of hand-to-hand fighting occurred before those who remained managed to scramble across a plank laid over the ditch and find safety behind the rampart. In what turned out to be a tragic case of "leading by example," right behind them came Rennie and two of his officers, who scaled the rampart. Looking back, Rennie shouted to his men, "Hurrah boys, the day is ours!" just as a volley from the New Orleans Rifles struck and killed all three men, who pitched headlong down into the ditch. Seeing this, the other redcoats fled in disorder, some along the levee, some along the road, and some along the riverbank. Captain Humphrey, with his eternal cigar, blasted them with his cannons, and so did Patterson's marine battery from across the river, until the riverbank was littered with dozens of dead and wounded British.

Historian Walker tells us that "a discussion arose" as to who had the honor of bringing down Colonel Rennie. "Mr. Withers, a merchant of New Orleans, and the crack shot of the company, settled the controversy by remarking: 'If he isn't hit above the eyebrows, it wasn't my shot.' "

Rennie's body was dragged out of the ditch, and "it was found that the fatal wound was in the forehead." Withers, therefore, was assigned the quaint custom of sending Rennie's watch and other valuables to his widow, who was among the wives aboard ship with the fleet off Lake Borgne.

Right about this time Captain Cooke, who was nearby behind the redoubt from which Rennie's men were retreating, observed that "at this momentous crisis a droll occurrence took place; a company of blacks emerged out of the mist carrying ladders, which were intended for the three light companies on the left of the attack." But, Cooke continues, "they were so confounded by the multiplicity of noises that they dropped the ladders and fell flat on their faces"; then he launched into a long dissertation on the proper employment of scaling ladders by men under fire, concluding that "only the very elite of an army" should be used for such a critical and dangerous enterprise.

By this time the battle was at its most pitiless intensity. According to Cooke, "The echo of the cannonade and musketry was so tremendous that the vibration seemed as if the earth was cracking and tumbling to pieces [and] the heavens were rent asunder by the most terrific peals of thunder that ever rumbled and produced an intermingled roar surpassing strange."

Cooke remembered seeing one of his friends, a Lieutenant Duncan Campbell, "running about in circles" and falling down only to get up again and run in more circles. It turned out that a grapeshot had torn open his forehead and rendered him blind. He was carried off to the rear, Cooke tells us, "and in a state of delirium and suffering he lived for a few days."

Back over on the British right, where the main attack under Gibbs had been expected to fall, a terrible and dangerous situation had developed, and the thousand tartan-clad Scotsmen of the 93rd Highlanders were beginning to undergo an ordeal of horrifying proportions.

When Colonel Dale was shot, right after ordering the regiment to halt, nobody in the subordinate command appeared to know what to do next. So the men remained there, in perfect marching formation, "standing like statues" with their regimental flags fluttering in the thin breeze, right in front of Jackson's rampart, while the American gunners and riflemen blasted away at them. They were not even told to fire back.

"The American batteries were playing upon them with awful effect, cutting great lanes through the column from front to rear, and huge gaps in their flanks." Some 600 of the Scotsmen were killed or wounded.

Meantime, Gibbs's other regiments were running up against a perfect firestorm from Carroll's and Coffee's Tennesseans and Kentuckians that no soldier on earth could long withstand. One of the Kentuckians, a man with the wonderful name of Ambrose Odd, was so short that he could not see over the rampart, and so he jumped atop it and began to fire at the British soldiers. When a colonel told him to get down, he replied, "Well, I'd like to know how I can shoot until I can see something!"

At one point Jackson ordered his artillery batteries to cease firing for a few minutes and let the clouds of smoke blow away, in order to fix the British troops clearly for more of the same. In Battery No. 3 he observed Captain Dominique You standing to his guns, his broad Gallic face beaming like a harvest moon. Though he was a short and squat man, he looked much larger now, his eyes burning and swelling from the powder smoke. Jackson declared, "If I were ordered to storm the gates of hell, with Captain Dominique as my lieutenant, I would have no misgivings of the result." During this momentary lull a strange incongruity occurred: the band of Beale's New Orleans Rifles resounded up and down the line playing "Yankee Doodle" and "Hail, Columbia"—in fact, throughout the entire engagement this band would play continuously every patriotic tune in its repertoire, though much of it could not be heard over the noise of the battle.

As the men in Jackson's line looked over the rampart at the stunned British host before them, the Americans were astonished at the number of red-coated lumps lying on the field. The morning was so humid and still that the gunpowder smoke did not drift away in the wind as Jackson had hoped, but "simply pancaked lazily toward the ground, as if the very air itself was exhausted."

Soon the order was received to recommence firing, and the "horrid concert" erupted once again.

"Stand to your guns!" Jackson roared. "Don't waste your ammunition. See that every shot tells! Give it to them, boys; let us finish the business today!" he told them.

Pakenham had watched in mortification as the deflated soldiers of the 44th and 21st Regiments streamed back toward the rear and declared, "Lost from want of courage!" When he rode out in front and tried to get them turned around, General Gibbs clattered up in a towering rage: "I cannot control my men!" he claimed. "They won't obey me!" Pakenham began rallying them "with reminders of the glory they had acquired in Egypt and elsewhere," leading them himself into the gloom and roar of battle. Along the way they passed by hundreds of men in little bunches, cringing in depressions or drainage ditches from the American fire.

"Shame! Shame!" the general called to them as he rode past. "Recollect that you are British. Forward, gentlemen, forward." At this point, one British officer tells us, "the American line looked like a row of fiery furnaces."

As he neared the fray, Pakenham was hit in the right arm by a bullet, while another killed his horse. He immediately took the horse of one of his aides, Captain Duncan MacDougall, and proceeded forward, with MacDougall leading it by the bridle and Pakenham, waving his plumed hat in his one good hand, exhorting his men all the while, "with appeals to their ancient fame." On reaching the battle area, Pakenham gave his final order, to bring up General Lambert's reserve, but as the bugler was blowing the call, a missile of some sort struck his arm and the message was never received.

Then grapeshot from one of Carroll's batteries tore into Pakenham's thigh and killed this second horse out from under him. As his aides were lifting the young commanding general up, another blast of grapeshot hit him in the stomach. The wound was mortal. Pakenham was carried to the rear and placed under a lone oak tree standing far back in the center of the field, where he died a short time afterward—"perished thus ingloriously in a war of unjust invasion against his own race and kindred," in the opinion of Judge Walker, who also recorded that "the old oak still stands, bent and twisted—a melancholy monument of that great disaster of the British arms!"

A lieutenant and a major from the 21st Regiment and about twenty men got across the ditch and managed to scale the rampart by standing on one another's shoulders, but when the major, whose name was Wilkinson, raised himself above the top, he was greeted by a blast of rifle fire. The Kentuckians, however, were so moved by Wilkinson's courage that they pulled him to safety behind the rampart. Walker tells us that a Major Smiley attempted to minister to the Englishman, saying, "Bear up, my dear fellow. You are too brave a man to die."

But Wilkinson fully understood his fate: "I thank you from the bottom of my heart," he replied. "It is all over for me. You can render me a favor; it is to communicate to my commander that I fell on your parapet and died like a soldier and a true Englishman."

After Wilkinson expired, the Kentuckians covered his body with their own flag. His was a particular English inconsistency "that did not seem to bother them in the least." The reasoning behind it seemed to be that if a man has to go, he may as well go cheerfully, and in good spirits, while most Americans so wounded—being a more practical people— would have railed in curses and lamentations at the imminent prospect of their death.

The lieutenant, whose name was Leavock, had meantime gotten over the rampart untouched, only to find himself in the unwelcome company of two Kentucky officers, whom he attempted to take as prisoners. The Kentuckians just laughed at him, however, and made him a prisoner instead, while the astonished lieutenant looked back to find that none of his brother soldiers had followed him but were cowering down in Jackson's ditch. Later, when he was finally released, Leavock claimed to fellow officers that when he rose up over the rampart all the Americans—except for the two officers who captured him—had run away, but this does not seem to square with reality.

By now General Keane had been critically shot in the neck and carried off the field. Also, according to accounts, General Gibbs had become like a man possessed, "riding around in circles," shouting at and abjuring his scattered men, when he was struck simultaneously by several American bullets and mortally wounded. He, too, was carried from the field in pain and agony, still cursing not only his present situation but Colonel Mullins's incompetence, the bad turn of the battle, and, some say, Pakenham himself; he died the next day.

The British army had lost all three of its active field generals, seven colonels, and seventy-five other officers—that is, practically its whole officer corps.

As an example of sublime naïveté, Lieutenant Gleig complained that the British soldiers "fell by the hands of men they could not see; for the Americans, without so much as lifting their faces above the rampart, swung their firelocks by one arm over the wall, and discharged them directly upon their [British] heads. The whole of the guns, likewise, from the opposite bank, kept up a well-directed and deadly cannonade upon their flank; and thus were they [the British army] destroyed without an opportunity being given of displaying their valor, or obtaining so much as revenge."

Gleig's problem seems to be, as it was with the rest of the British apologists then present, that the Americans did not play by European rules of warfare. Paraphrasing Walker, perhaps the British should have thought about that before they came to invade somebody else's country, and adjusted their lofty military customs accordingly.

Some of the fleeing soldiers exclaimed to others that they had heard an order to retreat, but that did not seem to be the case either; by now the entire British army was in irredeemable disarray. The hapless Scotsmen of the 93rd were still standing in the field when "that thirty-two pounder, filled to the muzzle with musket balls, poured its charge directly, at point blank range, right into the head of the column, literally leveling it with the plain"—laying low, as was afterward computed, 200 men. Finally the Scotsmen had stood all they could stand and fled to save themselves, leaving behind them two-thirds of their number, dead or bleeding on the field. The battle was only twenty-five minutes old from the opening shots, and already from the British standpoint it had become a shambles.

Most of the British army had by now run back out of cannon and rifle range, but there were still large numbers of fleeing soldiers who had taken refuge in drainage ditches or shallow depressions in the ground, or behind the trees at the edge of the swamp. With the withdrawal of the bulk of their associates, those who remained behind attracted the undivided attention of American shooters. For these unfortunate souls, there was nothing under the sun to appeal to, neither mercy nor justice nor, for that matter, even common decency; the Americans shot at them relentlessly, and even the smallest flash of red moving above ground would bring a dozen bullets whistling overhead. If they tried to run for it, they were invariably shot down.

One retreating British soldier was particularly annoying to the Americans because, as he got what he thought was a safe distance away, he "would every now and then stop and display some gestures toward us that were rather uncomplimentary (patting his butt at us!)." A number of men were shooting at him, a Kentuckian said, but they were ineffective. In the Kentuckian's outfit was a superior marksman known as Paleface, and the others urged him to take aim at the offending redcoat, which he did, killing him with a shot between the shoulder blades at a range of nearly three hundred yards.

Captain John Cooke, of the 43rd Regiment, remembered, "A wounded soldier who was lying amongst the slain two hundred yards behind us, continued without any cessation for two hours, to raise his arm up and down with a convulsive motion, which excited the most painful sensations amongst us; and as the enemy's balls every now and then killed or maimed some soldiers, we could not help casting our eyes towards the moving arm, which really was a *dreadful magnet* of attraction: it even caught the attention of the enemy who, without seeing the body, fired several round shot at it."

Other abominations starkly emerged. "A black soldier lay near us, who had received a blow from a cannon-ball which had obliterated all his features; and although blind, and suffering the most terrible anguish, he was employing himself in scratching out a hole to put his money into." Cooke saw one officer of his regiment, "when a *grape shot* passed through both of his knees; at first he sank back faintly, but at length opening his eyes and looking at his wounds, he said, 'Carry me away, I am chilled to death'; and as he was hoisted on the men's shoulders, more grape shot passed his head; taking off his cap, he waved it; and after many narrow escapes he got out of range, suffered amputation of both legs, but died of his wounds on board ship, after enduring all the pain of the surgical operation and passing down the lake in an open boat."

For the Americans, gazing over the rampart at the hideous mementos, the sight beggared the imagination, like a scene from the depths of Dante. The air stank of hot metal and gunpowder, of flesh and blood. A soldier from Kentucky wrote, "When the smoke had cleared and we could obtain a fair view of the field, it looked at first glance like a sea of blood. It was not blood itself, but the red coats in which the British soldiers were dressed. The field was entirely covered in prostrate bodies. In some places they were laying in piles of several, one on top of the other . . . in every possible attitude. Some laying quite dead, others mortally wounded, pitching and tumbling about in the agonies of death. Some had their heads shot off, some their legs, some their arms."

Even Jackson was flabbergasted by the sight. "I never had so grand and awful an idea of the resurrection as on that day," he later wrote, as scores of redcoats rose up like dim purgatorial souls with their hands in the air and began walking toward the American lines. "After the smoke of the battle had cleared off somewhat, I saw in the distance more than five hundred Britons emerging from the heaps of their dead comrades, all over the plain, rising up and coming forward and surrendering as prisoners of war to our soldiers." These people, Jackson concluded, had fallen at the first fire and then hidden themselves behind the bodies of their slain brethren.

One was a British major who walked into the Kentucky lines of Paleface and Ambrose Odd waving a white handkerchief. When a private told him to surrender his sword, the major balked, looking for a proper officer to surrender it to, instead of a private "who looked like a chimnysweep." But when the regiment's colonel came by—he was the same Colonel Smiley who had earlier tended to the brave dying major—he ordered the priggish major to "give it up" to the private, which he did.

Another soldier surrendering himself was a young Irishman from the 44th Regiment who came into the American lines. As soon as he got over the rampart, he was trying to take off his cartridge box when an American noticed a red spot of blood on his white shirt. Asked if he was wounded, the young soldier "replied that he was, and feared pretty badly." Several Americans began helping him remove his accoutrements when the soldier noticed one of the Tennesseans coming back from the river with a tin pot full of water, "and asked if he would please give him a drop." The Tennessean did so, and no sooner had the Irishman taken two or three mouthfuls than he sank back down, dead.

Fifteen

By midmorning most of the firing had ceased, except for an occasional American cannon that let off a roar every now and then, like a lion who simply wanted to let everyone know he was still there. Jean Laffite, who was returning from an inspection of his stores of powder and flints at the Temple, got there just as the battle ended, and as he reached the rear of his batteries he did not know who had won. "I heard the rumble of cannons raging in the distance," he said. When the gunfire slacked off, he remembered, "I feared that my supply of flints and powder were exhausted." Laffite moved as fast as he could to the rampart: "I was almost out of breath, running through the bushes and mud. My hands were bruised, my clothing torn, my feet soaked. I could not believe the result of the battle," he said, adding that "the spectacle presented before us by the battlefield was so horrible that we could not believe our eyes."

Because they were touched at the tremendous suffering that had come to pass all over the ground in front of them, many of the Americans went out to try and help the more seriously wounded redcoats. In several instances the wounded British soldiers mistook these gestures of kindness as being some sort of attempt to "finish them off," and several unarmed Americans were shot as a consequence.

Others went around collecting British muskets—a thousand or more—and sometimes the shoes of dead soldiers. Pakenham's spyglass was found, as was General Keane's elaborately embossed and engraved sword. A few weeks later, while still recovering from his wound aboard ship, Keane sent a letter to Jackson asking that his sword be returned to him, as it had sentimental value, and even offering to pay for it. Jackson, offended, ordered that the sword be returned, and it was.

Also by midmorning came a nasty little reminder of how fine the line is between glorious victory and ruinous defeat. A ruckus finally had broken out across the river on the west bank. Jackson, who was standing on the rampart with Major Latour, turned to see puffs of gun smoke and hear the racket of a battle in progress. Things had been so busy to his front this morning that he likely gave himself little time to worry about what was happening or going to happen over on the west bank. But now the proof was echoing back to him from across the river. At first it looked to Jackson as if the Americans were winning the battle. He could see some British sailors repelled from the American lines and heard the faint cheers of the American soldiers. Jackson called for three cheers from the men in his own line to answer and encourage them. These being delivered, it now seemed, upon closer study through the spyglass, that the British were winning, and indeed shortly thereafter there came to Jackson's ears the unwelcome but unmistakable cheers of the British force.

Like the recently deceased Colonel Rennie, Colonel William Thornton was one of the most outstanding and resourceful officers in the British army. Doubtless he would have wished to have had his entire 85th Light Infantry Regiment with him that day, instead of a mere one-third of its number, but orders were orders, and Thornton, like any good officer, found ways to accomplish them, rather than figuring out reasons why he could not.

The American general Morgan had stupidly sent the 200 Kentuckians to man a thin line about a mile south of his own, an especially foolish move since the Kentuckians were truly a sorry lot, dressed in rags and rotten shoes, and even their own commander admitted that they were in no condition to fight. They had been marched all night after crossing the river, sometimes in knee-deep mud, arriving at Morgan's position about four a.m. They had not eaten a meal in nearly twenty hours; worse, the weapons they had picked up in New Orleans were inferior—many of them were merely old fowling pieces or muskets with cartridges too large for the barrels. This was the kind of American "rabble" that the British had so long scorned and confidently expected to destroy.

Thornton and his men began landing just before daybreak about a mile south of where they had intended because their boats were caught in a strong river current. They made up for lost ground with a quick-time march, and soon came upon the Kentuckians and made short work of them. One of the boats with a carronade in its bow had rowed alongside the Americans' position and given them a blast of grapeshot in their flank. At the same time, Thornton had formed his column into a line and, with bayonets glinting, marched them straight at the American positions.

Those of the Kentuckians who had a weapon that would shoot fired a volley and then ran off in all directions, many into the swamps to hide. Given their poor condition, one could hardly blame them, except that it would certainly have been better, for appearances' sake if nothing else, if they had marched to their retreat in formation rather than in such disarray. It reminded Lieutenant Gleig, who was there, of the rout of the Americans before the nation's capital the previous summer.

Thornton then formed up for a march on Morgan's main force, which he found a mile up the river, manning their overly long line. He began stretching out his files so that they covered the entire American position, and at the same time he organized about 100 sailors who had rowed them over, armed with pistols and cutlasses, to storm a two-gun battery of American field artillery that commanded the road along the river.

With a great shout, Gleig tells us, the sailors rushed up the road toward the guns, "but were met by so heavy a discharge of grape and canister that for an instant they paused." This was apparently the action that Jackson and Latour had first witnessed from the rampart across the river, and that initially had made them think the Americans were winning.

When the rest of Thornton's 85th charged the American lines, the sailors recovered themselves and rushed the guns again; this time the whole position came apart. "A panic seized the Americans," Gleig wrote, "they lost their order and fled, leaving us in possession of their tents and of eighteen pieces of cannon."*

This was mostly true, except that there were only twelve cannons, the three in Morgan's line and the nine under Patterson's command in the rear, trained across the river. Luckily, Patterson was able to spike them and dump their powder into the water, before the British could gain control of them and turn them on Jackson's line. Patterson then retired up the road with his aide, "alternately denouncing the British and the Kentuckians."

Gleig notes, with apparent relief, that "in this affair our loss amounted to only three men killed and about forty wounded," but, unfortunately, "among the latter was Colonel Thornton." Gleig, however, was talking only about his own regiment; of the sailors, 4 were killed and 49 wounded, which reduced Thornton's detachment by nearly 20 percent.

Morgan, meantime, had ridden off in a tizzy, trying to reorganize his troops. At first it appeared they would run all the way up to New Orleans, but finally their officers got enough control to form them at a canal about a mile behind their original line, where they could perhaps make another stand. This, however, as we shall see, would become unnecessary.

After Pakenham was killed, his aide Major Sir John Tylden galloped back to find Major General Lambert, who was commanding the reserve, to inform him of the event and to notify him that he was now in command of the army. When he arrived at Lambert's position, Tylden also told Lambert, "Your Brigade must move on immediately," referring to Pakenham's last order to throw in the reserves. Major Sir Harry Smith, however, now serving as Lambert's military aide, had been watching the disorderly repulse of the British forces, and he reminded Tylden politely but firmly that "if Sir Edward [Pakenham] is

---

* One of these guns, a heavy bronze howitzer, had markings that identified it as having been captured from the British at the surrender of Yorktown thirty-four years earlier. How it got to New Orleans is anybody's guess.

killed, Sir John Lambert commands, and will judge of what is to be done." What Smith worried about most at this point was not that the attack had failed, but that the Americans would now form up and attack *them*, "as the French would have done," he added. He asked Lambert if he could take the brigade forward to cover this "most irregular retreat" until Lambert could ascertain the true state of affairs. Lambert agreed.

Having done this, Lambert ordered Smith and all the other staff officers to go to the rear and re-form the troops—"no easy matter in some cases," according to Smith. Lambert studied the situation, "wondering whether, under the circumstances, he ought to attack" with the reserve brigade; he concluded that "it was impossible, and withdrew the troops from under a most murderous fire of round shot."

The British admirals soon came to Lambert's field headquarters, "with faces as long as a flying jib," Smith remembers, for something resembling a council of war. Admiral Edward Codrington is mentioned, but one assumes Admirals Pultney Malcolm and Cochrane were there also. Codrington, whose job was to keep the men supplied with rations, stated, "The troops must attack or the whole would starve." Smith piped up "rather saucily," so he tells us, saying, "Kill plenty more, Admiral; fewer rations will be required." Smith and apparently other staff men gave it as their opinion, after having gone around to find out how the "pluck" of the troops stood, that those who had made the attack wanted no more of the Americans. "We know the enemy are three times our number," Smith told the council—getting the ratio of Americans to British soldiers wrong once again—and reiterated his conviction that Jackson was preparing to attack them. "Thornton's people ought to be brought back and brought into our line," Smith recommended. "The army is secure and no further disaster is to be apprehended."

Lambert agreed, and Colonel Dickson was sent to give the command for Thornton's return, which was why it was unnecessary for Morgan's men to make another stand.

Jackson, however, had been displeased with Morgan's performance.

He therefore sent across the river to finish the job several hundred reinforcements under the elderly French general Jean Robert Humbert, who had served in the French revolutionary army and who, in 1798, led the infamous force of French soldiers and adventurers in the unsuccessful invasion to expel the English from Ireland.

According to Judge Walker, Humbert was apparently something of a character. He never went anywhere dressed other than in his old French army uniform, with a French revolutionary military hat on his head and carrying his polished, inlaid sword under his arm. He spent his days drinking cognac and playing dominoes in one of the local coffeehouses. Sufficiently tanked up by the afternoon, he would march down the streets of New Orleans belting out "La Marseillaise" and other French martial tunes at the top of his lungs, with an army of cheerful children following after him.

Before Humbert's arrival, Jean Laffite was sent across the river with a message from Jackson to Morgan. It said:

> Sir:
>
> This will be handed to you by Mr. Lafitte whom I have sent to you as a man acquainted with the geography of the country on your side of the river, and will be able to afford you any information you may want with respect to the canals and bayous by which the enemy will attempt to penetrate. I have also sent Gen'l Humbert, a man in whose bravery I have unbound confidence, for the purpose of carrying the enemy if necessary at the point of the bayonet. It is my determination he shall be dislodged at all events and I rely upon you to accomplish it, they are not more than four hundred strong and your task not a difficult one. We have beat them here at all points with a loss on their side of at least a thousand men.
>
> > Brig-Gen. Morgan
> > right side of the river
> >
> > Andrew Jackson
> > Maj-Gen., Comdg.

The problem with Humbert's commanding the reinforcement was resentment at his being a Frenchman. It may also have had to do with his being "one of the characters" of the town, as has been described above.

As soon as the British danger had presented itself in early December, Humbert was among the first to volunteer his services, and after the British landing he would ride day in and day out personally scouting their positions in the face of flying bullets; serving as an aide to Jackson, he volunteered for anything the commanding general wanted him to do, no matter how dangerous. Jackson had not known the fifty-seven-year-old Humbert before coming to New Orleans, but in the weeks before the British actually landed, he came to realize that his new acquaintance was a general with real military experience in European wars—in fact, was the only fighting general among them all, when it came to anything more than battles with Indians—and Jackson would rely on him implicitly.

The trouble was, Morgan and Governor Claiborne did not agree on Humbert's replacing Morgan as commander on the right bank. A heated discussion ensued, with Morgan arguing that his militia officers would not follow a Frenchman with no formal commission in the U.S. Army and Claiborne apparently concurring.

When Humbert could produce no direct orders from Jackson relieving Morgan, the Louisiana general refused to relinquish command. Humbert, after dispersing his reinforcements to Morgan's lines, returned across the river in disgust, saying to Jackson that the American officers on the west bank had declined to serve under a Frenchman. This might have proved serious, even fatal, except that the British by then had been ordered to withdraw from the right bank, which they did in rude fashion, setting fire to a beautiful plantation château in order to mask their escape behind its smoke.

Late that afternoon, when the American cannonading had finally stopped, Lambert sent Sir Harry Smith over to the American lines to see if a truce could be arranged for the British to remove their dead and wounded. Smith arrived at a point about three hundred yards in front of the American rampart, where his orderly blew a bugle and waved a white flag to attract attention. Jackson sent out his aide Major Butler to find out what they wanted, and Smith gave Butler a letter for Jackson that was signed only "Lambert." When Butler took the letter back to the Macarty house, the general glanced it over in a lawyerly way and told him to return it to the messenger with the response that "he [Jackson] would be happy to treat with the commander-in-chief of the British army, but that the signer of the letter had forgotten to designate his authority and rank, which was necessary before any negotiations could be entered upon."

What Lambert evidently intended to accomplish here was to conceal the mortifying fact of Pakenham's death, but he could not fool Jackson with this sleight of hand, and presently Major Smith returned with another letter, this one designating John Lambert as commander in chief of the British forces.

Like the armistice letter itself, the negotiations were somewhat sticky. Jackson was worried about what a truce would mean to his beleaguered forces on the right bank of the river. Accordingly, he said he would agree to a truce until noon the next day, January 9, on the left bank, but not on the right bank, and only if Lambert would confirm that neither side was to reinforce its detachments on the right bank.

The next morning Smith went out with a "rather large" burial party, equipped with entrenching tools, as well as some surgeons to bring off the wounded. Since Jackson did not want a lot of British soldiers and officers near his lines—for fear they might do a little reconnoitering— the procedure was established that the Americans would bring the British dead to a spot on Bienvenue's plantation, which had been staked off near the place where Smith had originally come with his flag of truce. An "immense" grave was then dug by the burial party, while the Americans carried the bodies on the "clumsy and unwieldy" scaling ladders that the British had left on the field.

A somewhat solemn ceremony was observed, according to Smith, who was there to supervise. The Americans carefully laid the bodies on the ground on their side of the line, where they were received by the British burial party. They were straightened and the big toes tied together with string. Then they were thrown into the hole by the hundreds, "as fast as we could bring them," Smith said, adding, "A more appalling spectacle cannot be conceived than this common grave." It especially could not have gone well for the burial party, many of whom wept when they recognized friends or favorite officers.

Pleasant relations did not overtake the two enemies during this somber period. Smith had words with Major Butler, whom he later described as "a rough fellow," who came out "with a drawn sword and no scabbard." After Butler made a crack about the British dead and wounded, Smith retorted by telling him the British were going to attack again and drive the Americans out of their lines with bayonets. He then asked Butler why he carried a drawn sword with no scabbard.

"We have thrown away the scabbard," Butler told him, "so long as you Britishers are on our soil."

Smith then got into a contentious encounter with Captain Maunsel White, a wealthy plantation owner. Dismissing the heaps of British dead as "a skirmish, a mere skirmish," Smith seemed to be downplaying the defeat to the American officer.

"One more such skirmish," White told him coldly, "and devilish few of you will get back home to tell the story."

Lieutenant Gleig nearly had a run-in as well. Since he had been on the right bank with Thornton, he had gone to the scene of the burial to see for himself the magnitude of the failure. He took note that "an American officer [probably either Captain Humphrey or Captain White] stood by, smoking a cigar, and apparently counting the slain with a look of savage exultation, and repeating over and over to each individual that approached him, their loss amounted only to eight men killed and fourteen wounded.

"I had every inclination to pick a quarrel [duel]," Gleig wrote later, "but he was on duty and an armistice existed."

The curious thing about these exchanges and so many others like them during the engagement is that the British officers appeared to view war as a sort of game, with rules and niceties and an etiquette all their own, a sentiment embodied perhaps in the droll remark later attributed to Wellington after his final victory over Napoleon: "The Battle of Waterloo was won on the playing fields of Eton."

These soldiers of the American South knew precious little about any of that, beginning with Jackson himself, who had seen "Butcher" Tarleton's British marauders during the American Revolution hang, rape, burn, and kill, including members of his own family. Jackson's Americans might have been rude, but they were certainly not barbarians, and they also did not regard the conflict as some kind of gentlemen's tea party arrayed with guns. Instead they viewed the Englishmen as contemptuous invaders and intruders in their country, and on their own soil; from everything they'd heard and read, the British had been the perpetrators of the vilest acts of cruelty against an American people who simply wished to be let alone. The British might respond by saying that this was only a matter of perspective, and perhaps it was, but the Americans—especially Andrew Jackson himself—did not see it that way and would not rest until the enemy was ejected once and for all.

The day had become gray and clammy and was covered in a light fog. Back in the British lines, the mood of the men matched the weather. Everyone was blaming the 44th Regiment for failing to bring up the scaling ladders and fascines. Many of these dead cats were thrown at Colonel Mullins himself, who was placed under arrest and sent back to the fleet in disgrace until a court-martial could be convened. Gleig remembered that "if you attempted to converse [with the soldiers] on the subject of the late defeat, they would end with a bitter curse upon those to whose misconduct they attributed their losses." Not only that, but some of the soldiers were so venomous that they seized the deserter Galvez, the Creole Spaniard, on the theory that he must be an American spy, since he had told them that the part of Jackson's line they assaulted was weak and manned only by untrained militia. They dragged him to a tree and hanged him.

On the other side of the river, where the truce had never been declared, Patterson had got his batteries working again and even moved some of the guns closer to the British position, from which he hurled cannonballs at them all day and night.

The hospital, located in the De la Ronde plantation house, presented ghastly sounds and sights, including, according to one officer, "a basket nearly full of legs severed from these fine fellows, most of which were still covered with their hose." General Keane suffered from his wounds in the same room where the bodies of Pakenham and Gibbs were laid out side by side.

Jackson was not at all satisfied by the results of the January 8 repulse, and never would be, so long as there was a British soldier left on American soil. He viewed his enemy as a wounded lion—hurt, but still very dangerous. As the British major Sir Harry Smith had feared, Jackson by now had determined to attack the British, with hatchets and tomahawks if need be, but since he had collected so many of their muskets from the battlefield, he could now arm his whole army.* Yet when Jackson asked for the advice of his aides and generals, the consensus was a resounding "no."

"Your object is gained. The city is saved," said Edward Livingston, who went on to argue that it would not be worthwhile to risk the lives of its "worthiest citizens and rob so many families of their heads!"

"If we were beaten back," cautioned General Adair, "it would be with great loss of both officers and men, and might encourage the enemy to renew the attack. Most of our men are militia and without discipline, and if once beaten they could not be relied upon again."

Livingston had made a lawyer's argument, and Adair a general's, but in the end the conclusions were the same.

Jackson accepted this sage advice and returned to his old tactics of shelling the British by day and conducting his "hunting parties" by

* The thousand or so British muskets collected were just about the number Jackson needed to arm the Kentuckians and those of the militia who were poorly armed. He also figured the arms loss subtracted at least that number of British soldiers who could be brought against him.

night, which became even more effective after the disheartening repulse of January 8. "Of the extreme unpleasantness of our situation," wrote Lieutenant Gleig, "it is hardly possible to convey any adequate conception.

"We never closed our eyes in peace," he complained. "Tents we had none, and heavy rains now set in, accompanied by violent storms of thunder and lightning which, lasting during the entire day usually ceased towards dark and gave place to keen frosts. Thus were we alternately wet and frozen. The outposts [pickets] were attacked and compelled to maintain their ground by dint of hard fighting."

Captain Cooke's recollections did not come off any better. He complained bitterly of the American shelling, including that following a funeral for a fellow officer who had died of wounds. "The night after this burial a shell exploded over a hut in which two officers of our regiment were sleeping, which cut off the feet of Lieutenant D'Arcy. One of his feet was driven so deep into the soft mold [mud?] that it was obliged to be dug out the following day.

"On some days we did not taste food, and when we did it was served out in such small quantities as only to tantalize our appetites," Cooke remembered. If that weren't enough, one morning before daylight a great rush of water into everyone's blankets announced that the Mississippi had overflowed, due to all the recent rains, and "nothing but a sheet of water was to be seen." All day and into the night, Cooke reported, the men, "enveloped in blankets, shivering, stood around like polar bears on their hind legs."

Jackson spared them nothing, not even psychological warfare. Lieutenant Gleig recalls that "inducements such as printed papers, offering lands and money were held out by the enemy to desert," and that "many desertions began daily to take place and became before long so frequent, that the evil rose to be of a serious nature. In the course of a week many men quitted their colours, and fled to the enemy."

Still, it was going to take more than a bit of cold and damp and artillery harassment for Cochrane and the other British admirals to give up their dream. Doubtless they could almost *smell* all that fabulous booty in New Orleans, out of which their own cuts would be large enough to ensure them each a comfortable retirement. Of course, they also had their reputations to protect. How poorly it would reflect on these vaunted admirals to have sailed a large British army of professional veterans halfway around the world only to have it repulsed by American militia is anybody's guess, but one can assume that the Admiralty would be displeased, if not distressed. Since it was apparent that another march against Jackson's line had now become a practical impossibility, the navy men concocted yet another scheme.

As early as January 1 they had sent such of their ships as could ascend the Mississippi to do so and, bristling with big guns—more than a hundred of them—to blow Jackson and his army off of their imposing rampart, or to land large numbers of troops behind him, or to sail up and shell New Orleans itself into capitulation, or a combination of all three.

To effect this, they had already captured the Balize, a small, weak American fort on the southeast pass of the river, where it finally empties into the gulf. On January 9, the morning after the battle at the ditch, the vanguard of this fleet appeared off Fort St. Philip, a critical installation located on a bend about seventy river miles below Jackson's battlefield on the left bank. It then proceeded to bombard the American bastion with the obvious mind of reducing it so that their ships could pass by unmolested.

The fort was commanded, however, by Major Walter Overton, a U.S. Army regular, who had other ideas entirely.

Fort St. Philip, it will be remembered, was the fort that Jackson had ordered significantly strengthened. Overton had dispersed his powder and ammunition magazines all over the fort, so that if one was blown up he could use another. He had removed anything combustible to guard against fire and built bomb shelters for the men. The fort commanded fields of fire both up and down the river, and, because it was surrounded by "an impenetrable morass," was virtually impervious to ground attack. Fort St. Philip boasted thirty-four guns: two big thirty-two-pounders, twenty-nine twenty-four-pounders, a huge thirteen-inch mortar, and two howitzers of lesser caliber. It was manned by 406 soldiers and sailors, including detachments of regulars from the United States artillery and the 7th Infantry Regiment, a company of Louisiana volunteers and a company of free men of color, as well as the only gunboat that had not been captured on Lake Borgne, with its forty-man crew.

At ten-fifteen a.m. five British warships were sighted. They anchored two and a quarter miles downriver and sent out a pair of barges to within a mile of the fort, apparently to take soundings. Overton ordered the thirty-two-pounders and a few of the twenty-fours to open up on them, which they did, causing the two boats to retire. But now the British fleet had learned the range of the American guns—which was about a mile and a half—and maneuvered their own ships until they were just outside of it. Then two bomb vessels—large barges— moved forward and anchored, just out of American range, and opened fire on Fort St. Philip with their huge mortars. According to Latour, "The first shell from the enemy fell short, but the next burst over the interior of the fort." All that day and night the shelling continued, with only short intervals, generally a shell every two minutes. The next morning the firing continued, "with the same vivacity as on the former day, except that there was a cessation for lunch and suppertimes."

It was maddening for the Americans, because there was little else to do but sit there and take it. They had no gun that could reply in kind except their own thirteen-inch mortar, which had a range of two miles, but fuses for its ammunition proved to be defective and they had no tools to make others. The bombardment went on day after day, except for the noted lulls for lunch and dinner. Every day a few men would be killed or maimed, but not much structural damage was done. On January 11 a British shot hit the flagstaff and knocked down the American flag, causing a sailor "who was brave enough to stand on the cross-trees, exposed as a mark," to set the big star-spangled banner waving again. In frustration, Overton decided one day to let loose a huge blast from all his guns just to let the British know the Americans were still there. It didn't do any damage, but at least it made everybody feel better.

In the several days after the battle, the Americans had time to collect themselves, tidy up, and get about their chores, which also included continuing to strengthen Jackson's rampart. Many began setting down their impressions in letters to family and loved ones. On January 10, physician Avery, whose regiment had been sent to fight on the right side of the river under Morgan's command, wrote, still rather breathlessly, to his wife, Mary Ann, at Baton Rouge:

> I have just returned from the Camp, where I have been for several days—on Sunday the 8th, we had a most tremendous battle with the enemy, their loss in killed and wounded and prisoners according to the best information, is 14 to 15 hundred, the ground in front of our lines may be said to [be] litteraly covered with their dead, while our loss is only 4 men killed and about 30 wounded and those very slightly, the action commenced a little after daylight and continued violent for about three hours, there was a continual and most dreadful roar of musketry, without one single moments intermission.
>
> Same morning between daylight and sunrise a part of the British army crossed over the river and commenced an attack on that side of the river and drove our men from our batteries, in great confusion, but they withdrew the same day about 4 o'clock, as [it] is since learned; the day was thick and rainey, in the afternoon, they crossed the river in consequence of the great and unexpected loss they sustained on the Orleans [Jackson's] side; the order of attack was that three thousand should cross and attack on this side at the same time of the attack on the Orleans side, but in consequence of their defeat, which actually happened, to their great loss, they withdrew their troops from this side, the next morning after the action they sent in a flag, with a request, that hostilities cease for three days.

General Jackson answered that he would give them until half past one o'clock to bury their dead and no longer, and they accordingly sent a great number of men for that purpose, nothing of importance has happened since, the enemy have five vessels in the river below fort Placquemine [Fort St. Philip], we have heard a heavy cannonade today in that direction, if they should pass that fort, all our efforts here I am afraid will be unavailing, there would be but little to prevent them after from coming to Orleans, the place is very strong, and they will meet with great difficult—their first Genl and commander in Chief Pickingham and Genl Gibbs second are both killed, and Kean 3rd in command is wounded and said to be mortal—Cochran is now Commander in Chief.

> Please give my respects to all
> my friends and believe me,
> Dudley Avery.

While some of his facts may be incorrect, from the tone of his letter it is clear that two days after the battle Avery, like many others, remained astonished at all the things he had seen and heard.

The bombardment continued on the twelfth, thirteenth, and fourteenth "with the usual intervals." The enemy had finally decided that the best method of harming the Americans was to rig their shells for air bursts. One American was killed and another lost his leg, but this merely caused Overton's men to collect all the timber they had removed from the fort previously and return it in the form of heavy-timbered overhead shelters. For a solid week they had been receiving about two hundred shell blasts every day.

On the evening of the fifteenth supplies arrived by boat from New Orleans, including new fuses for the thirteen-inch mortar, which was finally able "to return fire with considerable effect." After several days of this back and forth, on the morning of January 18 the Americans woke up expecting more of the same, but, when they looked over the parapet, the British had lifted anchor and sailed away in the night, defeated yet again.

Latour calculated that during the nine days of bombardment the fort had been hit by no less than a thousand shells (seventy tons' worth, so he said) and that the British had "expended more than twenty thousand pounds of gunpowder." Much of the fort was in ruins, and "the ground outside was torn up in every direction," he said, but the British had finally concluded that they couldn't drive the Americans out of their positions. Especially after Major Overton's frustrating display of barrage power, the British command realized that going upriver and against the current there was simply no way their ships could get past the fire from this determined little bastion. So Overton and the Americans had prevailed after all.

On that same day General Lambert, who by then had concluded that further prosecution of the battle was incompatible with reality, began his evacuation of the British army from Louisiana. "Failure, failure everywhere to this imposing expedition," crowed James Parton, Jackson's early biographer.

Sixteen

Retreat in the face of an enemy is generally considered one of the two most dangerous military maneuvers (the other is an opposed amphibious landing).

Lambert had not put much faith in Cochrane's attack on Fort St. Philip and had been planning a retirement ever since the results of January 8 became so painfully apparent. Since the fleet still did not have enough boats to load up the army all at once, his staff worked out a scheme that they hoped could succeed.

It was more than *nine miles* from their present position at the Villeré plantation to the mouth of Bayou St. John. During the invasion the British had been able to ferry the troops to within two miles of the sugar plantations, but that was before the Americans discovered them. Now, however, they were being watched most carefully, and speed and stealth would be necessary to avoid being attacked and destroyed in detail during the process of their withdrawal.

Accordingly, British engineering parties, along with battalions of infantry, were sent out to build bridges over all the multitudinous streams, creeks, and bayous that emptied into Bayou St. John; sometimes using timbers, sometimes strung-together boats, but mostly using bound-together cane reeds from the swamps to form what they hoped would be a kind of dry footing, they fashioned a seven-mile-long path along the right bank of the bayou down to the Spanish Fishermen's Village.

At intervals in this gross morass they also fashioned redoubts, or forts, from which a pursuing enemy, confined by necessity to the narrow path, could be held off by concentrated cannon and rifle fire. The troops could then wait on the shores of Lake Borgne for the boats to come and pick them up, or so the operation was conceived. It took a full nine days, with thousands of men working around the clock, to complete this marvel of military engineering on what for eons had been only a trackless quagmire.

Meantime, Lambert had ordered a Major Wylly, his military aide, to accompany the remains of General Pakenham (grotesquely preserved in a barrel of rum) back to England for a proper burial, taking along with him "dispatches of the lamentable disaster" that would inform Whitehall and the Admiralty of what had happened.

During the week prior to the British evacuation, negotiations for a prisoner exchange had been taking place. Harry Smith again spoke for the British, but this time the jovial Edward Livingston represented Jackson, instead of Colonel Butler, whom Smith had found distasteful. Smith enjoyed Livingston immensely and praised him as "a gentleman and a very able man." Jackson initially had resisted a prisoner exchange because, he told Lambert in a note, the British had not been forthcoming in sending a list of the names of those American prisoners they had captured. When this was finally produced, Jackson agreed, and it was decided that the exchange would take place on the afternoon of January 18.

It became a notable event in itself, with the fashionable New Orleans Rifles marching out to the dividing line near where the British mass grave was located to escort some sixty of its members back into the ranks. As we know, these people represented the cream of influential and wealthy men of the city, and there was great cheering and boisterousness on the occasion of their return, associated, one suspects, with not a little drinking.

As soon as it got dark that night, Major Smith recalled, "our troops began to move off and [by] midnight we were well off and the pickets were retired." Lieutenant Gleig said that the British army stole away in the most surreptitious manner, "tending their cooking fires until the last moment, arranging things in the same order as if no change were to take place. The most profound silence was maintained; not a cough nor any other noise was to be heard from the head to the rear of the column." Apparently rumors of the British withdrawal had reached the Americans anyway, or so Gleig believed, "for we found them of late watchful and prying, whereas they had been formerly content to look only to themselves."

The wounded were the first to be moved, a few days earlier, with some of the black units, and it must have been a terrible strain on them, since the path was slip-and-stumble over its entire seven-mile length. The trail was bad enough for the leading elements, but as more and more men entered the swamp, it became a mire again, difficult enough to traverse in daytime, let alone in the freezing night with no moon and only stars to light the way. Lieutenant Gleig claims he fell up to his waist in mud and that he saw a man actually disappear beneath some sort of muddy quicksand.

Captain Cooke said he was terrified when he watched an alligator, "with a mouth large enough to swallow an elephant's leg," emerge from the water and penetrate into the swamp of reeds. "The very idea of the monster prowling about in the stagnant swamp took possession of my mind in a most forcible manner," Cooke remembered.

As they floundered on, Gleig, in the rear of the column, said that "all trace of a way had entirely disappeared" and everything was "trodden into the consistency of mud. Every step sank us to the knees, and frequently higher." This went on all night and into the next morning, as thousands of British soldiers slogged along and made their way in gloomy and disappointed silence away from the land of "beauty and booty."

When dawn finally lit the sky, Gleig remembered, the men were surprised to find themselves on the edges of Lake Borgne, in a "perfect ocean of reeds" as far as the eye could see, with the thin beaches and ponds along the lakefront rimmed with winter ice. They had had nothing to eat along their trek other than what they had brought themselves, and there was nothing here, either, so Gleig shot some ducks, which were plentiful at that time of year in southern Louisiana. But the ducks fell into the water, and Gleig did not want to swim in after them, as there was no way to get dried off afterward. "The only fuel," he said, was the reeds, "which blaze and flare up like straw," after which all warmth is gone.*

The army stayed put for two days, cold and starving, until the boats of the fleet finally returned and fetched them off in another cramped and wretched sixty-mile row across the lake in rain and cold. One can only imagine the atmosphere aboard ship then, compared with the day the fleet had first sailed into the Mississippi Sound less than a month earlier. Lieutenant Gleig sums it up as well as any, and seems to have said it for all of them: "We had set out in the surest confidence of glory, and, I may add of emolument, and were brought back dispirited and dejected. Our ranks were woefully thinned, our chiefs slain, our clothing tattered and filthy and even our discipline in some degree injured." It was enough, he said, "to prove the short-sightedness of human hope and human prudence."

The next morning, bright and early, Jackson and some of his staff, including General Humbert, were up at the observation post on the top floor of the Macarty house. Jackson scanned the British position, and things looked fairly normal: sentinels seemed to be posted as usual and British flags were flying. Something seemed strange, however; they could see none of the busy activity that they had so often observed. There were no horseback riders, and it was odd that thousands of men could be so still; there was no smoke from cooking fires. Then the eagle-eyed Humbert stepped forward and took a turn at the telescope.

"They are gone," he announced.

---

* Finally Gleig decided to go into the frigid water after his dead ducks. He took off his clothes, he said, but for some mysterious reason not his thick woolen socks, and he lost one of them in the mud. In his narrative Gleig carries on about the lost sock as if it were somehow more significant than the lost victory before New Orleans. I raise this point only to demonstrate that there is no telling what young lieutenants in the field might do or think after a battle.

"How do you know?" Jackson asked.

Humbert motioned for Jackson to look through the glass, which he had trained on a crow hovering above one of the British "sentinels," almost as if it intended to alight on him.

"The proximity of the crow showed that the sentinel was a 'dummy,' and so ill-made, that it was not even a good scarecrow."

The British had gone, and were doubtless on their way back to the fleet by now, but what would they do next? Come back for another try from a more promising invasion route? Attack Mobile and return from there? The calculus was varied, and maddening. Jackson could not have known it then, except perhaps intuitively, but the British army had just been reinforced by two more regiments, which had arrived from Europe—1,500 more men, which made good many of the losses suffered on January 8—and there was every possibility that they would renew their campaign in some other venue.

Jackson ordered Major Hinds and his dragoons to organize a scouting party and investigate what had become of the enemy, and, if possible, do damage to them. This force had not even had time to form when a British medical officer appeared on the plain waving a white flag. He carried with him a letter from Lambert, "which announced his departure," and asked Jackson in the name of humanity if the Americans would care for some eighty British soldiers whose wounds were such that they could not be taken along.

Jackson sent for his surgeon-general and along with him and his staff rode over into the British camp. "He saw that, indeed, they had departed and that his own triumph was complete and irreversible," says James Parton. They had taken much with them, but also left much behind, including fourteen cannons, which they had spiked and whose carriages they had ruined. Three thousand cannonballs were gathered up by the men and taken to the American lines.

Jackson went to the hospital in the De la Ronde mansion and "assured the wounded officers and soldiers of his protection and care." It did not take long for word to get back to New Orleans of the plight of the wounded redcoats, and soon many ladies rode down in their carriages "with such articles as were deemed necessary to the comfort of the unfortunates." According to Judge Walker, a British surgeon who had been left behind met and fell in love with one of these ladies, "a bell of the city," and not long afterward the two were married and settled in New Orleans to raise a large family.

The soldiers were removed from the rude plantation hospital and taken into town, but between them and the wounded, who had been captured on January 8, the New Orleans hospitals were full and accommodations few and far between. Many were taken in by the Ursuline nuns in their convent; more were lodged in the regular army barracks; others were parceled out to mulatto women, who traditionally ministered to New Orleanians during fever epidemics. Still others were taken in by fashionable Creole or American families, including the Livingstons.

From January 8 to January 21 the American army remained in its positions, not knowing what the British would do next. It rained almost every day, and soon this nearly two weeks of inundation presented the American line with a hideous tableau: out of the shallow mass grave in which the hundreds of British had been buried, bloated arms, legs, heads, and sometimes whole bodies began to arise from the soft ground—and remained in this attitude, silent except for the buzz of a swarm of winter blackflies, which cast a disturbing pall over the entire plain, with an accompanying horrifying smell. With the prospect of diseases such as cholera always associated with putrefying dead, Jackson realized he ought not keep his thousands of men in the lines much longer.

The butcher's bill for the Battle of New Orleans was among the most lopsided and outrageous in the history of organized warfare up until then, except perhaps for some of those biblical-style battles in which no prisoners were taken. The British suffered approximately 3,750 casualties: 850 killed or died of wounds (most of these on January 8); 1,200 wounded and disabled; 1,200 wounded and returned to duty; and 500 prisoners. The American casualty total was 333, with 55 killed, 185 wounded, and 93 prisoners.

The same day that Jackson visited the abandoned British camp he sent a dispatch to Abbé Guillaume Dubourg, head of the Catholic diocese in Louisiana and the Floridas, asking the bishop to announce a "service of public thanksgiving" at the cathedral; then he prepared to lead his army out of the soggy and miasmic cane fields and into the city.

On the morning of January 21 Jackson's army assembled in the mud field that passed for a parade ground behind the rampart, where the general gave a short address, "recounting in glowing words the major events of the campaign, and taunting the enemy with the miserable frustration of their designs. He also used the occasion to laud the bravery of Major Joseph Savary, a Free Man of Color from Haiti who had performed spectacularly during the fight."* Then, with bands playing, they marched in formation up to New Orleans, where the entire city turned out to greet and shower them with petals from camellias and such other winter flowers as were in bloom. There was cheering and yelling and laughter and tears, all to the tunes of "Yankee Doodle," "Hail, Columbia," and other American airs, as well as the inevitable "Marseillaise." To most it was a sight to behold: all of these diverse and divided New Orleanians, transformed in a single swift month into Americans, one and all. It was as if the stars danced in the Louisiana sky.

On January 23 an orgy of celebration overtook the city. It began with a chanting of the Te Deum in the cathedral, "and the citizens had prepared for the occasion a splendid pageant, which displayed the talent of the French in devising emblematic shows," wrote Latour. In the middle of the Place d'Armes, facing the cathedral, they had erected a great triumphal arch supported by six columns. The balconies and windows of

---

* A day earlier he had written an account to Secretary of War Monroe in which he summed up the entire action and singled out numerous individuals for special praise. It was in this document that my great-great-great-grandfather Major Montgomery was "mentioned in dispatches."

all the buildings and hotels surrounding the square were filled with people, the ladies waving handkerchiefs and the men hoisting glasses and cheering.

Jackson's army, with all its uniforms clean at last, and led by the New Orleans battalions of Plauché and Beale, was drawn up on three sides of the parade ground. The dirty-shirt Tennesseans and Kaintucks were there, too, as were Laffite's red-shirted Baratarian buccaneers, who had seldom if ever witnessed such formal grandeur, let alone been feted by it. Bands were playing and church bells pealing, and a celebratory cannonade began roaring off from the banks of the levee. New Orleans was perfectly awash in gratitude, and speeches of appreciation were delivered from almost every street corner. Jackson was the hero of the hour, and one might assume that at least the politician in him must have been pleased.

Beneath the triumphal arch, "on the right was a young lady representing Justice, and on the left another representing Liberty. Two young children were also under the arch, on pedestals, holding a crown of laurel. The walkway from the arch to the church entrance was lined with young ladies of New Orleans, each dressed in white and wearing a white transparent veil with a silver star in the center." Each was meant to represent one of the United States and its territories, and "each carried in her right hand a flag, inscribed with the name of the state she represented, and in her left hand was a basket trimmed with blue ribands and full of flowers. Behind each was a shield suspended on a lance stuck in the ground, inscribed with the name of a State or territory.

"General Jackson, accompanied by the officers of his staff, arrived at the entrance of the square, where he was requested to proceed to the church by the walkway prepared for him. As he passed under the arch he received the crown of laurel from the two children, and was congratulated in an address prepared by Miss Kerr, who represented the state of Louisiana. The general then proceeded to the cathedral, amidst the salutations of the young ladies representing the different States, who strewed his passage with flowers." So observed the general's military engineer A. Lacarrière Latour.

Jean Laffite, apparently astonished at himself, recorded later that "it was the first day of my life to appear and be recognized by the general public," which was not exactly the case, but he was probably referring to the ladies of New Orleans society.* Still, he felt a particular gratitude "at seeing my two elder brothers and some of my officers lined up in the parade . . . whom the public admired and praised with elegies and honor for their valor as expert cannoneers."

That evening, the victory party got into full swing. There were numerous banquets, balls, and a great deal of drinking. The fanciest celebration, the one attended by "the principal, eminent citizens," was thrown at the French consulate. Jean Laffite was there, as well as brothers Pierre and Dominique You, but they left after the banquet. However, according to Jean Laffite, who by now was becoming a sort of mysterious folk hero, "Many people encouraged me to stay for the ball afterward. I danced two dances. General Jackson and I attracted stares and were the most noticed," he remembered somewhat immodestly. "Many ladies with their husbands asked each other many questions. The youngest ladies looked at me, questioned one another, and passed answers back and forth to each other. General Jackson and his officers were amused by it; they were filled with enthusiasm by the questions and answers.

"It pleased me greatly," Jean went on. "It was my first time in such a large social event; I was completely unaccustomed to large crowds and kept my reserve during long conversations, limiting myself to reply very briefly to questions so as not to reveal my true personality or my privateering enterprises to everyone, for I was preoccupied at the thought of the enemy in retreat, who was boarding ship to leave the country. The night was ending; many began to leave before midnight. I left at

---

* Including, one presumes, the governor's wife, Madam Claiborne, who had declared him "the most remarkable man she had ever met," after having been introduced to him a few weeks earlier as the mysterious "Monsieur Clement" by the hostess of the Elmwood plantation above New Orleans.

two o'clock of that morning. I rose at a [forgotten?] hour of the same morning."

Wars, campaigns, and battles between great armies do not often simply terminate with a victory after which everybody goes home. So it was with the Battle of New Orleans.

First there came to Jackson's attention the issue of slaves, several hundred of whom either had found themselves within the British lines from the beginning or had come over during the campaign. When it was apparent that the British were about to retreat, the slaves became distraught, fearing repercussions from their owners, now that the ultimate freedom the British had promised them was no longer to be forthcoming.

Many of the slaves had attached themselves to British officers, and the prospects now before them appeared cloudy. One British captain recalled the agony of his serving boy, who moaned that he would be whipped to death if he was left behind and had vowed to swim across Lake Borgne if necessary. In the end, many of the slaves, encouraged or not, followed the British on their muddy path of retreat, and when they found themselves on the shores of Lake Borgne, the navy—despite "a general order intimating that no slave should be taken away or liberated by the British force"—put them in boats and rowed them to the fleet anyway. Interestingly, in all the literature of the campaign, nothing seems to be mentioned as to what became of the Indians who accompanied the Britannic expedition. One assumes they were allowed simply to drift back to their homes in any way they could.

On the other hand, the planters upon whose land the battle was fought soon became anxious to get their "property" back; in this they were referring, of course, to slaves. The going price for a bondsman was between $1,000 and $1,500, so that a planter owning twenty or thirty or fifty, or perhaps a hundred slaves, would have been out a considerable amount of money, plus the damage to his property caused during the fighting. Jackson, a slave owner himself, could sympathize with them, and to that end he dispatched his aide Edward Livingston to the British fleet, which had by then arrived at the head of Mobile Bay. His mission was to see if he could work something out vis-à-vis the slaves, as well as to tie up loose ends in the unfinished prisoner exchange.

Livingston, who by all accounts was an amicable personality, was received cordially by the British command and invited to dine at the table of the admirals and generals aboard the *Tonnant,* Admiral Cochrane's flagship. The prisoner exchange question was routinely sorted out to the satisfaction of both sides, but the slave matter remained murky. Cochrane suggested that any of the slaves who *wanted* to return to their masters in Louisiana could do so, but he told lawyer Livingston that it was presently the intention of His Majesty's government to distribute those slaves who did not wish to return to various British-held Caribbean islands. Whether this was a humanitarian gesture on Cochrane's part, or merely a bargaining chip, has never been made clear. In any case, Livingston was allowed to stay aboard the fleet and make his own arguments.

The reason the British fleet was at the head of Mobile Bay was that Cochrane was determined to wrest some kind of victory out of what thus far had been an entirely humiliating defeat. It will be remembered that four months earlier a smaller force with several ships of the British navy and some 100 British marines along with a band of 600 Indians had attacked Fort Bowyer, at the mouth of Mobile Bay, and was ingloriously repulsed by the 300 American soldiers defending it. But now the British had arrived with the real deal: some sixty armed ships and nearly 10,000 soldiers, including the recent reinforcements.

Unaware of the results of the peace negotiations at Ghent, Cochrane next intended to take Mobile and possibly have another go at New Orleans. All he knew for sure was that with these ships, and an army aboard them, and a war going on, he was going to have to employ them somehow against the Americans, and Fort Bowyer seemed like a good place to start. The fort would have to be reduced before the fleet could sail up to Mobile, where, Cochrane assumed, while not as valuable a prize as New Orleans, there still might be worthwhile things to plunder.

The troops were disembarked on Dauphine Island, just across the channel from Fort Bowyer, where they set up a camp complete with tents and kitchens. Immediately upon arrival they proceeded to steal the hogs and cows of a man named "Mr. Cooney, of Irish extraction, who had been banished to that island for some misdemeanor committed in the American navy." On February 8, Lambert's brigade—three regiments, including the disgraced 44th—was ferried over to Mobile Point, just in front of Fort Bowyer, to begin a siege. Behind them were off-loaded four eighteen-pounder and two six-pounder cannons, as well as two heavy howitzers and eight mortars. Three days later the guns were in place and the army had trenched in the soft sand to within twenty-five yards of Fort Bowyer.

Sir Harry Smith was dispatched in his usual role of communicator with the enemy, and under a flag of truce he was received by Fort Bowyer's commander, Major William Lawrence, who, according to Smith, "was as civil as a vulgar fellow could be." Smith spelled out Lawrence's situation for him, which was full of gloom—as if Lawrence couldn't see this for himself. He was surrounded by a force nearly ten times his size, outgunned, and cooped up in a flimsy wooden fort with little or no overhead protection against mortar fire. There were also women and children involved.

"If you do not surrender at discretion within one hour," Smith concluded, "we will blow up the fort and burn your wooden walls about your ears."

There was no reason to doubt that he meant it, but Lawrence stalled for time, knowing that he had sent to Mobile for a relief force. He told Smith he would surrender but would do so the next day, at noon. Smith, however, was having none of it. "I could see the major had some object in view," he said.

After some haggling, Lawrence, who was in a hopeless position, agreed to open the gates to the fort and let the British inside. In return it was agreed that he could save some small amount of face by waiting until the next day for the formal surrender, which came off as planned, with 370 U.S. soldiers and 16 women and children marching out of the stockade. Ill winds prevented the American relief force from arriving, and Fort Bowyer was taken without a shot being fired.

Before Cochrane could organize his expedition against Mobile, the British man-of-war *Brazen* arrived with big news: on Christmas Eve, December 24, 1814, the commissions at Ghent, Belgium, had signed a treaty of peace between the United States and Great Britain, the very day after the first action of the Battle of New Orleans—the one fought at night. For the soldiers in Cochrane's fleet, these must have been bitter tidings, considering all the suffering and death they had been exposed to since the treaty was signed. But there was relief, too. When Admiral Malcolm opened and read the notice of peace, he turned to Livingston and said, "I am delighted. I have hated this war from the beginning."

For the Americans it was bittersweet as well, since the treaty was not a good one—it didn't even address the questions of impressment or sailors' rights, and it resolved the remaining issues on the basis of *status quo ante bellum*, meaning that the Americans would get no new territory. The only good thing that came of it was that the British had been negotiating right up until the last minute on the basis of *uti possidetis*, which would have meant that the British could keep any lands they possessed at the signing of the treaty, and that would have included most of what is now the state of Maine and, presumably, by now, Louisiana.

Ironically, January 23, the day of the great victory celebration in New Orleans, was also a day of dire fears and consternation in Washington and other cities along the east coast. In Washington it was felt most keenly because the city still lay in ruins, and members of Congress were as fractious as ever. New England newspapers were filled with what Jackson doubtless would have viewed as treason. At the least they recommended that the region pay no taxes to the federal government until Madison ended the war.

A terrific blizzard in the capital had blocked roads and halted traffic of all kinds, including the mails, and all the citizens knew was that the British fleet had finally appeared off of New Orleans. There had been no news since J. C. Ingersoll, a Republican member of Congress, had discussed the siege of New Orleans with a naval officer, studying maps and comparing armies. In the end, the officer concluded that New Orleans was indefensible.

Into this black mood a packet of mail finally arrived in Washington. It contained dispatches from Jackson, one dated December 15, detailing the disastrous gunboat battle on Lake Borgne, and a second describing the night attack of December 23. Later that day another packet arrived describing Pakenham's reconnaissance attack on December 28 and the artillery duel on New Year's Day. The news was somewhat encouraging, but few gave Jackson much of a chance. His only opportunity, or so the thinking went, would have been if the Americans could have repelled the British as they attempted to land. But now that they were before the gates of New Orleans, most Easterners believed that Louisiana was a goner. For another week the sword hung over the citizens of the east coast as they waited "in the most painful solicitude" for information from the South.

Then, on February 4, welcome news arrived. Secretary of War Monroe read Jackson's account of the battle of January 8 and rushed with it to President Madison. "Washington was wild with delight," reported historian Parton. "How many things have been demonstrated to be impossible just before they were done!"

People ran shouting into the streets with the good news. The mayor ordered the city to be illuminated, and that evening throngs crowded the streets and serenaded and cheered the residences of the president and his cabinet. There wasn't even elbow room in the taverns; the lines for whisky were five and six deep. The *National Intelligencer* headlined: ALMOST INCREDIBLE VICTORY.

Overnight, Jackson became a great national hero. Celebrations and illuminations were in order at every city, town, and village as the news spread. Barely had the jubilation over Jackson's victory settled than even more momentous news arrived on a ship that had just crossed the Atlantic. "Peace!" was the word of the day. Cities were relit, and cannons were fired off at batteries from Washington to Philadelphia to New York to Boston to Baltimore, where people spilled into the streets carrying lamps, torches, and candles and shouting "Peace! Peace! Peace!" at anyone who would listen. As Parton notes, "No victory ever so electrified the nation as the news of this peace. Old enemies rushed into each other's arms; every house was a revel." Nobody even thought to ask about the terms of the peace treaty; for all they knew or cared, it could have given away New York or Pennsylvania. "We had got peace; that was enough."

The news had other repercussions, especially in the business world, where large fortunes suddenly were made and lost overnight. The price of sugar, which had been at $26 a hundredweight, plummeted by one-half, now that Louisiana's ports were open. The price of tea likewise dropped by half, and tin went from $80 a box to one-quarter the price. On the other hand, U.S. Treasury notes skyrocketed, as did bank stocks.

News of the peace treaty was received with rejoicing in New Orleans, but like many events of great import, it also precipitated a crisis, one that had been building ever since the parade of thanksgiving. Most people, soldiers and civilians alike, assumed Jackson would dissolve martial law and disband the army once the British had gone; now they found out that this was the furthest thing from his mind. Before the treaty could take effect, it would have to be ratified by the U.S. Senate; perhaps its terms would prove too harsh and it would be rejected. In any event, it would take a month or more to find out, and, in the meantime, Jackson still considered himself at war. In the days after the victory parade, the troops were drilled relentlessly; resentment began to fester; many soldiers had families who were suffering from their absences.

Jackson's rationale was, of course, that the British might yet return to do them harm; there was simply no predicting it, and Jackson wasn't taking any chances. He had himself an army, and he intended to keep it intact until he was certain they were out of danger. His confidence that he was doing the right thing was reinforced when, on February 19, word reached him of the demise of Fort Bowyer and the imminent fall of Mobile. The seeming indifference of the people of New Orleans to this news made Jackson irate.

On February 21 Livingston returned and brought with him reports of the peace treaty. It would not be official, however, until it was ratified by Congress and signed by the president, so Jackson remained on his guard. News of the treaty quickly spread and was made public by the *Louisiana Gazette*, but Jackson demanded a retraction and published a proclamation of his own in which he cautioned that the report might only be a ruse "by an artful enemy," to throw the Americans off their guard.

Despite this, the militia became even more restless, and desertions mounted. Governor Claiborne pleaded with Jackson to release the militia; even Abbé Dubourg came to him with stories of starving wives and children in Terre aux Boeufs, below the battlefield. The weather had warmed somewhat, and more than 1,000 soldiers contracted yellow fever; many perished from it. The French consul began issuing nationality papers to French and French Creole soldiers so that they could get discharged. When Jackson heard of this, Latour said, "he banished the consul and everyone to whom he had given discharges to Baton Rouge."

On March 3 an unsigned article appeared in a local French newspaper taking Jackson to task and reminding him that the French Creoles were largely responsible for his victory. In part, this stirred up a mutiny among several groups of militia, and when Jackson found that the author of the newspaper article was one Louis Louailler, a member of the legislature, he had him arrested for "abetting and inciting mutiny." When Louailler's lawyer attempted to spring him from the calaboose on a writ of habeas corpus, Jackson caused the federal judge who had issued the writ, the Honorable Dominick Hall, also to be arrested and put into the same cell as Louailler.

To many, Jackson was seen as being high-handed. Even Jean Laffite was unhappy with the general's harsh behavior. "The General was beginning to take secret measures like dictating bellicose orders and imprisonments," Laffite wrote. "He was excessively emotional and was inclined to a mental defect of forgetting past favors." For his part, Jackson considered the Louisianans ungrateful and naive with respect to the enemy's intentions.

Laffite had his own hands full trying to regain the property that had been confiscated by Commodore Patterson and Colonel Ross following their September raid on Grand Terre. In this endeavor he was represented not only by Livingston but by the able district attorney John Randolph Grymes, who had resigned his position (enticed, some said, by a $20,000 fee—or bribe—from Laffite) to pursue the recovery of Laffite's property, which included a dozen or so large sailing vessels as well as goods and riches of every description that had been piling up on Grand Terre for years.

On February 6 President Madison sent out a proclamation pardoning Laffite and all the other Baratarians who had fought with the army. Laffite assumed that since this had apparently cleared him of being a criminal, it also freed him to recover the property that he had accumulated during a perfectly legal privateering enterprise, or so he claimed. Patterson and Ross disagreed; they had the property now and were backed up by the army and the navy. Laffite's lawyers filed suit, but Ross and Patterson began to auction off the property anyway. It caused Laffite to become bitter against the government and resulted in a return to his old ways.

Seventeen

The British, in the meantime, were languishing on Dauphine Island, at the mouth of Mobile Bay. Like Jackson's, Cochrane's interpretation of the Treaty of Ghent was that there would be no formal peace until he had received official word that it was ratified; until such time as he received that news, he was determined to keep his forces in American waters and attack when feasible. For the redcoats, Dauphine Island was certainly a great improvement over the miseries of Villeré's plantation, and they began to set up housekeeping. Major Harry Smith remembered that they fabricated baking ovens out of a liquid mortar combining oyster shells and sand,* and that to amuse themselves they organized theatrical productions.

With the warming of the weather, however, came a plague of unpleasantries. First, as in New Orleans, mosquitoes brought yellow fever and malaria, and soon hundreds of British soldiers and seamen were stricken. Latour wrote after the British had gone, "We are not sure of the exact number of them that died, but from the graves on Dauphine Island there must have been a great many." Then the sand flies hatched, making life even more miserable.

Worse, the warm weather brought out "multitudes of snakes from their lurking places," according to Lieutenant Gleig, "which infested the camp, making their way in some instances into our very beds." Alarmingly, many of these would have been rattlesnakes and water moccasins.

---

* Along the Carolina coast this construction is known as "tabby."

"That was bad enough," Gleig continued, "but the alligators, which during the winter months lie in a dormant state, now began to awaken, and created no little alarm and agitation. At first these monsters confined themselves to the marshy part of the island, but becoming by degrees more familiar, they soon ventured to approach the very precincts of the camp. One of them entered a tent, in which only a woman and child chanced to be, and having stared round as if in amazement, walked out again without offering to commit any violence."

Nevertheless, this reptilian visit, Gleig recalled, "was of too serious a nature to be overlooked," so hunting parties were organized in which "it was common, upon their return, instead of asking how many birds, to demand how many snakes and alligators they had shot." Harry Smith noted that some of the younger men skinned, cooked, and ate small alligators: "I tasted one once; the meat was white, and the flavour was like coursely-fed pork."

Finally, on March 5, confirmation of the treaty ratification was received, and the fleet prepared to embark. After all their ordeals, at last they were going home, and it was reported that many shed tears of joy. Alas most—though they did not yet know it—would not be going home after all. Since they had been away, Napoleon had escaped from his banishment on the Isle of Elba and was on the loose in Europe again with another Grand Armée of "citizen soldiers." The Duke of Wellington was preparing for his Waterloo, and he needed all the army he could find, including the one in Cochrane's fleet.

Confirmation of the treaty did not arrive in New Orleans for another week, and Jackson was yet enduring all the complaints of an indignant city under martial law. More arrests were made on his orders; to many he seemed on the verge of becoming a tyrant. Then, at about this time, news of what Parton called "the catastrophe" reached the city. Two weeks earlier, "six coffins were placed in a row, several feet apart, in an open place near the village of Mobile." It was an occasion that signaled one of the greatest mistakes Jackson ever made, overshadowing even his infamous duels.

On September 19, 1814, the same day that the British fleet sailed for America, a mutiny had occurred at Fort Jackson, above Mobile, in which a number of Tennessee troops began to march north toward home. At issue was whether or not the militiamen had been enlisted for three or six months. The Tennesseans believed it was three, and they were correct, except that the secretary of war had extended their term to six. Even though this new order had been widely published in their camp, they considered it unfair, and the six men selected for court-martial had been singled out because they were the ones who had been the most vociferous in inciting and complaining.

Jackson had ordered a court-martial to be formed from Tennessee officers only, and then proceeded about his business, which included the defense of Mobile, the first attack on Fort Bowyer, the attack and occupation of Pensacola, and the British invasion of Louisiana. On November 22, he left Mobile for New Orleans and was, of course, preoccupied from that point on.

The court-martial took testimony on, and from, each of the six defendants, beginning on December 5, 1814. Most of the evidence against the men was that they had been "grousing" about having to exceed their anticipated enlistment expiration; there were no acts of violence. Even though the soldiers pleaded that they had misunderstood the enlistment orders, the court concluded that they were guilty as charged and ordered that they "receive the punishment of death by shooting."

Some two hundred others were accused of lesser charges, but, after learning the fate of those six who had tried to defend themselves, they pleaded guilty and were sentenced to a dock in pay and, at the end of their enlistments, to have half the hair on their heads shaved off and be drummed out of camp in disgrace. These were harsh times, but, even so, few believed Jackson would actually go through with the executions. Nevertheless, on the day before the victory parade and church service, Jackson affirmed the death sentences for the six men.

The condemned were brought in a wagon to the execution grounds at Mobile and paraded before nearly 1,500 soldiers, who had been drawn up in a square for this instructive lesson. They were ordered to get out of the wagon and stand by their coffins, while a Colonel Russell stood before them and said in an undertone, "You are about to die by the sentence of a court-martial. Die like men—like soldiers. You have been brave in the field. Do no discredit to your country or dishonor to the army or yourselves by any unmanly fears. Meet your fate with courage."

It must have been a truly dreadful scene. Most of the condemned stood straight and showed no visible emotion. "But one of the prisoners, John Harris, by name, a poor illiterate Baptist preacher, the father of nine children, several of whom were very young, a weak, heavy-laden man who had enlisted for the purpose of accompanying his son to the wars, was still unable to control his emotions. He continued to apologize for what he had done and wept bitterly as he spoke." Only the most heartless person could have felt nothing for him.

The previous night Harris had sent a pitiable letter to his wife, probably penned by his son, who was in the same regiment, in which he said, "I did not expect to have had this awful news to write to you. But my sentence is come and tomorrow I have to encounter death. Tomorrow by twelve o'clock, which is a terrible thing to think of. And I know your tenderness to me as a wife to a husband has been so great that it must be a grief to you and as such I wish you to meet it with as much fortitude as possible.

"It grieves me hard to have to part with you all. But I must resign to God; and we all have to part some time. I hope you will bring my little son up in the fear of God and my little daughters also. My mind is pestered, so I cannot write as I would wish. Remember me to all inquiring friends. So, my dear wife and children, I bid you adieu. This from your loving husband and father until death."

There is no record of whether the soldier son was forced to watch his father's fate before the firing squad.

The prisoners were then blindfolded and made to kneel upon their coffins. "Thirty-six soldiers were detailed, and drawn up before them; six to fire at each. The signal was given, the bloody deed was done."

All of the prisoners fell dead except a soldier named Lewis, who, "though pierced with four balls, raised his head and, finally crawled upon his coffin. The officer in command approached him."

"Colonel," the man said, "I am not killed but I am sadly cut and mangled. Colonel, did I not behave well?"

"Yes, like a man," replied the colonel with a faltering voice.

"Well sir, haven't I atoned for my offense? Shall I not live?"

The colonel, with cruel kindness, granted the poor fellow's prayer, but the case was past surgery. He lingered some four days in extreme agony and then died.*

What on earth had possessed Jackson at the time he signed those death warrants is not recorded; later, though, during his political campaigns, he wrote several letters justifying his action on grounds that the six had inspired mutiny and desertion during a time of war, and also that "it will be recollected in the Revolutionary war, at a time of great trial, General Washington ordered deserters shot without trial."

Jackson had just gone through an exhausting ordeal against the British army. Doubtless he had been hardened by the death and horror he'd been a part of, and he must have been suffering as well from the emotional strain of contemplating another British attack. But a man of his intellect, an attorney and judge by trade, in the light of meditating on these men's crimes, which weren't even crimes in civilian life—and these were civilian soldiers—surely might have, and should have, been disposed to grant them some sort of leniency, at least not to have them shot dead in cold blood. This blight on Jackson's escutcheon would follow him across the years and nearly cost him the presidency. Nor did it make him any more popular in New Orleans.

In early March M. Louailler went on trial for "abetting and inciting a mutiny, spying," and other charges, and was promptly acquitted by a jury of his peers—meaning that they were Creoles. Jackson was furious,

---

* This account of the execution of the militiamen is taken entirely from James Parton's *Life of Andrew Jackson*, which seems to offer the most accurate and extensive report.

but on March 11 he ordered that Judge Hall be released from the guard-house and banished from New Orleans "until the radification of the peace is regularly announced."

This occurred two days later, March 13, when a courier arrived from Washington with a copy of the treaty and the ratification. Jackson immediately rescinded martial law, prepared to discharge his militia, and issued another proclamation.

"And in order that the general joy attending this event may extend to all manner of persons," he concluded, "the commanding general pro-claims and orders a pardon for all military offenses heretofore commit-ted in this district." It is a poignant irony and a pity, in a war filled with irony and pity, that the Senate had ratified the peace treaty on February 16, five days before the execution of the six militiamen, for they surely would have been set free with the rest.

When he dismissed his army, Jackson issued yet another proclama-tion of the flowery variety, wrapped in sentences such as this: "Go then my brave companions, to your homes, to those tender connections and those blissful scenes which render life so dear—full of honor and crowned with laurels which will never fade." One can almost imagine the expression of serenity on his face as he penned such lines.

With the peace, the relief from martial law, and the dissolution of the army, New Orleans society began once again to preen. The city seemed to have forgiven Jackson, and he was again their great hero, feted at dinners and balls.

Into all this joy and relief descended plump, homely Rachel Jackson with their adopted son Andrew Jr., age seven. An intensely religious woman, Rachel was shocked at "the wickedness, the idolatry of this place! unspeakable the riches and splendor. Great Babylon has come up before me."

A number of Creole ladies, led by Livingston's elegant wife, attempted to entertain Mrs. Jackson, whom they found likable and amusing and who had never been to a city outside Nashville. Rachel admitted to them that she knew nothing about fine company and fine clothes "and had no resource but to throw herself upon the guidance of her friends." Mrs. Livingston therefore "undertook the task of selecting for her suitable dresses for the various public occasions on which she was expected to appear."

The ladies even raised a subscription to buy her jewelry worth $4,000. The subscriptions fell short, but the jewels were bought anyway. Rachel was dazzled at one of the banquets held in her and her husband's honor, on Washington's birthday, by "the splendor, the brilliant assemblage the Magnificence of the supper and orniments of the room," adding that, "ther[e] was a gold ham on the table."

Vincent Nolte was present, and recorded, "After supper we were treated to a most delicious *pas de deux*" by Jackson and poor Rachel, whom he snippily referred to as "an emigrant of the lower classes.

"To see these two figures," Nolte wrote, "the general a long, haggard man, with limbs like a skeleton, and Madame la Generale, a short fat dumpling, bobbing opposite each other like half-drunken Indians, to the wild melody of *Possum up de Gum Tree* and endeavoring to make a spring into the air, was very remarkable, and far more edifying a spectacle than any European ballet could possibly have furnished."

One person who had not forgiven Jackson, however, was dour old Judge Dominick Hall. No sooner had he returned to the city than he issued an arrest warrant for Jackson for contempt of court, for disregarding the writ of habeas corpus in the case of Louis Louailler, and "for having imprisoned the honorable judge of this court."

Jackson was now vulnerable, since he had revoked his rule of martial law. Livingston drew up a defense, but it was an uphill battle; an angry federal judge was a very troublesome individual to confront. On March 31 Jackson appeared for his trial, accompanied by the voices of "nearly a thousand excited people." This must be an exaggeration, but the courtroom was indeed packed, mostly, we are told, by Baratarians, who had learned to worship their general during the battle and had come to support him now. Wearing civilian clothes, Jackson acted with lawyerly decorum and silenced the rough privateers, reminding them that they were in a court of law.

It was a peculiar trial, even for those days. Judge Hall had rejected, and refused even to read, Livingston's pleadings, in which he and Jackson had tried to explain the general's position regarding the arrests in terms of his powers under martial law. Instead Hall had the district attorney draw up a list of nineteen questions (*viz:* "Did you not arrest the judge of this court?"), to which Jackson was apparently supposed to answer yes or no, with no explanation. Jackson was smart enough to see where this was headed and refused to answer them. He told the judge to just go ahead and sentence him, which Hall did, fining him $1,000.

At this the Baratarians could restrain themselves no longer and began cheering Jackson and booing (or whatever passed for booing in the day) Judge Hall. Then they carried Jackson out of the courthouse on their shoulders to a nearby coffeehouse, where drinks flowed all around. Jackson's "hellish banditi" offered to pay the fine for him, but he declined. He had not always been so universally admired.

Eighteen

The Battle of New Orleans became a defining event of the American nineteenth century, ranking in the nation's history with Bunker Hill and, later, Gettysburg, with which it has eerie parallels.

Great infantry or cavalry charges are as often remembered for the ones that failed as for the ones that succeeded. On July 3, 1863, General Robert E. Lee sent 15,000 Confederate infantry under George Pickett charging into the Union lines at Gettysburg. The resulting failure presaged the decline of the Confederacy. A decade earlier, England's Lord Cardigan had dispatched his light brigade of cavalry to charge against a strong Russian position during the Crimean War, and nearly all were killed or wounded; this became the stuff that poems were made of. In World War I, millions of soldiers were killed in frontal infantry assaults; it was likewise with the Japanese in World War II, who died by the tens of thousands in pointless banzai charges.

The psychology of the tactic was a leftover from the days of the rock, the club, the spear, and the sword, in which battles were won or lost in close combat with one side ultimately overwhelming and terrifying the other by dint of sheer audacity and ferocity. With the evolution of gunpowder and weapons of distance—rifles, cannons, and the like—personal physical prowess had become less and less important. Still, as military scholars continue to emphasize, most wars are fought on the strategies and tactics gleaned from the previous one, yet men commanding warriors of the nineteenth and even the twentieth century were slow to understand this.

By the early nineteenth century it was generally understood that it was risky business to charge a heavily fortified line, and Pakenham had to have known this. After the Americans had brazenly and savagely attacked General Keane on the first night the British arrived, Pakenham at least ought to have concluded that he was not dealing with the kind of ineffective American militia the British had so far encountered in the war. Certainly, in his reconnaissance attack of December 28, he got a good look at Jackson's rampart and must have realized that the Americans would continue fortifying more and more every day, so that the line he had faced on the twenty-eighth would doubtless be much stronger when he tried again eleven days later. And after the artillery duel of New Year's Day, Pakenham should have understood that even all the newly arrived British artillery was no match for the American guns behind Jackson's line.

What is more, he should have noticed that he was being sucked into what amounted to a funnel, for while his own lines at the Villeré plantation were nearly a mile wide from the river to the swamp, the passable fields were so narrowed by the time he got to Jackson's rampart that he could not employ his troops in line, only in column, which made them all the more vulnerable—a single cannonball could wipe out dozens of men.

The smart move for Pakenham at that point probably would have been to send for the boats from the fleet and reembark to fight another day and at another place. Apparently, pride stood in his way. We have no record of what Pakenham thought of Jackson's army, but he had certainly been tested by it so far. One may imagine that he simply refused to believe that his veteran soldiers could not rout a band of untrained militia. Cornwallis had made the same mistake at Yorktown thirty-four years earlier, a lesson apparently lost on the Duke of Wellington's brother-in-law.

Another strategy might have been to fix and hold Jackson's army with a part of his command and somehow try a night crossing of the Mississippi by a much larger force, say, 4,000 men. To do this, of course, would have meant that his canal project would have to be successful, as it had not been on January 8. If this had worked out as planned, Pakenham would have had an overwhelming superiority on the west bank and could easily have marched the seven or eight miles up to the river opposite New Orleans. The problem then, of course, would be how to get across, since the river there is more than half a mile wide. One way would have been for the boats, as they disembarked the infantry, to row up the river and be waiting to ferry the men across when they came opposite New Orleans.

If this scheme had worked, occupying New Orleans should have been fairly easy, since there were virtually no troops in the city itself to defend it. On the other hand, it, too, would have been a risky business, for Pakenham would have divided his army. But if the British had reached New Orleans, Jackson likely would have felt compelled to come out from behind his rampart to deal with them, thus exposing himself to open-field combat, which was a British strength, not an American one. Or the British could have marched through the city, down the levee road, and come up behind the American rampart, while the other force attacked it from the south in a pincers movement.

It is also probably worth contemplating what might have happened if the 44th Infantry Regiment had not forgotten the fascines and scaling ladders and, in the dim light of dawn, before the Americans could see them clearly, had rushed forward and breached the ditch. Surely some part of the British force would have been able to get into the American positions. Then there would have come a test of wills and courage. It is one thing to fight from behind a fortified rampart, but quite another when the enemy is right upon you. Would the American militia have broken and run, leaving a gap for more and more British arms to pour through?

When you consider the Americans' audacious behavior during the night battle of December 23, it seems unlikely; still, if the British ever stood a chance on January 8, that would have been it. Of course, this is all armchair generalship, but no less interesting to ponder.

As we have seen, the bodies of Generals Pakenham and Gibbs were eviscerated and shipped home. The viscera were allegedly buried under a pecan tree on Lacoste's plantation, and legend has it that the tree never again bore pecans. There is a persistence on the part of some writers to romanticize—if that is the word for it—Pakenham's death by suggesting that his new bride had accompanied him with the fleet, and that the poor woman had the dreadful experience of sailing home with the body of her husband preserved in a barrel of rum. That is nonsense; Pakenham was a bachelor.

In any case, both Pakenham and Gibbs were immortalized in a remarkable marble sculpture now in the hall of St. Paul's Cathedral in London. The statue depicts the two generals standing beside each other, with Gibbs's hand on Pakenham's shoulder, as if they were the closest of friends, watching the attack go forward. They each have a faraway gaze in their eyes that is quite touching.

Admiral Cochrane sailed his fleet back to England, no doubt despairing of the fabulous prize money that had slipped so narrowly from his grasp. He was made a full admiral in 1821 and took command of British naval headquarters at Portsmouth. In 1824 he retired to a life of leisure in the countryside and died in Paris in 1832.

Several months after the peace treaty was signed, and less than a month before the Battle of Waterloo, the Duke of Wellington, who was married to Pakenham's sister, Kitty, wrote a letter to Pakenham's brother, Lord Longford, lamenting his loss and blaming the British defeat on Cochrane. So disgusted was the Iron Duke that he condemned the whole campaign as a mere grab by Cochrane for plunder: "an evil design [that] defeated its own end."

Despite being reported by Judge Walker as killed at Waterloo, Major Sir Harry Smith stayed in the British army and became a lieutenant general. Later he was made a baron and appointed governor of the South African colony. After the Battle of New Orleans, he kept up an amicable correspondence with Edward Livingston, with whom he had negotiated on the fateful battlefield. He died in 1860.

Following the defeat of Napoleon at Waterloo, Lieutenant George Gleig went back to Oxford, where he received a bachelor of arts degree.

He later became an Anglican clergyman and ultimately chaplain-general to the British army; he died in 1888.

General Keane, having recovered from being shot in the neck, went on to become governor of Jamaica, where, we are told, he engaged in his favorite sport, "spearing alligators." Later he saw service in India, where he earned the title Lord Keane. He died on his estate in Ireland in 1845.

Major General Sir John Lambert was one of those tapped by Wellington to fight Napoleon at the Battle of Waterloo in June 1815. This he did at the head of his brigade, with distinction, and later he succeeded Keane as governor of Jamaica, where he died in 1848.

Colonel Mullins, commander of the ill-fated 44th Regiment, was court-martialed in Dublin, Ireland, in June 1815. He was acquitted of the most serious charge, cowardice, but convicted of dereliction of duty for "shamefully neglecting and disobeying the order he had received from the late Major-General Gibbs, to collect the fascines and ladders." From the transcript of his trial, it appears that Mullins was probably not guilty of much that he was accused of.

What emerges through a fog of nineteenth-century military legal rhetoric is that Keane had ordered a subordinate officer to ascertain from the engineers precisely where the fascines and scaling ladders were located. In fact, they were in a redoubt (a small fort, often protected by artillery) at the leading edge of the battlefield. But there was also an even more advanced British battery on the field, about a quarter of a mile ahead of the redoubt.

It seems that there was a confusion in terminology, for upon the subordinate's return the night before the battle, Mullins was left to understand that the ladders and fascines were in the advance battery, and not in the redoubt, which his regiment had passed right by on their way to the fight. The opinion of the court was that Mullins ought to have understood his orders more carefully and have gone personally to inspect the location of the scaling equipment, which he had been ordered to do, and that his remarks about his regiment being destined to become merely "a bridge of dead men across which the British army would cross" were proof enough that he was insufficiently enthusiastic about the attack.

In any case, Mullins was cashiered from the army in disgrace, and he retired to his estate in Ireland, but for the rest of his life he went about like the Ancient Mariner, telling his side of the story to anyone who would listen.

Of the Americans in the battle, Commodore Daniel Todd Patterson was made a captain and commanded the *Constitution*, "Old Ironsides," and later became commandant of the Washington Navy Yard, until his death in 1839. Lieutenant Thomas Ap Catesby Jones, who commanded the gunboats during the Battle of Lake Borgne, also remained in the navy, but with the onset of the Civil War he resigned and joined the Confederacy. He commanded the *Merrimac* after her captain was wounded during the fight with the *Monitor* in the celebrated Battle of the Ironclads at Hampton Roads in 1862. He was killed six months later and buried in Richmond's renowned Hollywood Cemetery.

General William Carroll returned to Tennessee, where he was twice elected governor. He died in Nashville in 1844. General John Coffee also went back to Tennessee, where he resumed work as a surveyor. He helped to found the city of Florence, Alabama, before his death in 1832. General John Adair was elected governor of Kentucky and later served in the U.S. Congress. He died in 1840. After the battle of January 8, Jackson condemned the disorderly retreat of the Kentuckians, to which Adair took exception, and the two former friends entered into a lengthy and acrimonious public dispute, demonstrating yet again the kind of pride between states that existed in that day.

General David B. Morgan, who had been in command of the west bank on January 8, returned to Louisiana politics. He, too, engaged in a protracted quarrel with Jackson, and others, over responsibility for the flight of American troops on the west bank. Jackson had blamed Morgan, who was in overall charge of the position, and Morgan, in turn, blamed the colonel of the Kentucky militia. Despite all the finger-pointing, the argument was, of course, moot: the battle was over; the Americans had won.

In April 1815, Andrew and Rachel Jackson left New Orleans for their home, the Hermitage, in Nashville. He remained in command of the Southern District but turned over most duties to subordinates and resumed his cotton planting and horse racing. However, a border crisis in 1817 led him to invade Florida the following year and wrest it from the Spanish, which precipitated a diplomatic crisis in Washington that threatened war. Jackson was in the clear when Secretary of State John Quincy Adams arranged for the purchase of that territory from Spain.

In 1823 Jackson was elected to the U.S. Senate, but his continuing hero status led a number of his friends to push him to run for president. In 1824 he was put up for president but lost to John Quincy Adams in an acrimonious political battle. In 1828 he ran again and won, although the acrimony was much more vicious and personal this time. Not only did Adams's supporters dredge up the old adultery charges regarding Rachel, which had inspired so many duels, but they published a broadsheet infamously known as the "coffin handbill," which depicted the six coffins of the Tennessee militiamen, along with inflammatory accusations from relatives of the executed men branding Jackson a cold blooded murderer.

Shortly after the presidential election, Rachel Jackson died at the Hermitage on December 22, 1828. Jackson had loved her all through the years, fought his duels over the honor of her name, watched her grow portly and loved her still, when he could have had more or less any woman he pleased after New Orleans, and did not. Rachel had been his rock, his anchor; and now he was alone. The personal attacks against Andrew during the political campaign had wounded Rachel and caused her to declare that she would "rather be a doorkeeper in the House of God" than live in the White House.

Andrew Jackson was inaugurated on March 4, 1829, the seventh president of the United States, and immediately the political and social climate in Washington underwent a wrenching change.

Jackson was an American original, whose world rested on moral principles as immutable as the laws of nature. He was the first populist president, the first to publicly and actively campaign in his own behalf, the first to come from west of the Appalachians—a rough country backwoodsman, dueler, and brawler, in stark contrast to the courtly Virginians and staid New Englanders who previously had held the office. The rumor mills ground out all kinds of unsavory reports: White House doors flung open to the rabble, and drinking, cursing, gambling, and brawling now become the hallmarks of America's highest office. It was claimed that the carpets of the president's mansion were muddied from the boots of the vulgar frontiersmen who were his friends, men who had never known a utensil besides a knife and who always ate at the dinner table with their fingers.

Yet Jackson's vision of America was as sweeping as the great prairies of the West. He saw the nation as a great, expanding panorama filled with appalling risks and soaring promise, and with wealth and happiness as its God-given design. He had grown up in poverty in the abominable Waxhaw canebreaks, lost his entire family to war, and then bootstrapped himself to become president of the United States. If he could do it, Jackson reasoned, then anybody could.

There were constant battles, as always. Jackson despised the notion of a national bank, which Alexander Hamilton and the Federalists had established, because he thought it would inevitably become corrupt, and this put him in direct contention with the monied interests. The abuses and intrigues of Washington were as unrelenting then as they are today, and Jackson soon found himself at odds even with members of his own party. In 1830 the powerful South Carolina firebrand John C. Calhoun, Jackson's own vice president, went on the stump against his leader over the issue of high protective tariffs imposed by a Federalist Congress. The South Carolinians declared the tariffs invalid under what they said was the theory of nullification (i.e., that the states were entitled to disregard any federal law they deemed to be against their interests). Jackson threatened to enforce the tariffs with federal troops, and the issue was defused. But here lay the underpinnings of the schism that eventually led to civil war, with the question of slavery only then beginning to insinuate itself seriously into the equation. If nothing else, Jackson had managed to postpone the inevitable for three more decades.

He was reelected in 1832, but not before he signed into law the still-controversial Indian Removal bill, which eventually resulted in some fifteen thousand Cherokees being rounded up from their eight million acres of territory in Georgia and force-marched nearly two thousand miles to what is now Oklahoma. (The Creeks and Chickasaws had already agreed to be moved, and had left their lands by then.) Nearly 20 percent of them died from starvation or exposure to rain, sleet, and snow in what became known as the Trail of Tears. There was an outcry of indignation against this harsh act, and many of Jackson's other policies were equally controversial, but when he departed office in 1837 he was, among other things, generally credited as being the father of the modern Democratic party.

He retired afterward to the Hermitage, where, though in ill health but much revered, he was ever open to political discussions. Many who came through Nashville wanted to see him, and he was always accommodating. He lived until 1845 and was buried in the garden next to Rachel.

In 1851 the Place d'Armes in New Orleans was renamed Jackson Square, and a few years later a life-size statue of the general was erected there, depicting Jackson sitting on his rearing horse and waving his hat. It is there today, and Jackson Square is almost always filled with tourists, a focal point of one of the world's cities of destination.

It is often noted that history is written by the victors, and this became a sore subject with Jean Laffite and at least some of the Baratarians. Although Jackson commended them, they did not feel that they received their due in the official reports, which of course were what the press studied to publicize the battle. Jean was especially incensed that none of Jackson's dispatches mentioned the large quantities of gunpowder, flints, and other armaments that he had donated to the campaign.

When Commodore Patterson and Colonel Ross began auctioning

off what Laffite claimed as his property, which among other things consisted of fifteen armed privateering ships, Jean persuaded his old partners—who remained among the wealthiest and most influential citizens of New Orleans—to surreptitiously repurchase them for him, which they did. While he was waiting for his lawsuit against the government to be settled (it was now before the U.S. Supreme Court), Laffite resumed his old activities, preying on Spanish shipping under letters of marque from Cartagena.

Since Patterson's raid on Grand Terre, it had become apparent to Jean that Barataria was no longer a safe place to conduct business, and he decided to relocate to what is now Galveston Island, about three hundred miles to the west. This he did in 1816 with some five hundred of his men. Others decided to stay on at Grand Terre and engage in the tamer pursuits of fishing and shrimping, with a little smuggling on the side, but not privateering. Some of their direct descendants lived on the island until the 1940s, and others reside in the general area today. Some of the Baratarians moved into town, including Louis Chighizola (Nez Coupe), who peddled fruit in the old French Market till the end of his days.

Galveston had certain advantages over Barataria in that it was much more remote and was also the subject of a diplomatic dispute between Spain, which claimed it was part of Mexico, and the United States, which asserted that it was part of the Louisiana Purchase. Neither nation, therefore, wanted to exercise a presence there for fear of upsetting the negotiations. Its disadvantages, however, were manifest. First, there was no ready outlet for disposing of captured goods as there had been in New Orleans. Also, the island was writhing with poisonous rattlesnakes and cottonmouth moccasins (it was at first called Snake Island). Not only that, but there was a fierce band of Indians, known as the Karankawa tribe, who over the centuries had come under the impression that the island belonged to them.

Nevertheless, after battling both snakes and Indians, Laffite and the Baratarians established themselves on what they had named Campeche, which soon would contain a boardinghouse, arsenal, shipyard, and a number of rude houses. A formal government was set up, complete with tax collectors, magistrate, notary, and secretary and with Laffite as its "governor." Laffite seems actually to have moved there, but his brothers Pierre and Dominique apparently kept residence in New Orleans and visited only when they went out on raids.

One possible reason Jean did not stay in New Orleans was that a nasty rumor had begun to circulate that among his "goods" being auctioned off by Patterson and Ross were certain pieces of jewelry that had been identified by New Orleans women as having belonged to a well-known widow who had gone on a trip to Europe and vanished without a trace. The implication, of course, was that she fell victim to pirates, and that here was the evidence, in Laffite's own cache of booty. All his life, Laffite maintained that he was a privateer and never a pirate and that he did not countenance piracy among his Baratarians. Yet here was this allegedly damning evidence, or rumor of evidence, and Laffite became thoroughly disgusted. He had done his best to save New Orleans, sent his men, his artillery, his munitions, risked his life—and now this ingratitude and innuendo.

The Galveston enterprise quickly became profitable, and by 1818 Laffite had made arrangements to sell his captured goods to various merchants in the interior, as far away as St. Louis, Missouri, where, on April 15 of that year, he received a receipt from one Jh. Robidoux for "Twenty slaves, mature, have good teeth. Males speak French; Twenty mirrors; Five Hundred big hatchets; Two Hundred butcher knives; Twenty-five cauldrons. Twenty-five silk ropes; One thousand steel and flints. Three hundred pieces of wool bands; Three thousand flints; Three hundred pounds glue; Three hundred muskets. Three hundred pounds powder; Five hundred blankets; Twenty pieces packing-canvas; Four casks wine; Two hundred pounds tobacco. Three hundred shirts; Five hundred pounds raw sugar." All of it worth, on the black market, $3,535.

Jean Laffite seemed to be one of those people for whom "trouble always rides behind and gallops with him." It wasn't long before the authorities in Washington got wind of the goings-on at Galveston; James Monroe, who had since become president, sent a message to the effect that Laffite and his crews must depart that place under threat of being evicted by U.S. troops.

Laffite then began to engage in a long-winded correspondence with the federal government over a period of months, which purported to establish his legitimacy in occupying Galveston but upon second reading appears merely to be a stall for time. Then, in late September 1818, a hurricane roared through Galveston Island, drowning a number of men, wrecking most of the ships, ruining the food stores and supplies, and wiping out most of the houses and buildings.

With all this difficulty, a more prudent man might have packed up and gone, but Laffite set about rebuilding and resumed writing letters to the authorities, which by now included the Spanish government, who had of necessity become involved in the thing, and who began characterizing Galveston as a *madriguera de malvado* (place of wickedness). Laffite managed through this gauzy and voluminous correspondence to keep the authorities at bay for another two years, but finally in 1821 he abandoned the commune. It was apparently not an impromptu decision; in the intervening time Laffite—no doubt recalling what had happened when Patterson raided Grand Terre—had been stashing his goods in numerous places, from Donaldsonville, Louisiana, to St. Louis.

When he finally left Galveston, Laffite for all intents disappeared. American naval officers who had come to see him off arrived with every expectation that they would confront a fierce, piratical-looking man, dressed in colored sashes, swashbuckle, the works. Instead they found Laffite wearing a handsome blue topcoat and forage cap, and aboard his sleek and elegant ink-black schooner. He invited them on the ship for a sumptuous supper and apparently charmed them. One of these officers later concluded a magazine piece about the encounter: "We made our adieus . . . with feelings far more interested for the gallant rover than either would have chosen to confess. We shook hands for the last time in this world."

What became of Laffite afterward has been the subject of much contradictory speculation. It was reported that he was killed in a sea battle, drowned in a hurricane, hanged by the Spanish, died of disease in

Mexico, and murdered by his own crew. If you believe his own journal (a discussion of that document appears in the Notes on Sources section at the end of this book), Laffite retired from the privateering business after Galveston and, according to family papers, went upriver to St. Louis, where he had considerable business connections. There, in 1832, he was remarried, to a young woman named Emma Mortimere, found God, and settled down to the life of a landlubber, fathering a son. During this period a spate of books and magazine stories appeared, most of them absurdly fictitious, which often characterized him as the bloodthirstiest kind of pirate and attributed to him deeds of the vilest nature. Chagrined, at some point Laffite, now turning portly, grew a beard and changed his name to John Lafflin.

During his later years, according to the purported memoirs, Laffite traveled widely, engaged in various "business transactions," and sometime in the early 1850s settled in Alton, Illinois, across the river from St. Louis, where he began writing a journal of his life. He lived there until his death in 1854 at the age of about seventy.

He never got over the shabby treatment he felt he had received from the federal government and from the city he had risked his life and treasure to defend. At one point he mused bitterly over what might have happened if he had instead taken the British offer of money and other emoluments and betrayed America. Answering his own hypothetical, he concluded that the Americans would have lost the battle, as well as Louisiana, and that there would have been no president of the United States named Andrew Jackson.

He makes some interesting points. First, Laffite and the Baratarians possessed the vital knowledge of the tides, shoals, and quirks of Barataria Bay and of all the tributaries, paths, and routes leading up to New Orleans. It is just possible that he could have guided the British up to the city without being noticed. His warning to New Orleans, even though it was not believed for a few days, certainly put the city on alert, when time was measured practically in precious minutes.

His offer of powder and flints may well have been critical to the outcome of the battle. New Orleans had inadequate munitions and, as we have seen, being so far in the West, acquiring them was a difficult proposition (the missing arms boats did not turn up until two weeks after the battle ended). It took a great deal of gunpowder in those days to fire a single cannon shot—sometimes up to twenty pounds—and since we know that on one morning during Pakenham's reconnaissance attack, the *Louisiana* alone fired some eight hundred rounds, that could have used up as much as ten thousand pounds of powder.

If the Americans had run out of gunpowder on the morning of January 8, who can determine the outcome? Likely it would not have been a good one. The same is true of the flints (made from a very hard type of stone). Muskets and rifles then were flintlocks, meaning that the shot was ignited by a spring-loaded hammer into which a flint had been inserted, striking a flashpan of gunpowder that, in turn, was set off by the resulting spark. But flints wore out fairly often. Some of the troops at first had to use pebbles for flints, the kind one finds on the ground, but naturally these did not work well most of the time.

It was Laffite's suggestion that the rampart on Jackson's left be strengthened and run nearly half a mile into the swamp. This was truly an astute observation, and while somebody else might have thought of it later, Laffite is the one who gets the credit in the history books. It is well that the matter was taken care of, too, because turning Jackson's left was precisely what the British had in mind.

Finally there were Laffite's Baratarian artillerists, who fought so hard and well at the guns on the rampart. Their absence alone might not have turned the tide of battle, but, when everything is taken into consideration, Laffite's contributions to the victory were substantial, if not crucial. When the government would not give him back what he considered his property, obtained legally under international law (though admittedly illegally smuggled), Laffite smoldered until the end of his days, though he always blamed "corrupt, dishonest officials," not the American nation herself.

After Galveston, Pierre Laffite is said to have joined Jean in the area around St. Louis. He died in 1844, in the small town of Crevecoeur,

Missouri, where he was buried in the local cemetery. Brother Dominique You bought a saloon on St. Anne Street in New Orleans, joined the Masons, and settled down to a calmer life. He died in 1830 and, after a large public funeral in which his casket was carried by the Masons, was buried in the fashionable St. Louis Cemetery No. 2 with full military honors, including an artillery salute.

Of the other characters in the drama:

Major Gabriel Villeré, who had neglected to block Bayou St. John, which was right behind his house, and thus let the British land unmolested, was court-martialed for dereliction of duty. Perhaps because his service during the rest of the campaign was stellar, or perhaps because of the outcome of the battle, he was acquitted "by a jury of his peers." He lived into old age; by the time of Judge Walker's recollections, he'd invariably get misty-eyed when he described how he had had to kill his favorite dog to keep from being recaptured by the British. His father, Major General Jacques Villeré, later became a governor of Louisiana.

The architect Arsene Lacarrière Latour, who was Jackson's chief military engineer, returned to New Orleans, where he became, of all things, a paid agent (spy) in the employ of Spain. He also began work on the first historical account of the battle, which was published in 1816. Latour's book is of inestimable value, since it is the first contemporary account and includes almost all of the pertinent documents surrounding the campaign, as well as his complete map atlas. Afterward Latour went to Cuba and resumed his architectural work, then in 1834 returned to France, where he lived with an old aunt until his death in 1837, during a flu epidemic.

Edward Livingston, Jackson's military secretary and composer of his dispatches to Washington, was already a well-known attorney at the time of the battle. Afterward he became a famous one, having written over a number of years what has come to be known as the Livingston code of criminal law. He served three terms in Congress before being elected senator from Louisiana in 1829. When Jackson assumed the presidency, he named Livingston his secretary of state and, later, ambassador to France. In 1836 he died at the family mansion on the

Hudson River in New York. Not long afterward, on Grand Terre, a substantial fort named Fort Livingston was erected by the United States. Right up until the end, Livingston continued to enjoy a correspondence with his old antagonist Sir Harry Smith.

Louisiana governor William Claiborne was elected to the U.S. Senate in 1816, but he died before he could take office. He remained angry that Jackson had not embraced him and had relegated him to lesser military roles, doing him out of a chance to share in the glory.

The French general Jean Robert Humbert, who fought so bravely as a volunteer with Jackson's army, had trouble making ends meet after the war. He tried teaching and at one point went to Mexico to get in on the revolution, but he arrived too late. He continued his daily excursions to the New Orleans coffeehouses, in full French uniform as usual, for dominoes and brandy, and "died of dissipation" in 1823. The city of New Orleans gave him a military hero's funeral.

The free men of color who had performed so bravely at the battle were given short shrift. One of their number, Captain Joseph Savary, was recognized for valor and voted a military pension of $30 a month by the Louisiana state legislature. Later he apparently led a group of fifty or sixty followers to Galveston to join Laffite. Another, Jordan B. Noble, who had been a teenage drummer boy, later became a drummer during the Mexican War. As a drummer for the Plauché Guards of the Confederate army, he was captured during the Civil War battle for New Orleans and switched sides to the Union army. For years "Old Jordan," as he was affectionately known, "became a fixture in the many city parades that marched down the years."

In a noteworthy act of ingratitude, however, after the British had been defeated, apparently few, if any, of these blacks were given their promised bounty or land and, in the words of one historian of the free men, "were forced to be content with honeyed words and stately phrases, which became empty phrases after the battle."

Most of the owners of the great plantation houses within the battle area returned to find their homes in ruins. Those that were not

destroyed or damaged by fire had been looted and ransacked. The owners began immediately to restore or rebuild, and many of these places lasted into the first half of the twentieth century, until sugarcane growing moved westward and high prices were being paid to buy up the area for industrial development. The proprietor of the Macarty plantation left many of the British cannonballs embedded in its walls and had them coated in gold as a conversation piece.

The big mansions are gone now, along with their formal gardens and luscious orange groves, replaced by large shipyards, which cut huge slips into the plantation grounds, as well as by cement factories, sugar and oil refineries, and other commercial enterprises.

Like Laffite and the Baratarians, the Creoles of Louisiana afterward felt that they had been overlooked in the military dispatches Jackson sent out in the weeks following the victory. There is some truth to this. Jackson, now a major general of federal troops, tended to heap most of his praise on the two regiments of U.S. Army regulars, as well as on his home-state Tennesseans, and so a false and painful impression was created in the minds of Americans that Louisiana and the United States had been saved mainly by the brave volunteers from Tennessee.

This was true, as far as it went, since the Tennesseans constituted some 5,000 of Jackson's 8,000-man army. But for years afterward the Louisianans, who had fought as bravely as anybody else—more so, perhaps, since they were defending their land, their homes, their wives and daughters—used every opportunity to convince the world otherwise.

Of the men who served with Jackson during the Creek War but were not at New Orleans, Davy Crockett went on to become a U.S. congressman and later, of course, was at the Alamo, where he passed into legend. Sam Houston also went west, where he performed deeds that resulted in his becoming the Father of Texas, and ultimately presided over the independence of what would soon become the Lone Star State.

Not much poetry, good or bad, came out of the battle, but several popular songs did. "The Hunters of Kentucky," a ribald ballad consist-

ing of nine stanzas, was composed by a Samuel Woodworth and sung to the air of "The Unfortunate Miss Bailey," which sounded a bit like "Yankee Doodle."

You've heard, I s'pose how New Orleans
Is fam'd for wealth and beauty,
There's girls of every hue it seems,
From snowy white to sooty.
So Pakenham he made his brags,
If he in fight was lucky,
He'd have their girls and cotton bags
In spite of old Kentucky.

CHORUS:
Oh Ken-tuck-y, the hunters of Ken-tuck-y!
Oh Ken-tuck-y, the hunters of Ken-tuck-y!

But Jackson he was wide awake
And was not scar'd at trifles,
For well he knew what aim we take
With our Kentucky rifles.
So he led us down to Cypress swamp
The ground was low and mucky,
There stood John Bull in martial pomp
And here was old Kentucky.

CHORUS.

The composer, a Bostonian, seems to have acquired an elevated concept of the Kentuckians' role in the battle.

In the America of that day, many of the prominent names that came out of the battle were stamped indelibly on the public mind. Perhaps it was because the nation was expanding so quickly, and there were so many new places to be named: among others, we have cities and counties named after Jackson and Houston, and for Montgomery, who was killed at the Battle of Horseshoe Bend; counties named for Carroll, Coffee, Adair, and, in Mississippi, for the gallant cavalryman Hinds. A national park has been named for Laffite, and a street and a hotel in New Orleans were named after Governor Claiborne. Also in the city

today, the Laffites' blacksmith shop is extant, and the tomb of Dominique You, the Old Absinthe House, where Jean and his crew hung out, as well as the calaboose are tourist attractions all.

There is another city park dedicated just to the battle itself, which is now run by the National Park Service. In the late spring and summer following the battle, many citizens of New Orleans began to visit the site. It was too soon, and what they saw was not pleasant. "At one place the ditch still retained a bloody stain and the smell was extremely offensive," wrote one early visitor.

Over the years the river began to erode the right side of the rampart nearest the levee, and before long it was gone. The architect and engineer Benjamin Latrobe, who had designed the U.S. Capitol, and whose son had fought in the battle, visited the site several years later and predicted that the whole line would be washed away by rains in the coming years, destroying "every vestige of a work which saved the city and the whole country . . . from conquest."

For years visitors were beseeched by local slaves to buy souvenir bullets, grapeshot, and cannonballs that they had picked up from the fields. And as these things were becoming more scarce, the relentless press of agriculture was removing many traces of the event. The American forward redoubt near where Colonel Rennie had died; the British forward batteries and their redoubts; indeed, Jackson's own line itself were all either obliterated or threatened to be, reverting back into sugarcane fields.

In 1839 a group of foresighted young New Orleans men proposed building a memorial on the battlefield, but they were unable to raise enough subscription money. The next year, however, was the twenty-fifth anniversary, and Jackson himself agreed to attend. This was only a few years before his death, and he was in ill health. If he had any impressions of the old rampart—known by then on battle maps as "Jackson's Line"—he kept them to himself.

In 1851 the mayor of New Orleans organized a committee to build a memorial, and the next year the state legislature appropriated $5,000 for a monument and also funds to purchase the surrounding land on Chalmette's plantation. It was decided that the monument would be an Egyptian obelisk 150 feet high, along the same lines as the Washington Monument, which was then under construction (but which would be more than 500 feet high).

The work was interrupted by the Civil War and thereafter, for thirty years, by a lack of funds, and the monument remained half finished and in dilapidated condition, an embarrassment to both the city and the state. City officials tried to cede it to the federal government, but Washington did not want it, and nobody seemed to know what to do next. Then some women got into the act.

A group of Louisiana ladies known as the United States Daughters of 1812 petitioned the governor of the state to do something—and he did. In 1894 he gave the monument to them, along with $2,000, and told them to get it finished if they could. Using funds from private donations and "with the meager revenue derived from the sale of pecans, wood and the rental of pastures [the society] built a keepers lodge, repaired old fences, cleared and drained the grounds, replaced twenty-one iron steps inside and placed a temporary top until such time as it could be completed."

Then they appealed to Congress for money, and waited, patiently, which was a good thing since it was a long wait—fourteen years, to be exact—but finally Congress appropriated the money and the Chalmette Monument was finished, seventy years after it was begun; it remains there today. People unacquainted with the area often mistake it for a lighthouse.

One thing is certain: if Tecumseh had never come to Alabama, and if William Weatherford had not been inspired by him to go on the warpath, and if Andrew Jackson had not led his militia to victory in the Creek Indian War, then Jackson would never have been commissioned a major general in the United States Army and ordered to take charge of the defense of New Orleans.

Instead, some hidebound bumbler such as General Wilkinson likely

266

would have been put in command merely because he held the rank, and the outcome probably would have been quite different.

In the overarching vault of military history, it almost seems as if nobody *other* than Jackson could have pulled it off. In a matter of a few weeks he cobbled together the most unlikely of armies—90 percent of them untrained—and by sheer dint of will he inspired these disparate men to cling to their rude dirt rampart like bats to a cliff and hold it in the face of a professional British army that had never tasted defeat.

Jean Laffite, like Andrew Jackson, had grown up on the edges of civilization, where life had taught him some harsh lessons. Also like Jackson, he was a natural leader of men and could be a killer when necessary. Confidence in imaginary possibilities was an enduring part of Laffite's thinking, but the British bribe of cash and commissions had adjusted his sense of reality, presenting him with a decision of brutal simplicity: either to warn the Americans, who wanted to arrest him, or to join with the British and take their bribe. He made his choice to become an American patriot.

Laffite was a complicated and mysterious man, as the writer J. Frank Dobie once suggested years ago when he wrote, "He must have been a puzzle even to himself." But at the Battle of New Orleans Jean Laffite was there when it counted. Jackson appreciated it, and that was enough.

Early on in the war, when fortune began to turn against the United States, most Americans looked into a lowering future and were frightened and disturbed by what they saw. After the British invaded Washington and rendered it to ashes, those same Americans immersed themselves in an orgy of shame and despair beyond their wildest fears. The effect of Jackson's victory can hardly be overstated. Even though the war had technically come to an end on Christmas Eve 1814, certainly nobody in the nation knew it then, and all indications are that if the British had prevailed at New Orleans, their alleged objective of booty and beauty would have been the least of America's problems.

It would have been very difficult, perhaps impossible, to dislodge them. They would have been able, as Jackson had, to engage any advancing army on ground of their own choosing; and if their fleet, or most of it, with its hundreds of heavy guns, could be sailed upriver, it would have presented an almost impregnable obstacle. From New Orleans, the British would have controlled the Mississippi River, all the way to Canada, and, as Lord Castlereagh had said, thus turned America into a mere island, isolated from herself and from the world. Who knows what the skittish New Englanders would have done then? Broken with the Union, perhaps, and declared themselves some sort of British protectorate? At least in that event they could have gotten back to business. And what about the rest of the Americans, humiliated, beaten down in a ruined economy? Would their newfangled democracy have broken under the strain? The possibilities are endless and uneasy to contemplate.

Yet it did not happen that way. The action at New Orleans not only inspired a wave of joy and self-esteem, it served to put some backbone into the citizens of a strange and brave new world; it changed the very way they thought of themselves and how they came to behave in the international arena. Jackson's victory at New Orleans—so total, so irrevocable, so *unexpected*—lifted them suddenly on a wave of patriotism and pride of nation, almost religious in fervor, that transcended even the great chasm of civil war and lasted well into the following century. It was called by historians then, and by many now, the "Second War of Independence," because it forever settled the question of whether democracy could work, and it confirmed that the United States was a legitimate sovereign power.

By the twentieth century the United States was a nation of steam and steel, of rail and iron; of telephones, radio, skyscrapers, airplanes, and widespread prosperity on a previously unimaginable scale. Also by then, of course, the men who fought the war of 1812 at the Battle of New Orleans had become mere shadows in time, the stuff of history and legend, but they remain today a stitch—perhaps a seam or two—in the fabric of the American character, and when they died their dust enriched the national trust.

◥ Notes on Sources & Acknowledgments ◤

The most striking feature of researching this book was the dismaying number of contradictions and conflicts in the various historical accounts. Practically everything seems to be in dispute: troop strength, number of cannons, length of battles, population of New Orleans, spelling of names, distance on the battlefield, width of the Mississippi, number of British dead, and who said or did what, when, where, and to whom and for what motives. Just about the only facts not in dispute are the outcome of the battle and the dates on which it occurred.

Having said that, I believe it is equally true that one can put together a fairly accurate account of the event. Official papers, especially the correspondence of Jackson with Secretary of War Monroe and with his officers, are the bedrock of the factual material. These I found in the book *Memoirs of Andrew Jackson*, a collection of the official dispatches, organized by S. Putnam Waldo, a Connecticut lawyer, in 1819, which is nothing more than a compilation of the Jackson correspondence found in his papers in the Library of Congress but just as valuable.

Likewise, a year after the battle Arsene Lacarrière Latour, Jackson's engineer, published most of these same documents, as well as additional immediate orders, in his running account of events, *Historical Memoir of the War in West Florida and Louisiana*, which includes a priceless atlas of maps of his own drawing that allow the reader to see in detailed close-up the battle areas in the various actions.

Jackson himself is the subject of many biographies, almost all of them useful. The earlier ones at times, for reasons of poor communication, lack of documentary materials, or sheer embellishment, occasionally skew the material. But this is usually counterbalanced by the fact that the biographer himself lived either during the age of Jackson or directly after it, and spoke personally with men who were present at the fight. Alexander Walker, for instance, had become a city judge in New Orleans when he wrote *Jackson and New Orleans* in 1856, forty-one years after the battle. He had the opportunity to interview veterans of the war, who would have been in their sixties or seventies, but he often records as fact their embroidery or faulty memories. The same is true of John Reid and John Eaton's *The Life of Andrew Jackson,* published in 1817. James Parton's *Life of Andrew Jackson* (1861) is a trained historian's account but frequently cites Walker's sometimes fanciful reportage as fact.

Of the more modern works on Jackson, Marquis James's *The Life of Andrew Jackson: The Border Captain* (1933), Burke Davis's *Old Hickory* (1977), and Robert Remini's *The Life of Andrew Jackson* (1988) are each entertaining and contain much useful factual information. In addition, Remini has written a lively and powerful account of the episode in *The Battle of New Orleans: Andrew Jackson and America's First Military Victory* (1999).

Major Howell Tatum's Journal, the recollections of another of Jackson's engineers, published by Smith College in 1922, has a straightforward, if bland, account of the battle but contains corroborative material. Vincent Nolte, the German cotton merchant, published *Fifty Years in Both Hemispheres* in 1854 and was an eyewitness, if a rather low-ranking one, to the fight. Benson Lossing's *Pictorial Field Book of the War of 1812* (published in 1867) is especially useful for its lovely pencil drawings of military sites, including the Rodriguez Canal, the Macarty house, De la Ronde's plantation, and so on.

The *Louisiana Historical Quarterly* is a fountain of useful information. Published by one of the nation's oldest historical societies, it contains countless memoirs, recollections, arguments, and accounts of the battle and events leading up to it. Miraculously, its issues, dating back to the nineteenth century, can be read and downloaded online simply by joining the Louisiana Historical Society for a very reasonable membership fee.

If the *Quarterly* is a fountain, the Williams Research Center in New Orleans is a perfect geyser. This wonderful facility, housed in an old former courthouse in the heart of the French Quarter, contains practically every original document, diary, and journal relating to the Battle of New Orleans and has an extremely polite, generous, knowledgeable, and helpful staff.

The British seem to have brought more diarists to the battlefield than did the Americans. There is, of course, the prolific Lieutenant George Gleig, who in 1827 published his first account, *The Campaigns of the British Army at Washington and New Orleans Under General Ross, Pakenham and Lambert;* his embarrassingly embellished revision of it was issued six years later in an American edition: *A Subaltern in America; Comprising His Narrative of the Campaigns of the British Army, at Baltimore, Washington, During the Late War.*

An excellent account by a high-ranking officer is that of Colonel Alexander Dickson, who was the chief of the British artillery during the invasion. His recollections are contained in the Dickson Papers at the Royal Artillery Institution at Woolwich. Also used extensively were the memoirs of Captain John Henry Cooke, *A Narrative of Events in the South of France and of the Attack on New Orleans in 1814 and 1815,* Benson Earl Hill's *Recollections of an Artillery Officer,* and the *Autobiography of Lieutenant-General Sir Harry Smith.*

Several modern British historians have written books or papers with a decidedly slanted point of view and occasionally take quarrelsome exception to the American accounts of such things as "booty and beauty" (untrue!), the intention of Pakenham's reconnaissance attack on December 28 (never intended as an actual attack), the relative strengths of the two armies (the British were outnumbered), and so on. Among these are Robin Reilly's *The British at the Gates* and the work of Carson I. A. Ritchie, who claims, among other things, that diarists Gleig, Hill, and Cooke gave unreliable accounts of the battle. Reilly's and Ritchie's are nevertheless well-written and instructive arguments and should be paid close attention.

Very useful for the Creek War segment were *The Amphibious Campaign for West Florida and Alabama,* by General Wilbert S. Brown; *Tecumseh,* by R. David Edmunds; and *Andrew Jackson and the Creek War* by James W. Holland. For the War of 1812 in general, see Donald R. Hickey's *War of 1812: A Forgotten Conflict;* Roger H. Brown's *The Republic in Peril;* Frank Owsley's *Struggle for the Gulf: The Creek War and the Battle of New Orleans;* and Walter Lord's *Dawn's Early Light.* For the Battle of New Orleans itself, the *Historic Research Study, Chalmette Unit, Jean Laffite National Park and Preserve,* by James A. Greene, is invaluable for meticulous and unvarnished research. Samuel Carter III's *Blaze of Glory* is a lively and entertaining account. And Tim Pickles has published a neat illustrated book on the subject for the English Osprey Series with many interesting facts and interpretations. Also, in 1965, the sesquicentennial of the battle, the Battle of New Orleans, 150th Anniversary Committee of Louisiana, caused to be published a series of nine little gems of pamphlets on specific aspects of the battle, addressing such topics as *The Weapons of the Battle of New Orleans, Negro Soldiers at the Battle of New Orleans, Plantation Houses at the Battle of New Orleans,* and the like.

The naval aspects of the campaign are well covered by Theodore Roosevelt in *The Naval War of 1812,* which is entertaining, instructive, insightful, and about as good as it gets on the subject.

The Life of Edward Livingston by Charles Havens Hunt, published in 1864, remains the best work on that interesting and vital individual.

Figures regarding the relative values of the American dollar and British pound during the period under examination, vis-à-vis what they would be worth today, were obtained from the Internet consortium of economists published jointly by Wake Forest University and the University of Miami. It can be accessed by typing into your search engine "How much is that?" The scholars who developed this resource are to be highly commended for providing a valuable, informative, and worthwhile service.

Jean Laffite and the Baratarians are most elusive and difficult to pin down—Laffite especially—up to and including the spelling of his name. Stories have him born in various places in France or in Haiti. Compounding the problem is the fact that people in Laffite's profession often played fast and loose with such particulars as their ages and even their identities. (Writers have often confused Pierre and Jean, because contemporary accounts frequently used only "Laffite," or "Lafitte," or "La Fite," or "LeFete," or "Lafite," or "Lafit," and so forth, leaving history to sort out just who was who.) Stories have him terrorizing the high seas off the coast of Spain and Africa. Other accounts have him cravenly offering his services to the United States in order to get his big brother out of jail; yet others have him offering the same services for purely patriotic reasons. Laffite is a slippery character.

Not long after the Battle of New Orleans Lord Byron memorialized Laffite in a poem, then various novelists either romanticized or villified him as they saw fit. One of the first attempts at biography was *Lafitte the Pirate* by Lyle Saxon, from 1930, which has its interesting aspects. In 1952 New Orleans historian Stanley Clisby Arthur wrote *Jean Laffite, Gentleman Rover*, in which we have, for the first time, at least the proper spelling of Laffite's name, which was taken from a safe-conduct pass into and out of Grand Terre that Laffite had given to a wealthy New Orleans merchant. Arthur's was also the first book to utilize the controversial *Memoirs of Jean Laffite*.

Next came the first biography by a trained historian, Dr. Jane Lucas De Grummond of Louisiana State University. *The Baratarians and the Battle of New Orleans* was published in 1961 by Louisiana State University Press. It, too, cited the disputed *Memoirs of Jean Laffite*, which subject we shall now open for discussion.

This document, and other papers purporting to pertain to Laffite, first surfaced in the possession of a man named John Andrechyne Laffite, who said his name was once John A. Lafflin, which allegedly was Jean Laffite's assumed name after he moved to Missouri following the war. The man said that he was the great-grandson of Jean Laffite; that his grandfather had willed him a trunk of family papers after he died; that the trunk contained, among other things, an autobiographical journal composed by Laffite in the 1840s and '50s, when he was an old man. (Most sources record Laffite's death as having occurred sometime in the late 1820s.)

In the 1950s John A. Laffite began trying to sell the documents and went to New Orleans to do so. He was immediately taken in by a married couple interested in the history of the period who introduced him to the leading historians of New Orleans and the War of 1812. The problem was that this Laffite seemed to be something of a crank, and people quickly tired of him. In 1955, likely at somebody else's suggestion, he sent samples of the memoirs to a well-known laboratory in Nebraska, which authenticated them as being "more than seventy-five years old," and the next year the Library of Congress informed him that the paper used appeared to have originated in the early nineteenth century.

Written in French over several hundred pages, the memoirs were poorly translated into English, possibly by the Ursuline nuns of New Orleans, and published in 1958 by Vantage Press as *The Journal of Jean Laffite*. Lafflin, or Laffite, as he now called himself, was a retired railroad engineer traveling on free passes and so turned up in many places, "making public appearances as the great-grandson of Jean Laffite; peculiar in personality; well liked by some, scoffed at by others."

Over the next two decades the original papers remained awash in controversy. They were bought by antiquarian manuscript dealers, sold, resold, and finally wound up being bought, personally, by the then governor of Texas, Price Daniel (who was interested because of the Galveston Island connection), and interred in 1977 at the Sam Houston Regional Library and Research Center, where they remain today.

The controversy over their provenance, however, proved a snake pit of antiquarian backbiting. For every expert who pronounced on their authenticity, another expert would dispute it. Finally the former Texas governor had had enough. The Laffite journal and papers were by then appraised at $75,000. In 1979 the ex-governor foolishly agreed to let one of the principal skeptics, an IRS employee and amateur pirate buff, have a professor at the University of New Orleans, who was reputed to be an expert in handwriting, examine the documents and render a final appraisal of their legitimacy.

This so-called expert soon concluded after a lengthy handwriting analysis, according to a New Orleans newspaper account of her findings, that the Laffite journal was "one of the biggest freehand forgeries in American history." All this went out on the wire services, was picked up by the TV networks, and was reported throughout the land: Jean Laffite's journal was nothing more than a crude hoax. And there the matter seemed to rest.

It turns out, though, that this handwriting expert was apparently someone who had only taken a class in graphology twenty years earlier as part of her course work in something called "art therapy," and had since developed her skills to teach a class at the University of New Orleans in the Continuing Education Department, in which she employed her "handwriting analysis" as a sort of palm-reading or tea-leaf-reading device to determine the compatibility of lovers. In other words, she was not exactly the FBI crime lab.

Yet the damage had been done; millions of Americans had now seen or heard of the alleged fraud, and Laffite's *Memoirs* fell into disrepute. The graphology teacher had even written her sponsor that she hoped the whole thing could be parlayed into a profitable exposé—a movie, television, or book deal—but this never happened.

The situation languished that way for nearly twenty years, until a Louisiana college history professor mentioned to a colleague who taught languages that there was this manuscript in French in Texas and would he be interested in translating it and seeing if it were genuine? He did, and thus a new edition of *The Memoirs of Jean Laffite* was published in 1999, including forty-two pages of scholarly discussion of its provenance. It is a fair argument on all sides, and just as inconclusive.

Laffite's writings have been used by any number of historians of the New Orleans battle, including the redoubtable Andrew Jackson scholar Dr. Robert Remini, although his *Memoirs* is rarely cited in their notes.

Because I chose not to annotate this story, I can hide behind that tree. In the various histories I have written I have both annotated and not annotated, or have used footnotes only to illuminate the story but not included the remorseless endnotes to prove somebody else's scholarship; if text is in quotations, that means somebody else wrote or said it. As pointed out previously, many of the issues in this book are so contradictory that it would serve nobody's interests, except those of confusion, to try and document them here in such a way.

The most recent Laffite biographer, William C. Davis, discounts the *Memoirs,* noting correctly that they are "disputed," and has done hard scholarly work to prove that Jean and Pierre were born in Bordeaux— which may be so, but even his fine book offers no absolute proof of this. Likewise, Davis concludes that Jean died after being wounded in a battle with Spanish ships in 1823 and was buried at sea near Honduras, and that Pierre had died of yellow fever in Mexico the previous year. But he also points out that there are varying accounts of the lives of the Laffites following the war, though he does not consider the one given in the *Memoirs.* Record keeping was poor and hard facts are dimmed through time; there are no absolutely reliable birth or death certificates or tombstones.

The reason I have used John A. Lafflin's, or Laffite's, so-called inherited journals (and I used them quite sparingly—mostly in trying to reconstruct Jean's early life and then his later years after leaving Galveston, but not in connection with the Battle of New Orleans) is one of simple deductive logic: as of right now they cannot be proved or disproved. The price estimated by the Sam Houston Research Center to have them authenticated by modern methods (FBI or other superscientific time-dating and handwriting laboratories) is probably upward of $25,000, and the center simply doesn't have the money at this time when so many other pressing human issues are awaiting attention in the Texas state budget.

Here is my opinion. If Laffite's *Memoirs* is a fake or forgery, then who on earth would have done it, and why, way back then, and then hidden it in a trunk not to be opened for nearly a hundred years? If, as the

Library of Congress apparently stated, the paper and ink date back to the nineteenth century, then why would anybody have taken such time to scrawl by hand several hundred pages of this—and in French? There are certainly entries that make one's flesh crawl, because they do not square with the known facts of Laffite's participation in the battle; actually, they appear to be the work of a boasting, angry personality, which goes against the popular notion of him as a smooth and suave gentleman privateer. But might they not be the outpouring of an embittered old man, looking back at his past through rose-colored glasses and seeing it in terms of a government that he indisputably helped in its time of need, and which he then believed had betrayed him by confiscating his years of privateering fortune? Also, from comparing the few proven writings of Laffite, the *Memoirs* seem to have his "voice" and, in addition, contain some of his familiar themes.*

History leads to many dead ends, and though I believe my interpretation is likely true, I'm willing to eat crow if I'm proven wrong. (Reminder: "If you have to eat crow, eat it while it's hot.") If one has to lean on odds, I would guess the odds at just better than even that Laffite's *Memoirs* is authentic; but until someone other than a handwriting fortune-teller from New Orleans proves conclusively that the thing is a fake, I'll stick by my guns.

There is also the matter of Edward A. Parsons, a New Orleans lawyer, Tulane professor, and antiquarian collector who kept a private reference library in a room of his home, which he entitled Bibliothèque Parsoniana, devoted mostly to original documents from the War of 1812 and, most especially, those pertaining to Jean Laffite. In the 1950s Parsons donated this valuable collection to the University of Texas, and it had long been my notion that it must contain priceless historical information on the life and times of the alleged pirate. Although there

---

* Namely, one that he expressed in a letter to President Madison when trying to get his privateering property back: that he had known of Patterson's intended raid on Barataria and could have loaded his valuables on his ships and sailed away, but because of the impending crisis he chose to stay and help fight the British, even though it meant the loss of all his ships and property. This is vintage Laffite.

is certainly solid, valuable information in the collection, it is mostly primary documentation of previously known facts and interpretations, and gives little fresh insight into the man himself.

I would especially like to thank Wren Murphy for her dogged location of research materials and for organizing them all in large categorized ring binders, which only she knew would make the work so much easier. As usual my wife, Anne-Clinton Groom, was, and remains, tireless in her efforts and support. A profound and grateful thanks for that. My literary agent, Theron Raines, gave invaluable support both to the project and to the manuscript, and Ash Green, my editor at Knopf, astonishes in his eagle eye for error and misuse of language.

ᖰ Index ᖱ

Abercrombie, James, 130
Adair, John, 178–81, 192, 195, 215, 252
Adams, Henry, 128
Adams, John, 19
Adams, John Quincy, 128*n*, 253
African Importation Act, 71
Armstrong, John, 25, 27–8, 35, 56, 60
Army, British
    Americans scorned by, 3, 7, 132, 141, 155, 207
    arrogance and pride of, 99, 173, 188, 193, 201, 214, 217, 225, 248
    at Bayou Bienvenue, 117, 121, 122–3
    campgrounds of, 133–4, 142, 216, 239–40
    casualties of, 139–40, 172, 196, 199, 201–4, 208, 211–13, 226–8, 239
    on Christmas Eve, 142–3
    Congreve rockets of, 153, 156
    December 28 attack by, 155–60
    defense of Canada by, 22–5
    desertions of, 216
    dreams of riches for, 95, 127, 149, 184, 217, 225
    experienced soldiers in, 6, 130, 172, 173, 175, 193, 217
    ferrying of, 115, 117, 134, 136, 143, 150, 174, 222, 225
    food for, 174–5
    at Fort Bowyer, 233–4
    44th Infantry Regiment, 183, 190, 195, 196, 199, 214, 233, 249
    gathering for attack on New Orleans, 96–9, 121, 125–6, 133–4, 188
    Great Reconnaissance of, 152
    horrors committed by, 56, 96, 135, 193, 214
    Maine occupied by, 55–6
    munitions for, 175
    New Year's Day attack by, 168–74
    93rd Highlanders, 97, 137–8, 140, 153, 159, 190, 196, 198, 202
    95th Rifles, 96–7, 153, 195
    numbers of, 131, 133, 154, 182, 209
    at Pea Island, 116–21
    at Pearl River, 114–21
    regiments of, 96–7, 153
    reinforcements for, 145, 173, 226
    retreat of, 195, 196, 197, 199, 201–2, 208–9, 211, 221, 222–5, 231
    at Rodriguez Canal, 175, 182–94, 195–204
    scaling ladders and fascines for, 173, 183, 190–1, 195, 196, 197, 214, 249, 251
    slaves working for, 144, 231–2
    Spanish allies of, 115, 117, 121, 125, 129
    surrender of, 203–4

279

❧ A Note About the Author ❧

Winston Groom is the author of fourteen books, including the acclaimed Vietnam War novel *Better Times Than These* and the prize-winning *As Summers Die,* and coauthored *Conversations with the Enemy,* which was nominated for a 1984 Pulitzer Prize. He is also the author of the *New York Times* No. 1 best seller *Forrest Gump.* Mr. Groom's *Shrouds of Glory,* an account of Confederate general John Bell Hood's decisive actions in the last great campaign of the U.S. Civil War, was published in 1995. He lives with his wife and daughter in Point Clear, Alabama.

❧ A Note on the Type ❧

This book was set in a version of Monotype Baskerville, the antecedent of which was a typeface designed by John Baskerville (1706–1775). Baskerville, a writing master in Birmingham, England, began experimenting around 1750 with type design and punch cutting. His first book, published in 1757 and set throughout in his new types, was a Virgil in royal quarto. It was followed by other famous editions from his press. Baskerville's types, which are distinctive and elegant in design, were a forerunner of what we know today as the "modern" group of typefaces.

Composed by North Market Street Graphics,
Lancaster, Pennsylvania
Printed and bound by Berryville Graphics,
Berryville, Virginia
Designed by Wesley Gott
Maps by Jeffrey L. Ward